Professional Development in Social Work

Social work practice in the twenty-first century is continually changing. Contemporary practitioners work in complex areas and have to do so quickly and competently. This text helps qualified social workers, as well as those about to qualify, to build on their initial studies in order to develop professionally.

The volume considers not only what you need to know to practise, but how you develop in criticality and capability – in particular, how you can respond effectively in times of uncertainty and change to become more effective. It examines new roles, identities and contexts, including some international perspectives and the impact of globalization. Each chapter discusses the contexts of practice (such as law, policies and theories); the contributions made both by those who practise social work and those who use its services; and the capabilities and skills that social workers need to develop in order to deal with complexity in social work.

Making use of The Open University's expertise in providing cutting-edge but accessible course materials and its distinct approach to social work practice, this textbook includes underpinning knowledge, practical applications and critical reflexivity. It includes questions for further reflection and application, plentiful examples and suggestions for further reading.

Aimed at the newly qualified practitioner and the developing professional, *Professional Development in Social Work* is written by a team of authors with extensive practice and teaching experience. It will be particularly useful to students undertaking post-qualifying training or in the final year of their qualifying studies.

Janet Seden is Senior Lecturer with the Faculty of Health and Social Care at The Open University, UK.

Sarah Matthews is Staff Tutor at The Open University. She was a Mental Health Act Commissioner and also runs a training and consultancy business.

Mick McCormick is Lecturer in social work with the Faculty of Health and Social Care at The Open University, UK.

Alun Morgan is Lecturer in social work with the Faculty of Health and Social Care at The Open University, UK.

Post-qualifying Social Work

Forthcoming titles:

Professional Development in Social Work
Complex issues in practice
Janet Seden, Sarah Matthews, Mick McCormick and Alun Morgan

Social Work with Children and Families
Developing advanced practice
Penelope Welbourne

Professional Development in Social Work

Complex issues in practice

Edited by Janet Seden,
Sarah Matthews, Mick McCormick
and Alun Morgan

First published 2011
by Routledge
2 Park Square, Milton Park, Abingdon, Oxon OX14 4RN

Simultaneously published in the USA and Canada
by Routledge
270 Madison Avenue, New York, NY 10016

Routledge is an imprint of the Taylor & Francis Group, an informa business

Typeset in Sabon by GreenGate Publishing Services, Tonbridge, Kent

Printed and bound in Great Britain by CPI Antony Rowe, Chippenham, Wiltshire

British Library Cataloguing in Publication Data
A catalogue record for this book is available from the British Library

Library of Congress Cataloging in Publication Data
Professional development in social work: complex issues in practice/edited by Janet Seden ... [*et al.*].
p. ; cm.
1. Social service--Vocational guidance. 2. Social workers. I. Seden, Janet, 1947–
[DNLM: 1. Social Work. 2. Professional Practice. HV 10.5 P964 2011]
HV10.5.P72 2011
361.3'2--dc22
2010011372

ISBN: 978-0-415-55335-3 (hbk)
ISBN: 978-0-415-55336-0 (pbk)
ISBN: 978-0-203-84298-0 (ebk)

Contents

List of contributors

Dr Jane Aldgate OBE is Professor of social care at The Open University and a researcher specializing in social work for children and families. She has an extensive national and international profile and has profoundly influenced policy and practice in children's services.

James Blewett is an independent consultant and trainer. He has substantial experience teaching in universities and delivering training for the children's workforce. He has also written and tutored for The Open University. He is Director of Making Research Count.

Dr Ian Buchanan lectures at York University and has been a manager in local authorities and a research associate at The Open University. He writes and teaches in the areas of learning disability, service user involvement and social policy.

Dr Barry Cooper is Lecturer in social work at The Open University. He is a qualified social worker and has practised, taught and researched in social work for thirty years. His writing and publications include critical and constructivist approaches to practice, education and assessment.

Roger Davis is Staff Tutor with The Open University in Scotland. He is involved in managing the professional social work programme and is researching the preparedness for practice of newly qualified social workers.

Dr Monica Dowling is Professor of social work at The Open University. She has research interests in children with disabilities and international adoption. She has also guest edited *Innovation in the Public Sector* – an international online journal.

Sue Dumbleton is Senior Lecturer and Staff Tutor at The Open University in Scotland. She has a long-standing interest in learning disability and has worked with people who have a learning disability in housing support, residential care and in further and adult education.

Dr Sandy Fraser is Senior Lecturer at The Open University. He edited *The Critical Practitioner in Social Work and Health Care* (2008). His research interests are comparative social work and the application of values and ethics.

Jean Gordon is Associate Lecturer on The Open University social work programme and is active in supporting work-based learning in Scotland. She has published research in mental health, Scottish law, social work practice and work-based learning.

Dr Richard Hester is Senior Lecturer at The Open University. His research interests include the teaching of youth justice practitioners and children's rights. His practice experience includes the posts of Assistant Director of the Rainer Foundation and Coordinator of Community Safety in Warwickshire.

Dr Caroline Holland is a research fellow in the Faculty of Health and Social Care at The Open University. She is a social gerontologist researching environments of ageing, including aspects of everyday discrimination and how it affects older people.

Sarah Matthews is Staff Tutor with The Open University. Sarah co-edited *The Critical Practitioner in Social Work and Health Care* (2008) and is now researching the impact of changes in mental health legislation on social work identity.

Mick McCormick is Lecturer in social work at The Open University. He has extensive experience of adult services and writes in the areas of learning disability and mental health. He is researching aspects of mental health in current contexts.

Mo McPhail is Head of Social Work (Scotland) with The Open University. She has developed a research and writing profile in the area of service user and carer involvement. She edited *User and Carer Involvement – Beyond Good Intentions* (2008), co-authored with a service user and carer.

Alun Morgan is Lecturer in social work at The Open University with substantial social work management and practice experience. His research and publishing interests are the use of ICT for communication and participation in children's services and the development and application of multimedia teaching methods in higher education.

Ingrid Nix is Lecturer in learning and teaching technologies in the Faculty of Health and Social Care at The Open University. Her role includes developing and evaluating technology-enhanced learning for social workers.

Dr Lucy Rai is Senior Lecturer at The Open University with an interest in the development of academic and professional writing in social work. She also took an academic lead in the BBC series *A Child of Our Time* and *Someone to Watch Over You*.

Wendy Rose OBE is a senior research fellow at The Open University and a former senior civil servant, with a national and international profile in child welfare research and development. This includes improving outcomes for children, policy development in child welfare and the practice and management of children's services.

Dr Janet Seden is a qualified social worker and Senior Lecturer at The Open University. She authored *Counselling Skills in Social Work Practice* (2005). She researches and publishes in the fields of child welfare, social work theories and methods and managing care.

Parissa Sextone is a qualified social worker who has worked in post-adoption and foster care. Current research interests include mental health, cognitive behavioural therapy and a special interest in refugee communities.

Sandy Sieminski is Lecturer at The Open University. She is researching the changing contexts for practice and current issues in social work education. She has an interest in person-centred planning for older people.

Gill Walker is Staff Tutor for The Open University in the West Midlands and an independent practice assessor. She has undertaken research into workplace placements for social work students.

Fran Wiles is Lecturer at The Open University and her research interest is defining some of the issues of changing identity for social workers in changing policy environments.

Foreword

I am delighted to introduce this collection of readings which comes from the research, scholarship and teaching of The Open University's social work programme. The authors represent those engaged in the programme. There are members of the distance learning social work academic team, based centrally in Milton Keynes and regionally across the UK, together with academic colleagues in health and social care and associate lecturer and research partners. The programme has been running successfully since 2004 and has become one of the largest educators of qualified professional social workers in the UK. At the time of writing, 660 candidates have already graduated, with 1,256 currently studying. This collection derives from some of The Open University's unique teaching materials. It also includes scholarship and research undertaken by staff. The aim of this book is to move concepts and ideas from the arena of the qualifying social workers into the world of continuing professional development with which our graduates will be already engaging. Achieving the best possible outcomes for those who use social work services depends on the quality of social work practice on offer. That practice needs to be evidence-based, with practitioners making sure they constantly update their knowledge and skills. This book provides some excellent contemporary ideas and materials to support practitioners in their endeavours.

Professor Jane Aldgate OBE

Acknowledgements

We would like to thank the following practitioners for reviewing and commenting on chapters: Louise Archer, Sarah Ball, Godfred Boahen, Fiona Coombs, Charlotte McCormick, Ged Durkin, Michaela Friend, Guillermo Garcia Maza, Jasmine Harvey, Julie-Anne Howard, Marianne Hughes, Sian Jones, Jackie Lelkes, Amanda Moore, Ann-Marie Mullin, Gordon Murray, Haydn Nelson, Amanda Rice, Wendy Saunders and Ayfer Secmezsoy-Dunn.

We would also like to record our thanks to Jo Ann Knight and Kyra Proctor for administrative support at The Open University.

Introduction

Complexity is a hallmark of social work in the twenty-first century and the authors of this book have attempted to capture and discuss some of the dilemmas and contradictions that arise and the issues this presents for social workers in practice. This volume is an edited collection of accessible but academic chapters, considering contexts for social work practice, contributions made by social work to society through their roles, relationships and responsibilities and challenges relating to professional practice in the workplace. Each chapter is written at an invitational level, where the reader is asked to consider a key aspect of social work and its complexities. It aims to be a collection of readings to support the newly qualified practitioner and the developing professional across a wide range of themes and issues. Each chapter gives an overview and poses some practice-related questions. Further reading for follow-up in more depth is indicated by an asterisk (*) in the main text.

The writers are all involved, or have been recently, in varying capacities with The Open University's social work degree, and so the book derives from The Open University's approach to teaching social work to open and distance learners. We hope it will contribute to building the confidence and effectiveness of those frontline professionals who read it by providing chapters relevant to their own practice, but also by encompassing a wide range of practice areas which contribute to their understanding of the concerns of other practitioners with whom they work in partnership.

The book is not, therefore, designed to be read from cover to cover, but aims to be a resource which busy practitioners may find scholarly, yet manageable and accessible. For each reader there will be a chapter relevant to their practice setting, but the book also provides chapters which will enable them to quickly come to grips with the issues confronting practitioners who work in other settings with different service groups and identify the commonalities and differences that exist. The aim is, therefore, to provide readings which outline key themes and also to point to other relevant research literature.

We have organized the writing to include some critical considerations which are important in modern social work practice. We are highly aware of the changing contexts for practice in the UK and internationally and related to that the complexities for individual practitioners. The Social Work Task

Force report comments that social workers deliver a contribution of great value to society:

> When people are made vulnerable – by poverty, bereavement, addiction, isolation, mental distress, disability, neglect, abuse or other circumstances – what happens next matters hugely. If outcomes are poor, if dependency becomes ingrained or harm goes unchecked, individuals, families, communities, and the economy can pay a heavy price. Good social workers can and do make a huge difference in these difficult situations.
>
> (DCSF 2009b: 1)

However, we are also aware that the contexts within which practitioners practise are not ideal. Fast-paced change, resource issues and the hardships that some members of society experience create their own pressures which contribute to the difficulties and dilemmas of practice. It can be argued that some social policy trends, government initiatives and budget reductions make the job harder. This is especially the case when government needs a quick response to public concerns and when media pressure distorts the realities of what can reasonably be expected from practitioners. We also believe that a vibrant social work profession is of great value to society and these chapters demonstrate how that is the case.

Following on from our concerns about changing contexts, we are also aware that practitioners have to take account of their own roles, responsibilities and relationships and what challenges in the workplace mean for practitioner capabilities. We have, therefore, asked authors, each in their own way, to include these themes. These interlinked issues are relevant to all four countries of the UK and more widely. Contexts change constantly and require flexible, professional and ethical responses. The contributions social workers make to society and those of the people who use the services need to be evaluated for their relevance and timeliness and are discussed mainly in Part II. The theme of capabilities (knowledge, communication skills, confidence, competence and values) is an important component for both qualifying students and for practitioners involved in personal professional development and the development of others. This is the focus of Part III, which looks at some of the challenges of the workplace and the learning journeys that practitioners embark on.

Finally, as the audience for this book is anticipated to be practitioners who are seeking to develop their professional practice, each chapter was reviewed by a practitioner. Some of their responses are used to introduce each chapter and to perhaps indicate what the learning therein might be. For example, a practitioner commented on Chapter 19, saying that is has 'great pointers for developing and improving practice – also excellent pointers to research and exemplars of good practice which can be followed up as a means of developing and improving practice'.

Janet Seden and Professor Monica Dowling

Part I

Complex contexts

Janet Seden

For Part I, we commissioned chapters which paint the bigger picture and consider the contexts within which social workers operate and the complexities of them. While social workers' daily practice is with individuals, this is always set in the complex context of the societal climate of the time. Thus, the way practice is organized and the ethics and values that underpin it depend heavily on the ideologies of governments, social and economic situations and public opinion. It can be argued that practice at the beginning of the twenty-first century has been particularly influenced by media criticism of its supposed failures, the impact of globalization changing communities and groupings with whom practitioners work and the managerialism which has taken hold of the agencies where social workers are employed. It is also set in the context of political philosophies which shape law and policy, postmodernism and modernity, concepts which several authors consider in this first section.

This book opens with a chapter on effective multi-agency work in children's services. This may, at first, seem a strange choice, but the criticisms of children's services following child abuse scandals has been the biggest driver for re-evaluating practice. The situation of 'Baby P' led directly to the Social Work Task Force (DCSF 2009b) and its examination of practice. It is on the assumed 'failures' of childcare professionals that the most media abuse has been focused, and where – given the tragedy of child deaths – public concern is most obvious. Given the almost ubiquitous finding of child death inquiries that professionals fail to work together to protect children, this seemed a good place to start.

Rose (Chapter 1) has contributed hugely to developments in children's services and here she identifies from research and literature that the aspiration of working together to protect children has been alive for the past fifty years. Despite the cynicism that this reflection might induce, she is able to suggest some grounds for optimism, identify some success factors and offer a fresh perspective on what is often seen as an intractable 'problem'. Inter-agency collaboration is also, of course, very important when working to improve the circumstances of adult service users and there may well be some transferable practice ideas. Multi-agency work with adults is also considered within the chapters in Part II.

Building on the theme of context, Buchanan (Chapter 2) seeks to capture some of the history of the political environment for social work and to bring that up to date with some thoughts on current social and political issues. He draws attention to the long-standing nature of some social ills, such as poverty, and reminds us that despite the uncertainties, the social work profession continues to strive for the rights of marginalized groups.

Cooper (Chapter 3), following a discussion of postmodern dilemmas, focuses on criticality and reflexivity to offer practitioners tools for responding to complex and changing environments. Given the widely held view that the only certainty in social work and care over the past few decades has been the certainty of change, it is critical that practitioners can find ways of responding which enable them to make sense of changing situations and environments. Uncertainty is a constant dilemma of practice and Cooper argues that criticality and reflexivity are the tools which enable social workers to provide a good-quality person-centred service, while handling the systems within which practitioners work. He concludes that best judgement in uncertain situations is the most that can be expected.

This is followed by a linked chapter which undertakes a similar brief in relation to values and ethics in which McCormick and Fraser (Chapter 4) argue that perhaps social workers' concern with values has been at the expense of exploring what is morally or ethically acceptable. Their discussion explores why this may be and considers how practitioners might find the space to examine their actions.

Social workers' values and ethics are clearly linked to suitability issues and registration. The question of who is suitable to be a social worker is ultimately a question of the character and values of professionals and the behaviours that society expects from them. Registration is a relatively new expectation for practitioners, but one with which they will continue to engage throughout their professional careers, and social workers will need to be consistently mindful of codes of practice and how their work adheres to these. Wiles (Chapter 5) draws from codes of practice, some controversies in the literature and her own research in order to explore the dilemmas of social work registration.

The final two chapters in this section look at the widest contexts of all – the impact of globalization and the international scene for social work. Morgan (Chapter 6) considers the inevitability of globalization, its impact on social work and the diversity of service users and workers now in the UK. This challenges social workers to make sure they act in anti-oppressive and anti-discriminatory ways, and also to develop a cultural competence that enables them to engage with and deliver appropriate services to service users with a wide range of backgrounds and perspectives.

Finally, Fraser (Chapter 7) examines the concept of 'international social work', discussing the exchange of ideas between different countries and social workers in different regimes. He argues that the views and practices of social workers from outside the UK both illuminate and enhance local practices. In considering the local and global, Chapters 6 and 7 remind us that the context and complexities of social work require a wider set of concepts and engagements.

1 Effective multi-agency work in children's services

Wendy Rose

> This chapter ... reinforces the centrality of multi-agency working and the difficulties in achieving this in practice ... offered a new perspective on an old and often intractable 'problem' and pointed me in the direction of exciting research and literature to inform and improve practice.
>
> (Independent social worker – Child Protection)

Introduction

This chapter focuses on frontline practice with children and families and explores why practitioners from different agencies and disciplines need to work together to achieve better outcomes for the most vulnerable children. The literature about multi-agency working underlines what a contested area it is – a football continuously in play between politicians, professions and service agencies. The chapter argues, however, that by starting with children and families and by taking a child's perspective, it is possible to develop a clearer understanding of its importance and how and why it is important and what can help professionals to work together more effectively. The chapter concludes with suggestions of how multi-agency work can be developed to be successful and have a positive impact on the lives of children and their families. The most persuasive advocates for agencies and practitioners working together are undoubtedly children and families themselves, and their perspectives illustrate their experience of contact with services and practitioners, and what they find makes a difference for them.

What is known about multi-agency work?

The current emphasis of governments on the importance of agencies working together in children's services is not new (Hallett and Birchall 1992). It has been a thread running through child welfare policy, research and practice for at least the past half-century. Hallett and Stevenson (1980: 1) cite a Home Office circular of 1950 on ill-treated children which recognizes that inter-agency cooperation is required to deal with the problems of child abuse and recommends setting up 'children's coordinating committees'.

Reinforced as a key principle in the Children Act 1989 it has received even more prominence and impetus in public policy guidance since the late 1990s (Allnock *et al.* 2006). Achieving effective multi-agency working, however, is not entirely straightforward and three broad reasons for this are discussed in this chapter.

First, inter-agency collaboration is generally regarded as a good thing but still remains conceptually and practically elusive. A plethora of different terms, such as *collaboration*, *joint working*, *coordination*, *consultation*, *communication*, *cooperation*, *partnership* and *teamwork* are employed to describe multi-agency work. Underpinning all these terms is the general idea that by working together, professionals can achieve 'an additive component (something more than the sum of their parts)' (Hallett and Birchall 1992: 8), which is likely to be effective and beneficial. This lack of specificity has the potential to create confusion and misunderstandings for practitioners about respective roles, responsibilities and expectations in collaborative activity with practitioners often using these terms 'interchangeably' (Horwath* 2009a: 12).

Second, effective multi-agency collaboration is notoriously difficult to achieve. Inquiries and reviews into the particular circumstances of children who have died or been seriously injured through maltreatment frequently identify the failure of professionals to work together to communicate and share information appropriately, and to acknowledge joint agency responsibility (Brandon *et al.* 2008; Rose and Barnes 2008). Studies which have examined interdisciplinary teams reveal a range of inhibitors to achieve effective professional collaboration (Hudson *et al.* 1999; Miller and Freeman 2003). Considerable consensus exists across the inter-professional literature about these inhibitors (McLean 2007). Sidebotham and Weeks* (2010: 100–3) build on earlier work by others to categorize the barriers as structural; procedural and financial; professional; barriers related to status and legitimacy; and personal barriers. These are enough to suggest caution is required in advocating more multi-agency practice without addressing what is already known to support or hinder its effectiveness. Hudson (2000: 253) observes that 'there is a paradox here, with "collaboration" seen as both problem *and* solution – failure to work together is the problem, therefore the solution is to work together better!'

The third challenge is that even if professionals are working well together, evidence of the positive difference that collaboration can make to outcomes for children is equivocal and often less than robust. Hallett and Birchall's (1992) literature review found no clear evidence that coordinated multi-agency practice resulted in better protection for vulnerable children. Two issues stood out: a 'pro-coordination bias' and little reporting of failures (1992: 324). They also found that studies identified more methodological difficulties in trying to establish outcomes than in examining process. More recently, Webb and Vulliamy's (2001) study of social work trained home–school support workers in secondary schools, and Wigfall and Moss's (2001) study of a multi-agency network of childcare services, express uncertainties about how far such multi-agency projects are meeting their aspirations and are capable of producing the desired benefits for children and their families. Further, Glissen and Hemmelgarn (1998) found that focusing on inter-agency coordination was likely to have less benefit in terms of outcomes for children than improving the organizational climate within agencies. Gardner (2003: 156) sums up the current position:

> While the vision and rationale for joint work between specialist groups are powerful, there is as yet insufficient evidence to argue that greater collaboration between services will necessarily produce better outcomes for all children and families.

This has led researchers such as Allnock *et al.* (2006: 36) to see the future as being 'to design and commission research that is capable of addressing both process *and* impact in the context of these increasingly complex multi-agency systems'.

Starting with the child and family's perspective

What happens if these uncertainties about multi-agency working are considered in the context of the contemporary experience of children and families? Sidebotham and Weeks (2010: 80) assert that 'children are complex social actors living in complex social worlds'. Layard and Dunn (2009) suggest that the current generation of UK children are generally facing a more difficult world than previous generations, despite the apparent overall improvement in prosperity. In their inquiry into contemporary childhood, they identify some of the multiple factors contributing to the complexity of the world children need to negotiate.

For example, there are major changes and transitions in family circumstances so that 'by 16 years old one in eight children has been through parental separation and is living with a "new" parent', and '20 per cent of children are currently living with a single parent' (Dunn 2008: 7). Many children also experience adversity in their homes, schools and neighbourhoods, such as substance misuse, mental illness and domestic violence within families; school pressures and bullying; and living in poverty and growing up in poor and rundown communities. In a UNICEF (2007) overview of child well-being, UK children, compared with a number of measures with children in twenty-one of the world's richest countries, had the lowest overall ranking.

All four nations of the UK have expressed their commitment to improving outcomes for children and ensuring priority is given to children's well-being in preparation for adult life. It is acknowledged that if improvement is to include all children and young people, special attention has to be given to helping those children who, for whatever reason, are likely to experience difficulties in doing well (DfES 2004a, b). This requires policies and structural building blocks that will help children flourish. For individual children and families policies aim for early identification of difficulties or concerns, before children reach crisis points, to protect them from 'slipping through the net'. Appropriate, proportionate and timely help should be offered so that all children can have the best possible start in life (DfES 2004a, b; Scottish Government 2008a).

The expectation is that this help is offered through improved inter-professional working, accountability across the public, private and voluntary sectors and through integrated service delivery. There is a strong political agenda behind the emphasis on inter-professional working and integrated service delivery (Allnock *et al.* 2006; Anning* *et al.* 2006) and also a powerful rationale for inter-professional working, grounded in theory and knowledge about how children develop. A developmental–ecological perspective emphasizes how a complex interplay of inner and outer world factors influences a child's development, including genetic, physical, psychological and family influences, as well as successively larger and more complex social groupings of friends, neighbourhood and cultural influences (Rose 2010).

If children are beginning to experience difficulties in one or more aspect of their well-being, they are likely to have contact with universal health and/or education services which may be able to provide them or their families with the additional help they need. Some children, though, are very vulnerable and have serious and complex circumstances which may require a range of targeted and/or specialist help from several different agencies at the same time. Their parents or carers may also be experiencing their own difficulties which may have an impact on their capacity to meet their children's needs and may need help in their own right from one or more adult services (Cleaver *et al.* 2007). This means that the number of agencies involved with a family may increase very quickly. In these complex situations, social workers have a distinctive contribution to bring to multi-agency work, through their knowledge and skills, in coordinating assessment, planning and intervention with children and families, and reviewing how well children are doing:

> What social workers do inevitably overlaps with what other workers do. This blurring of operational boundaries is a real strength as people's lives cannot be defined within organizational boundaries. Social workers are skilled navigators and coordinators of services across these boundaries.
>
> (Scottish Executive 2006b: 29)

Families' experiences of multiple service providers vary – some report excellent, well-coordinated help, while others talk about a fragmented and unpredictable set of services, multiple assessments according to each agency's protocols, duplication or absence of help when it is needed, and their alienation and exclusion from the process of developing and managing a plan of services to help them. A frequent concern of families is that agencies appear to be working independently of each other, without sharing information and communicating with each other, in what has come to be termed as *working in silos* (Marchant and Jones 2000). Perhaps the clearest message from children and families is that working together means working in partnership with them and not just improved working between practitioners of different agencies (Gardner 2003).

Succeeding in multi-agency practice

Starting with the experience of children and families, acknowledging the complex world in which children are growing up and keeping children at the centre of professional practice provides the foundation for multi-agency work. Thus it does not become an end in itself, but is an essential part of helping all children. It requires a shared understanding between professionals about the purpose and objectives of their joint involvement, and an agreed framework to guide how they will work together (Scottish Government 2008a).

Gardner (2003: 157) suggests, from her review of research and practice, four critical factors which can help to overcome some difficulties in providing effective multi-agency practice:

1 Commitment and leadership in each organization.
2 Good communication *within* as well as between collaborating agencies.
3 Consultation, training, planning and reflection time.
4 An infrastructure to deliver these key elements of support.

These four factors probably need to coexist as part of a developing strategy for multi-agency practice. For instance, even if there is strong leadership and high-level commitment to collaborative working, it does not necessarily guarantee effective translation into practice. It requires the vision and objectives for multi-agency collaboration to be clearly communicated and understood at strategic and operational levels of all the agencies involved (Stradling *et al.* 2009).

Hudson (2002: 7) also warns against reliance solely on the development of an infrastructure as the answer:

> To some extent, the assumption seems to be that if interagency partnership policies, processes and structures are established, then frontline partnerships between a range of traditionally separate professions will fall into place.

Furthermore, developing an appropriate infrastructure for multi-agency work has sometimes been interpreted as restructuring or bringing services together under one roof. However, Baginsky (2008) and others argue that the task is more about putting building blocks in place to support effective joint working and that the emphasis on continued restructuring is misplaced.

Baginsky (2008: 183) concludes:

> Delivering improved services depends on how policies are *implemented* rather than just how they are *structured*. Integrated services require shared vision, a commitment to learn from each other, willingness to compromise and a clear focus on what those using the service need.
>
> (emphasis added)

A rush to restructure without really addressing some of the underlying issues will not work. Perhaps most importantly, research suggests that the development and transmission of a shared culture and values, supported by middle management, within each organization is critically important (Glissen and Hemmelgarn 1998). Middle managers can have a pivotal role in mediating and sustaining the organizations' aims and approach in frontline practice (Rose *et al.* 2007). The importance of shared culture, values, language and systems is illustrated by Stradling and colleagues in their evaluation of a whole system's change in a Scottish Local Authority. Even at an early stage, families are able to report:

> They are now more aware of when things are happening and what the processes are likely to involve. They are kept better informed. Families know they have access to someone with a clearly identified lead role who is responsible for their plan and there is emerging evidence that this is appreciated.
>
> (Stradling *et al.* 2009: 60–1)

Finally and not least, Hudson provides a salutary reminder that inter-agency work is about human relationships and cannot be reduced to mechanistic or electronic communication. He suggests the development of trust between practitioners from different agencies is essential to collaborative success, as 'inter-organizational relationships are largely built upon *human* relationships' (2000: 254).

Conclusions and reflections

Nearly fifty years ago, Stevenson commented in a talk to former social work students that 'some of us have been feeling recently that this topic of coordination and cooperation in social work has become a little stale' (1963: 208). She also acknowledged the very real difficulties by examining in detail 'a fairly commonplace example with no outstandingly unusual features' which demonstrated why multi-agency cooperation is essential to working with families in need 'whom we so often fail through our clouded perception of the processes in which we are involved' (1963: 212).

With the contemporary policy emphasis on the importance of multi-agency work in delivering improved outcomes for children and families, and the practical challenges to achieving this encountered by frontline professionals, it is as relevant today to remind ourselves of the wider objectives of services for children and families in need. There are sound reasons for joint working between professionals, grounded in theory and knowledge, and children and families have said they find this helpful, even in the most difficult circumstances, such as allegations of abuse and maltreatment. However, effective multi-agency work is difficult to achieve – the obstacles are well identified and, understandably, this leads to a sceptical if not pessimistic view about some aspects of the current policy rhetoric.

It has been argued here that, by starting with children and families at the centre of our concerns and by building culture, systems and practice around the child, based on a common set of values and principles shared by all agencies, it is possible to find signs of more efficient and effective working and positive benefit to children and their families. Research evidence is still not robust about the benefits of joint working for children and families, but when carried out within a whole systems approach there is room for optimism, and some 'green shoots' of progress are being identified in evaluative studies (Stradling *et al.* 2009).

Gardner (2003: 140) is among those who are prepared to take a more optimistic view, concluding that 'in spite of acknowledged problems, joint working does have the potential to provide positive outcomes in services for children and families'. Since the rationale for multi-agency working which emerges from a child-centred approach is, to use McLean's phrase (2007: 342), so compelling, the challenge is 'how to maximize the likelihood of success in this endeavour'.

Helpful literature is available to practitioners. Anning *et al.* (2006) discuss the dilemmas common to multi-professional teamwork and suggest ways forward. Horwath (2009b) and Sidebotham and Weeks (2010) provide key pointers for multi-agency working in the context of safeguarding practice and of assessing children in need. Horwath (2009a: 131–2) provides some practical questions to assist practitioners who are working together to meet the needs of children. This work shows how some of the acknowledged barriers to the process of inter-professional working outlined in this chapter can be overcome and progress made in a complex and changing world.

Questions for reflection

What issues has this chapter raised for you in relation to your own practice and experience?

What do you need to do to achieve better collaborative practice in your agency?

2 Policy swings and roundabouts

Social work in shifting social and economic contexts

Ian Buchanan

> The discussions on user involvement and emancipation remind us that despite the uncertainty, the profession continues to strive for the rights of marginalized citizens whilst being true to the 'old' values of service-user emancipation.
>
> (Social worker – Referral and Assessment Team)

Context – policy and practice in response to risk and uncertainty

The uncertainty that the social work profession faces in the early twenty-first century is entirely typical of its development. The profession has a long lineage but its modern reincarnation came with the creation of local authority social services departments. The new departments were recommended by the Seebohm Report (1968) and the enactment of the Social Services Act (1970) brought training and a recognized national qualification for social workers. This final piece of legislation associated with the reforms of the 1960s saw social work emerge as a profession, in a way consistent with the social concerns of the time. More than any other profession, social work sets out to address what Mills (1970: 14–15) refers to as 'personal troubles and public issues'. Social work is an expression of the belief that some personal troubles can only be addressed adequately when seen in the widest social context as public issues. Changes in policy may appear to be the source of uncertainty but policy and practice, although often apparently developing separately, are subject to the same influences.

Some of the economic, political and social challenges that face social workers and social care agencies in the twenty-first century first became evident in the newly enhanced profession's formative years. Post-Seebohm euphoria was barely over when Britain entered an economic recession brought on by the 'oil crisis' of 1973–4 and ambitions for personal social services were curtailed by severe cuts in public expenditure. Policy critiques of the post-war welfare settlement emerged before the new profession had found its feet. These came from across the ideological spectrum drawing on the rediscovery of poverty and the subsequent realization of its intractability and the climate of economic uncertainty (Klein 1993). Moreover, before social work could tackle the impact of *Cathy Come Home* (an influential television documentary that drew the plight of homeless families to public attention) and the reaction to the troubled, complex, vulnerable lives that it showed, it was confronted by another source of contention, the emergence of child abuse and child death (manslaughter and murder) into the public arena (Howitt 1992). The publication of the report on Maria Caldwell's death in 1973, while she was under the care and supervision of a social services department, came to have a sustained and growing impact on public policy and social work practice. The death of Maria Caldwell was among the first of a series of 'crises', not all related to childcare (Butler and Drakeford 2003), that raised questions about policy and progressively brought social work practice under the continuous public scrutiny, which led to professional self-doubt.

The familiarity of recession, political scrutiny, public concern and self-questioning to present-day social workers is misleading. Enduring issues do not signify an unchanged or unchanging world. The spirit of the age (*Zeitgeist*) in the twenty-first century differs from that of the 1970s. It is that of an ever-changing world, understood in very different ways; in relation to globalization, consumerism, individuation and rights. The ambiguities that are engendered in this 'runaway world' (Giddens 2002) complicate both the making of policy and social intervention, including social work. One reaction to this challenge is the pursuit of radical alternatives to 'reclaim' social work (Ferguson 2008b). While the radical tradition has been influential in relation to ideas, it has been less so in relation to practice and professional development (Powell 2001). Policy and practice are both bedevilled by prevailing uncertainty. Social workers are faced with intractable public expectations in relation to complex, value-laden issues and pressure to respond. This is not an entirely rational process and the outcomes are often contested and judged. Accordingly, this chapter attempts to shape a critical focus on policy as it develops alongside societal change and its implications for present and future professional development and practice.

Runaway change and the uncertainty that it engenders is associated with the 'risk society' and as an important factor in the reconfiguration of the post-war welfare state it has been of significance in social work (Beck 1992; Giddens 2002). Rapid change and the uncertainty and complexity that it produces expose risk, making risk a preoccupation of individuals. The impossibility of dealing adequately with such risk has called expertise into question by fragmenting and democratizing sources of action. People demand action from government but no longer rely on it, which legitimizes the distrust of government and its agencies, including social care agencies and the social work profession. Faced with irreconcilable demands, government has resorted to the expansion of accountability systems in order to be seen to act. Kemshall* (2002), therefore, refers to the shift of social work practice away from welfare towards risk. The change has been produced by the proliferation of managerialist rule systems, a defensive action with the primary aim of protecting government welfare agencies and their agents, including social workers. Recourse to bureaucratic systems associated with Weberian modernist sociology is an interesting and apparently contradictory response by welfare systems to a global world that is characterized by rapid change and flexible structures (Webb* 2006). The contradiction stems from government's need to be accountable and be seen to act and take or fix responsibility. In an uncertain and rapidly changing world, reducing risk implies implementing prevention strategies and what has been termed 'responsibilization' (Rose 1996). Enabling practice is, to some extent, a product of this shift in welfare agencies from solving to managing problems with consent or in partnership.

Social work practice in the runaway world

While policy swings and roundabouts concern problems that are recognizable from the early days of the modern profession, we can see that the situation that the profession now finds itself in is much changed and new approaches have developed. This is clearest in childcare. Child abuse brought forth protection and safeguarding systems that have signally failed to predict or to prevent. The inquiry into the murder of Victoria Climbié provided the stimulus for a reconfiguration of children's services in England (Cm 3760 2003). The government's response, the Green Paper *Every Child Matters* (DfES 2004a) and its post-consultation document *Every Child Matters: Next Steps* (DfES 2004b) led to the passing of the Children Act 2004. The new law instigated a concerted attempt to gain control over children's welfare that shifted the emphasis of policy beyond the traditional welfare/protection debate. National and local governmental systems were brought into alignment through the creation of the Department for Children Schools and Families with responsibility for virtually all children's policy and services (notably education and children's social care).

The threshold for preventive intervention became 'any cause for concern' under the 1989 Children Act, a much broader category than 'a child in need', and the most significant challenge to the traditional view of the family as part of the private as opposed to governmental spheres when there are no special circumstances. Information holding and exchange is at a premium in the new regime and perhaps the best illustration of the scope and extent of the changes is the *Integrated Children's System*, a national database combining records from across all public services on every child in the country. While there are civil libertarian objections to the level and extent of surveillance, Parton (2006: 187) raises doubts over the practicalities of what he terms 'the Preventive State', fearing that 'the intensity of the government of childhood' may fail to make children safer or emancipate them. At the very least there must be concern that a universal system may lead to a loss of focus on the greatest risk.

The culmination of fourty years of high-profile abuse cases and the attendant attention is an inauspicious foundation for a discussion of the profession's practices as contributions to improvements in the lives of many other vulnerable individuals and families. The preoccupation with risk and its elimination in the collective thinking which crystallizes in the determination that similar tragedies 'must never happen again', reinforces the association of child murder with the failure of social work in the public mind. However, that part of the policy agenda is not the whole story. Social work retains its overarching purpose of addressing 'personal troubles' and 'public issues'. The association of the risk society or the 'runaway world' only with risk averse practice is, it can be argued, wrong. It is also associated with uncertainty, opportunity and the possibility of transformative change (Giddens 2002). Confronting demands that are not easy to reconcile in the face of uncertainty has not been confined to the proliferation of managerialist rule systems in social work and social care agencies. Significant change has resulted from commitment to engagement in partnership working with other professionals and service users and carers that represent an important and continuing development that parallels an increasing emphasis on reflexive practice and knowledge-based practice.

The extent of the changes is apparent when comparing the Barclay report, an early enquiry to establish the profession's role and tasks, with the General Social Care Council's (GSCC) recent similar project. Barclay's advocacy of both community and neighbourhood approaches has been superseded by the importance the GSCC gives to the service user voice (Barclay 1982; GSCC 2002a). This a product of consumerism and rights coming to prominence in parallel in the 1990s, cemented in the National Health Service and Community Care Act (1989) (NHS and CC Act) and the Children Act (1990). The stimulus to listen to and engage in different ways with service users and carers was acted on quickly in adult and child social care. In adult care it was first established in drawing up community care plans and widely used later in systematic engagement between agencies, professionals and service users. Similarly, the Children Act was drafted with a view to children's rights to protection, to education and to participation which were codified in parallel in the United Nations Convention on the Rights of the Child (UNCRC 1989). The rights agenda is also codified in social work codes of ethics and practice nationally and internationally (BASW 2002; GSCC 2002a; IFSW 2002).

There is contention about social workers involving service users in their practice. Sheppard (2006) argues against emancipatory or politicized social work practice. He does not dispute that participation in a political struggle, as some service users do, may have personal benefits. However, he does not believe that this is the function of social workers in their relations with individual service users. He contends that realistic objectives for social workers in relation to service users are to help them cope in their lives or maintain a family's viability. These are tenable objectives in work with chaotic and troubled individuals and families that are not incompatible with a rights agenda or consumerism. Service user involvement remains important despite Sheppard's criticism of emancipation because enabling practice, helping people to control their own lives as far as possible, cannot be achieved without the active involvement of the individual or family. The argument holds even in statutory work where individual liberty is sometimes removed to protect the individual, family members or the public.

Policy futures and social work practice

The post-Climbié reforms have been partially overtaken by a subsequent harrowing murder of a child under the protection of the same local authority, Haringey. The 'Baby P' case (Ahmed 2009) has resulted in a review aimed at prescribing a 'comprehensive reform programme' with implications for training and professional development for the profession (DCSF 2009b). These are worrying times for social work, increasing the already severe scrutiny that it is under. The unprecedented sight of the Prime Minister and the Leader of the Opposition crossing swords in the House of Commons over the 'Baby P' case may have been the product of electoral politics, but it was also an indication of how far the political stakes have been raised. Furthermore, in the midst of the greatest economic recession for almost eighty years and the prospect of sustained cuts in public spending, resources to back reform are unlikely to be generous. It seems certain that health care will continue to be a greater public spending priority than social care for both adults and children.

Social work is also faced with significant challenges in adult care where the personalization agenda and individual budgets signal changes in practice. The individual choice that is central to personalization appears likely to move responsibility for the purchasing (micro-commissioning) of service packages that has been the mainstay of care management to service users. At the same time, but not coincidentally, adult safeguarding has been introduced. Personalization is a response to criticism of care management's ability to meet individual choice and it may be regarded both as a further step towards fuller lives for adult care service users, a widely accepted policy objective since the NHS and CC Act (1989), and as a policy response that 'responsibilizes' service users. Community care reform is an exemplar of the shift from need to risk that Kemshall (2002) has identified as part of the responsibilization of welfare. Risk and eligibility is mainly a concern of agencies in managing problems that they have difficulty in solving with scarce resources, whereas social work's concern remains with the 'personal troubles' in complex relationships found in disorganized and chaotic lives that constitute 'issues' and the associated social work values that still underpin the profession. The social care agencies that employ social workers have a focus on risk and, while risk (to and from service users) and vulnerability are very important to social workers, social work's future in an uncertain runaway world also depends on its values and in maintaining its purpose of working with those least advantaged in society on the basis of principles of social justice.

Social work's continuing concern with the least advantaged in society is shaped by society's attitudes to disadvantage. With their overriding concern with the control and reduction of public expenditure, the Thatcher government of the 1980s shifted the approach to public issues in ways that can be partly understood in terms of later accounts of the runaway world and individual opportunity and responsibility. Poverty was recast as a problem that is not amenable to redistribution of income and services were transformed to deal with personal troubles through support for individuals and families to help themselves. The enabling state giving opportunity and actively pursuing equality of access rather than equality of outcome is now the conventional wisdom. However, the ideas of the 1980s were often articulated as part of an exclusive social analysis. Poverty was reconceptualized in terms of cycles of deprivation and the (re)emergence of an underclass, rather than as a product of structural disadvantage. An underclass gives a particular coherence to social problems because its existence implies the perpetuation of deviance and disadvantage located within failed or failing families across generations (Mann 1992). The high unemployment among a generation of young people in the early 1980s became a significant public issue which has seen the widespread association of youth with danger and deviance.

Such an analysis poses a significant challenge to social work values which are predicated on the possibility of change in the lives of individuals and families. However, the idea of the underclass and the demonization that is associated with it retreated in the face of a decade and a half of unbroken economic growth after 1992 which brought prosperity that transformed these public issues through the inclusion agenda. The end of this prosperity in a severe recession that is likely to have repercussions lasting into the foreseeable future will challenge social workers in their dealings with their service users (predominantly the poorest in society) in what seems set to be a climate of hardening social attitudes to deviance with reduced resources to pursue inclusion.

Values are on the England Task Force's agenda. The review is led from within the profession and emphasizes that 'the strong moral purpose of social work remains'. It 'sees social work as one profession' and 'wants ... [it] ... to become more confident and more effective where it counts: on the front line' (DCSF 2009b: 4). However, its primary task is externally driven and quite clear, 'keeping the children in our most troubled families out of harm'. This is the political and societal priority and the review is concerned that 'The core functions of social work have become unclear in the minds of some and reduced to simple enforcement in others' (DCSF 2009b: 3). For Webb (2006), values (within rather than as an alternative to professional change) are also the crucial issue in and for the future of social work in the policy context of the times. The importance of values means that the engagement of social work with a much changed policy context may still be a question of swings and roundabouts, within which individual practitioners will need to negotiate their particular position for action.

Questions for reflection

What is the balance in your practice between welfare and concerns about risk?

Given the law and policy which guides your practice, what space and/or managerial support do you have for negotiating that balance?

3 Criticality and reflexivity

Best practice in uncertain environments

Barry Cooper

This chapter has given me access to theories that assist me to conceptualize and explore the challenges I am experiencing in newly qualified social work practice and has also reminded me that assessments and intervention based upon my best judgement are the best I can do in any given situation.

(Social worker – Adults' Services)

Introduction

Social work operates across those boundaries where public services impact upon private lives. It is a risky business, in changing and uncertain environments, and social workers meet the very different demands of institutions and the needs of individuals who depend upon the services they provide. These two perspectives, institutional and individual, are often conflicting and in recent years efforts to improve confidence in the effectiveness of institutional 'systems' have taken priority over regard to the personal, relationship-based services that traditionally characterized a social work service.

Much energy still focuses on the organizational and systemic structures that support social work and foundational legislative changes continue to modernize, raise standards and increase the quality of social work (Department of Health 1998, 2000b; DCSF 2009b) while raising the profile of service user involvement. The underlying rationale of regulation is to modernize and standardize social work procedures through the increased use of schedules and ICT recording systems, to try and provide a greater consistency of service through threshold criteria and benchmarking and, overall, to increase a service user perspective that aims to rebalance the inherent risks of professional interventions into private lives. On the surface it seems counterproductive, if not positively Canute-like, to argue against attempts to 'modernize' and deliver risk-free certitude and assurance. However, I argue that such an approach cannot be the sole road to success without the necessarily challenging and risky professional social work practices of criticality and reflexivity. It is the central paradox of social work that an acceptance of creative ambiguity offers the only sustainable basis for best professional social work practice in times of uncertainty.

Contexts

To understand why current times are described as 'uncertain', some explanation is required of how the 'grand theories' of modernity and postmodernity are relevant to social work. A detailed explanation is beyond the scope of this chapter, but Parton* (1994, 1996) provides a good introduction. As argued in Chapter 2, social work in the UK is firmly located at the interface between the state and private lives. It is thus concerned with social policy and social welfare and this 'embeddedness' within economic and political spheres of influence and operational contexts is profound enough to lead to arguments that social work 'has virtually no role or identity outside the welfare institutions where it is located' (Yelloly and Henkel 1995: 9). This creates a conflict, as any analysis of social work *as a practice* reveals it to have core characteristics that are distinctly postmodern.

Howe (1996) draws upon Wagner's (1994) prime distinctions of 'liberty' and 'discipline' to identify a key existential consequence of the modernist project. The capability to act upon and shape the world necessarily entails a responsibility for whatever is created. This dilemma is an existential one through experiencing 'the modern condition of freedom and choice on the one hand and responsibility and insecurity on the other' (Howe 1996: 79). Howe argues that the social transformations brought about through the scientific and commercial revolutions of the Enlightenment inevitably worsened the existing problems of poverty. These transformations, in turn, gave rise to dissatisfaction with the realities of the relative impoverishment for large numbers of people. The emergence of the social sciences and a growing welfare state were a response to growing aspirations to address social injustice and inequity. It was a belief of modernity in the nineteenth century that the ability to act upon and transform the physical world could be replicated so that 'solidity and certainty could be re-established into the social fabric' (Wagner 1994: 59). The price of this attempt to create 'solidity and certainty' in the social realm was 'discipline'. Transgressions from the discipline of a social order would result in 'correction' or 'punishment' through social systems, structures and processes made up of institutionalized networks of power (Foucault 1975).

From this perspective in UK social history, social work emerges at the forefront of the drive to create a modernist social order through state action within the social domain. However, the social realm is characterized by ambiguity and power. The power potential of social work's position emanates from its emergence as the profession where the state penetrates the world of private relationships. Its locus of application is the social (Donzelot 1988) between private and public. Individual acts of social work intervention are carried out within a complex and detailed nexus of legislative duties and obligations. Social workers operating within this field carry enormous potential power through an authority which is not clear cut. The social field is one of great indeterminacy. Publicly sanctioned interventions into private and interpersonal arenas require the professional social worker to both judge the actions of others through an implicit or explicit assessment *and* to seek to treat those actions. As Howe (1996: 81) puts it in his analysis of social work's role:

> Social work formed under the double perspective of control and cure, as it embraced both the judicial and the therapeutic in single acts of intervention.

This juxtaposition of potent yet potentially conflicting professional mandates creates a core ambiguity of purpose and activity. The only way that these elemental ambiguities can be productively worked with is through practices that are both critical and reflexive. Criticality and reflexivity are the core contributions of professional social workers and these complex concepts and activities are explored in the next section.

Contributions

'Critical practice' and the academic notion of 'criticality' are common requirements for social work students and newly qualified practitioners engaged in post-qualification studies. In the pressured and frequently uncomfortable professional contexts of rapid change and uncertainty, social workers have to be secure in not knowing all the answers (Glaister 2008), but nonetheless feel confident in having the skills to initiate and follow through with enquiries into challenging situations and to construct assessments to help resolve doubt and ambiguity. Lord Laming, in the Victoria Climbié Inquiry (Cm 5730 2003: 205), describes this approach of mindful enquiry as 'respectful uncertainty'. This approach to practice critically examines situations and keeps them under constant re-evaluation in recognition of changing circumstances and the dynamic nature of social work knowledge. However, as this and other inquiries have repeatedly identified, the basic tasks of social welfare work should be done, and much of the time when things go wrong, they have not been done. So, the basic competences of communication and recording within complex multi-agency systems are also necessary building blocks but not sufficient alone. Individual critical judgements and reflexive attention to self, others and feelings arising from interactions are the vital professional architecture that has to be constructed upon basic foundations.

A critical approach to practice does not accept situations at face level or take things for granted. A critical practitioner questions the assumptions that underpin 'the way things are' and, if necessary, 'problematizes' the given or received wisdom about situations. Underlying this approach is an understanding that social work is essentially about power and that interventions into others' lives is an intervention into networks of power relationships. It is the structures of power and powerlessness that produce both the problems and the potential solutions. However, a definition of what is the problem is itself recognized as essentially problematic in social work. The people involved, workers as well as service users, each have different perspectives upon situations and a consensus about what the problem is, or even whether there is a problem at all, has to be explored and negotiated to reach agreement. Similarly, any potential solution to identified problems must be negotiated and agreed in partnership with those affected in order to include people in plans and, if possible, avoid imposing upon them. Social work is about the judicious and ethical use of power and authority and the accompanying professional responsibilities.

This use of power and authority and the contributions of skilled social work as best practice is set out and discussed in Jones *et al.* (2008). Cooper (2008a, b) illustrates and extensively analyses the critical and reflexive power plays of social work interviewing. In Cooper's two chapters a best-practice analysis reveals how a skilled social worker balances the competing demands of personal challenge, multi-agency child protection and risk assessment, while maintaining the basis for a constructive, working relationship. These are the highly skilled workings of reflexive practice in action. Critical reflection helps to highlight the dynamic processes that link individual practitioners with their initiation of interventions and the monitoring and development of the ensuing and evolving practices. The following shows a newly qualified practitioner reflecting upon these complexities and changes in their practice:

> I know that I'm drawing on different theories, and I'm drawing on different approaches – I'm seeing a difference. Or sometimes I'm not – and then I'm thinking right, okay that didn't work – I need to go back to the drawing board here, [...] I would never have thought of that three years ago.
>
> (Cooper and Nix 2009)

These core social work insights into the fluid and contestable nature of defining social problems and possible solutions highlight the central paradox of social work identified in the introduction to this chapter. Parton (2007: 145) describes this as a 'major conundrum':

> For while the world has taken on many of the characteristics associated with postmodernity in terms of its complexity, fluidity, and uncertainty, mainstream policy and practice has responded in even more modernist and rationalist ways.

Social work practitioners continually confront this quandary in their attempts to meet the espoused professional values of responsive, personalized, relationship-based service provision within growing and prescriptive systems of audit, accountability and risk management that are becoming more standardized and demanding of their time. The increased systemization through information and communication technology, ushered in by the Department of Health (1998), has led to a situation where social workers arguably spend more time at their desks inputting into systems for recording than they do in face-to-face interaction with people who use services. This profound change in the balance of tasks undertaken by professionally qualified social workers has a pervasive impact upon how the profession is becoming understood by managers and practitioners. What, then, are the capabilities needed by practitioners on this frontline between system demands and professional values, and how does reflexivity help?

Capabilities

The capabilities of reflexive social workers are captured through an ability to demonstrate expertise in action. O'Reilly *et al.* (1999: 1) describe the flexibility needed as

> helping people develop as capable practitioners equal to the challenges of fluid environments and unpredictable change, taking responsibility for their careers and their learning, and able to exercise the kind of practical judgement and systemic wisdom needed for a sustainable future.

The capability approach assumes that professional practices are initiated and enacted by individual people, as part of social relationships, within complex situated environments. It is a critical and reflexive attitude that regards continuing professional development as an opportunity for lifelong learning, challenge and growth (Cooper* 2008c). On the surface there is no argument that the nature of social work is such that communication and engagement, through relationships with individuals and their families in the uniqueness of their cultures and communities, is the means through which the work happens. However, this definition of social work is now under threat. The requirements of ICT-driven systems make growing demands upon practitioners' time. Further, White *et al.* (2009) suggest that the pervasive nature of ICT systems (e.g. *Common Assessment Framework*, DfES 2007) insidiously attempts to standardize children's social work services, and by shaping the epistemology of professional judgements can 'be seen to reconfigure professional practice in quite profound ways'. In recognition of this very modern dilemma, I argue for the value of re-introducing diversity into the systems of social work through personal, interpersonal and consciously self-aware reflexivity. It is no quick or easy solution as social work is difficult and challenging and, as a concept, reflexivity mirrors this complexity. Nonetheless, at its essence, reflexivity is about self-awareness, the conscious awareness of one's self as the overriding 'tool' in working with others through relationships.

Taylor (2006: 74) describes reflexivity as a 'slippery' term. One reason is that it focuses attention upon the processes which we ordinarily choose to ignore for the sake of convenience. In social work, we have a professional duty to override this habitual way of filtering out complexity. Howe (2009: 171) neatly describes the basic processes of reflexivity as

> the interesting realization that as we observe and engage with other people, we affect them, and as they are affected by us, in turn they affect us, and so on in an evolving dynamic of interpersonal transactions.

Awareness of these everyday processes helps us towards a better understanding of the philosophical issues at the heart of the postmodernity debate. The concept of reflexivity captures how, as ordinary individuals and as professional practitioners, we do not just participate in an objective world. Rather, because we cause and initiate actions as well as responding to others, we actually *create* our views of ourselves and others in our different subjective and intersubjective guises and identities. Therefore reflexivity is essentially a constructivist concept, showing that who we are and what we bring to our interactions influences what we see in others and our understanding of both ourselves and of others. On this analysis, the relevance for social work couldn't be greater. Reflexivity is about reciprocal interaction. It is what we do all the time in our everyday lives. In an earlier paper (Cooper 2001) I described it as 'participative practice' and argued for a constructivist approach as a viable basis for practice and continuing professional development in social work.

A focus upon the individual's perspective as part of the constructive discourse has been strangely underplayed in social work and a fuller understanding allows a constructive approach to become a conducive one (Cooper and Broadfoot 2006). A constructivist approach is conducive insofar as it foregrounds the creative capacity of the people involved in the interaction. A conducive assessment process in social work, for example, acknowledges the psychological dimensions through which social interactions have to be negotiated. This interpersonal assumption of different individual perceptions, of a foundational individuality, demands engagement in a relationship in order that the assessment can be ethical, empowering and participative. A conducive assessment is thus both empowering of individuality whilst recognizing the social and commonality dimensions of an existential intervention into another's life. A conducive professionalism thereby balances the realities of working within an instrumental system alongside a fully reflexive, individualized, communicative approach to practice. These are taxing demands of the highest order and government conceptions of social work have rarely reflected its complexities or its pivotal public policy position.

As argued earlier, social work operates on the boundaries of social field ambiguities and as such is, or should be, the postmodern profession par excellence. Barnett (1997: 143) makes the conducive case when he outlines the complexities and asserts that a

> [Post]modern professional faces the challenge of the management of incoherence. The self is the crucial and underplayed aspect of this as the professional needs to engage in a continuing process of 'ontological reconstruction' to define, defend and redefine the professional self within a professional peer culture and professional selves within multiple discourse.

It is the critical and reflexive 'self' in professional social work that requires rehabilitation not just to 'manage incoherence' but to actively co-construct coherence with others.

Conclusion

The critical practitioner in social work understands that proficiency in the core tasks of practice is a necessary foundation for competent practice. However, 'modernization' that attempts to standardize and systematize the uncertainties and risks of interventions into people's lives cannot be an acceptable approach for social work. I have argued that this cannot be 'best practice' or sufficient to sustain social work as a profession. The sine qua non of professional practice necessitates criticality and reflexivity. The paradox of social work is that uncertain times require a stance of creative ambiguity. Questioning, reflecting, re-evaluating and living with the contingencies of professional assessments are the core of social work practice. The only certainty entails being sure of your best judgement in particular situations at particular moments in time and with the fully considered evidence of incomplete knowledge so that you can defend and justify your assessments, plans and interventions. It is the best that you can do.

Questions for reflection

What makes critical and reflexive practice a solution to the dilemmas of change and complexity in twenty-first century social work practice?

What particular dilemmas in your setting does the approach apply to and how?

4 Reflections on values and ethics in social work practice

Mick McCormick and Sandy Fraser

> For me the most useful part of this chapter was the discussion on discursive space, and I need to think about where I can find this space in my busy work schedule.
>
> (Social worker – Community Mental Health Team)

Introduction

Since social work became a unified profession in 1970 (Scotland) and 1971 (England) there have been various attempts through a variety of publications to inject distinctly ethical thinking into social work education and practice. Examples are Bowles* *et al.* (2006) and notably the work of Banks* (1998, 2004, 2006, 2008). Nevertheless, we argue here that there has been a failure to use *ethics* as opposed to 'value-talk' in social work practice (Clark 2000). This chapter will explore some reasons why there has been a failure to engage in ethics and suggest that ethical discussion and argument offer a powerful support to critical social work practice and professional discretion.

For example, if practitioners wish to liberate themselves from being subject to a wide variety of arguably negative organizational trends in their practice environment, such as unnecessary routine, proceduralism and managerialism, then bringing an ethical argument to support their own professional discretion will be helpful. Banks (1995: 139) recognizes this issue when she argues that

> we need to guard against the preoccupation which the bureaucratic approach encourages with the distribution of existing resources, and think about arguing for more resources for service users.

In this next section we discuss three possible broad reasons why ethics has failed to sufficiently penetrate practice environments. These are pragmatic barriers, anti-ethics environments and a poverty of discursive space.

Pragmatic barriers

Moral dilemmas arise when tangible harm will result from any possible choice, and/or where there are differences in values between the service user and the professional and/or between professionals. Yet, the kind of moral or ethical debate that might be helpful to resolve these can be crowded out by the day-to-day realities of practice pressure. For example, in the practice window between the Laming report on the death of Victoria Climbié (Cm 5730 2003) and the case of 'Baby P' (Ahmed 2009) a social worker in Haringey who spoke out about what she considered to be poor practice, in the interests of 'doing right' for a family of children came into conflict with the council.

'Doing right' in this case was what she and other practitioners wished to achieve in their practice, yet standing out resulted in disciplinary procedures (Bingham 2008). It is noticeable that political and inter-agency wrangling obscured the primary task of ensuring child welfare.

We argue that that it would be unusual to find a practitioner applying a moral philosophy to practice dilemmas to underpin their view of 'doing right' and that there are a number of non-ethical methods of dealing with dilemmas and moral problems which avoid ethical thinking. Typically this will result in postponing and/or collectivizing a decision. Action concerning a dilemma then becomes refocused on how to progress decision making while the practitioner has not discerned the 'right' thing to do in the circumstances. There is nothing necessarily entirely *un*ethical about engaging in such practices, but they are not the result of direct ethical thinking by practitioner or managers – and there may be times when the unthinking following of custom/procedure will lead to poor practice and mistakes.

This pragmatic and current context for bureaucratic process in social work delivery often creates a barrier to the ethical exploration that arguably underpins best practice (Prynn 2008).

Anti-ethics environments

Ethics can be described as a way to think about and analyse what our values are (Eby and Gallagher* 2008). Traditionally this activity was called moral philosophy and it was often tied to religion. Generally speaking religion no longer has the status of 'think-tank' for our society, although a range of faith-based ethical positions are held by many practitioners which they may conscientiously wrestle with in practice (Adams 2008). Ethics, however, cannot disassociate itself from all of the traditional concerns that moral philosophy has highlighted over thousands of years.

Despite modern conditions, some of the moral choices that we face today could easily have been faced by Aristotle – whether it is right or wrong to tell a lie for good intentions is not a particularly new question. There is a long history of moral philosophy which can be drawn upon to help with current concerns and dilemmas. For example, Banks (1995: 9) argues that much of social work 'involves making moral decisions or judgements'.

Despite the age-old nature of ethical questions, we are doubtful if social work practice has really embraced ethical knowledge in any deep or sustained way and a combination of anti-intellectualism and the prominence of politically-based values have marginalized ethical thought. Additionally, there has been a pervasive anti-intellectual strand in social work – the idea that caring is 'commonsense' and that 'theory' has no real place in social work practice (Jones 1996).

Left wing anti-ethics

When social work combined to form a single generic profession it brought together different strands of thought about what social work was – at a time when post-war social democracy was attempting to renew itself. It was a period in which social work was validated both by the 'Old Left' of Harold Wilson and of the 'New Left' of the late 1960s. The 'Old Left' could see social work as a kind of fulfilment of Beveridge's vision and it could also be seen as one of the new ways to 'socially administer' the newly perceived social problems that Beveridge's policies were failing to address. The influence of the 'New Left' suggested that social workers could adopt a radical, challenging stance in relation to the oppressive elements of the establishment (Seed 1973). Left-wing debates and divisions featured attention to new social forces – feminism and anti-racist politics increased their legitimacy and effectiveness. The 1960s preoccupation with the individual *psyche* gave way to preoccupation with the *social* and political.

During the 1970s, traditional left-wing analyses based on class led to wider interpretations of oppression centred on gender, race and disability. This involved debate between opposed brands of left-wing traditionalism on the one hand and of the advocates of gender-based, race-based, sexuality-based political advocates on the other (Gamble 1991). These different political concerns embedded themselves in social work practice during the 1970s and early 1980s. At the same time the consensus that gave rise to professional social work began to unravel. The economic crises of the 1970s led to a crisis of ideas on the political left. The 'Old Left' was seen as ideologically bankrupt and more radical left-wing alternative perspectives found it difficult to achieve any kind of lasting consensus or effective political alliance to effectively challenge the 'New Right'. The inception of professional social work in the 1970s saw the end of social work's organizational fragmentation, but through the course of the 1970s the ideas which had supported its birth were in crisis and splintered in different directions (Prynn 2008).

The crisis of ideas on the political left led to a series of concerns within social work which remain with us today (Davis 2006). Political analyses, not ethical analyses, were used to distinguish ideologically correct ways of thinking and practising social work. Ethics was seen as an associate of individualist rather than collectivist thinking and a concern for politics drove out, or at least diminished, ethical thinking in social work practice until fairly recently.

Right-wing anti-ethics

Thatcherism's primary political goals were not focused on social work but rather with defeating the political power of trade unionism and with that an attack on the ideas which had supported various aspects of the post-war settlement. The values of Thatcherism simply dismissed the 'social' while promoting individual responsibility and a market approach to social care (Thatcher 1987). Business values were brought into social work, edging out and transforming the left-wing agenda of the 1970s and early 1980s. These moves toward managerialism and market in social care tended to marginalize the way ethical thought was valued and were consolidated under New Labour after 1997 (Harris 2003). Here is the logic: if social work agencies can be likened to firms in the marketplace then the same types of organization and culture which are appropriate to businesses can be applied to the business of social care. If that is true then managers can and should apply the same market-oriented values and yet the *value* of, for example, 'the customer is always right' only displaces and avoids the question of what the practitioner thinks is morally right or wrong.

The growth and crisis of ideas that marked social work in the late 1970s also brought forth another reaction in the 1980s which grew in the 1990s and peaked in the early part of this decade – 'evidence-based practice' (Keeping 2008). This developed from a concern that, however, fashionable Feminist or Black Liberationist (for example) ideas were, they were no guarantees that the practice they inspired actually worked, either in their own terms or 'objectively' (Sheldon 1978). This also fitted with an increasing recognition that professional knowledge bases were not an adequate or legitimate basis for practice.

During the latter part of the 1980s and throughout the 1990s the position of the social work 'client' became likened to that of a consumer (Dalrymple and Burke 2006). This was allied to social movements whose origins were in the 1960s and 1970s and which politicized the role of the 'patient' and the 'client'. Users of health and social work services became empowered as 'experts by experience' in a way which challenged professionals who were experts by knowledge base. Evidence-based practice appeared to form a bridge between the perspectives of service users and different types of professional (Keeping 2008). Solid knowledge, as revealed by empirical research concerned with 'what works', was unfavourably contrasted with 'ideology' and 'values'. Evidence-based practice thus promised to yield the 'correct' answers to problems faced in practice. Indeed attention to, and employment of, the results of empirical research about social problems and social work practice is currently embedded into the National Occupational Standards for Social Work (GSCC 2002a).

Poverty of discursive space

Ethical thinking can be seen as a type of 'generative discourse' as described by Parton (2003: 9):

> Generative discourses ... simultaneously challenge existing traditions of understanding and at the same time offer new possibilities for action and change.

This means that individual practitioners as well as agencies have to ask the question: What is the right thing to do? This is different from asking questions like: What is the most *effective and efficient* thing to do? What is the most *anti-racist* thing to do? What is the most *anti-oppressive* thing to do? These questions can be answered in their own terms but it is also reasonable to ask: What makes an effective and efficient course of action ethical? What makes an anti-racist action ethical? What makes an anti-oppressive action ethical?

This is not to suggest that such actions are *un*ethical. What we suggest is that to understand the values which drive efficiency, effectiveness, anti-racism, anti-oppressiveness and so on, attention to the ethics implied by those values ought to be important. What makes any proposed action or practice the morally right thing to do? While empirical evidence may support a morally right practice, it cannot determine its moral status. The systematic investigation of the values that underpin the practice can do this and if social work is to return to values-based practice then it is appropriate for social workers to examine the reasons for their values.

We argue here that ethical thought requires discursive space. Ethical ideas always have to be contextualized and that requires discussion with both service users and peers. So the context in which practice occurs ought to support discursive space for ethical thinking. This is not just a matter of managers and peers being open to and permissive about ethical thinking – it is also a matter of having an adequate ethical language. These two issues can be frustratingly entangled. Ethical thought and language is not new and has gone on in various fields for thousands of years. Real innovation in ethics takes place over time, and certainly more slowly than changes to law and government policy.

We therefore suggest that these kinds of development are consistent with a renaissance of values-based social work. They are also part of a reaction against all forms of practice that avoid justification in terms of what is morally right. Critical social work practice cannot allow anti-intellectualism, legalism, proceduralism, evidence-based practice or particular political enthusiasm to displace the distinctively ethical justification of practice.

Conclusion

Ethical theory draws heavily upon concepts of morality and explanations of how our behaviour affects others, and while some ethical choices appear relatively easy to make, in many cases it is not possible to reach a straightforward decision about whether an action is right or wrong, good or bad. In social work practice, practitioners can often feel under pressure to move quickly from problem to solution and thus have limited time to consider ethical approaches to their practice, as Adams and Payne argue, 'Haste is the enemy of ethical practice' (2009: 87).

But there is a balance to be struck and Fitzpatrick suggests that ethics can provide 'tools and guidance designed to influence a social climate' (2008: 4). As a social work practitioner, you may find that considering ethics and ethical approaches to your practice will help to develop reflective skills (Chapters 3 and 26) which you can use on a daily basis and that will provide you with a framework to enhance your ability to work at your thinking and decision making.

Eby and Gallagher (2008) warn against understanding ethics in a vacuum and encourage practitioners to get together to discuss practice-related ethics. How do you do this in practice? It may be that you negotiate time in your formal supervision sessions (Chapter 24) to consider ethical approaches to your practice. Similarly, you may consider peer group support – either with social work colleagues and/or colleagues from other professions with whom you are working.

Work in a multi-agency team can provide a valuable platform for discussing complex issues which can be considered from a number of different professional perspectives, and it is almost inevitable that some conflict will arise from these different perspectives. Reel and Hutchings (2007) stress how important it is that team members are aware of different ethical approaches to practice and they encourage 'willing participation', involving mutual support, respect and an appreciation of differences in practice, as means to resolve conflict.

Use of professional journals and books which consider values and ethics would be a good place to start. Similarly, Seedhouse (2009b) has developed a 'values exchange' (Chapter 22) which enables practitioners from a range of settings to examine ethical problems and give responses based on ethical decision-making tools. The 'values exchange' tool is designed to help both health and social care professionals in their decision making.

There is no definite answer to the question of what ethical position we should adopt in our day-to-day work, but it is the questions you consider which will see you develop as a critically reflective practitioner.

Questions for reflection

How much time do I spend thinking about ethical approaches and responses in my work?

Where do I go to discuss this – where is my discursive space?

5 A social worker 'in work or outside work'

The benefits and dilemmas of registration

Fran Wiles

This chapter has encouraged me to be consistently and actively mindful of the codes of practice in my everyday work, and use this in supervision to examine my decisions and actions.

(Social worker – Adults' Services)

Introduction

Since 2005 it has been illegal to call yourself a social worker if you are not registered with the care councils. 'Protection of title' is a milestone in the history of the UK's social work profession. In 2003 when registration was launched on a voluntary basis, Alexander, then Head of the Scottish Social Services Council (SSSC) said it 'provides public recognition that workers are committed to, and will be held to meeting, high standards of practice, something that doctors and nurses have enjoyed for years' (Batty 2003). Social work registration departs from existing models of professional *self*-regulation (McInnes and Lawson-Brown 2007) and has the interests of service users at its heart (Department of Health 1998: paragraph 15). Registering with the care council requires a serious commitment to professional standards for each individual entering and remaining in the profession. This chapter explores some dilemmas for registration in England, making comparisons with regulation across the UK, drawing from literature and research.

Why registration?

Modernising Social Services (Department of Health 1998: executive summary) argued that there were 'too many examples of problems and failures in social services. As a result of these, there is very low public confidence in our social services'. In response, the Care Standards Act 2000 introduced measures to build competence and strengthen social workers' accountability to the public. Four nation-specific regulatory bodies, 'care councils', were created, the qualifying diploma was replaced by the degree and in 2005, compulsory registration was introduced.

The key purpose of registration is to protect the rights and well-being of service users. Stevens, an independent disability trainer and consultant (with personal experience of care services) comments that 'Social workers have huge amounts of power over a service user's quality of life and this often ad hoc relationship can be brilliant or a living hell' (Gillen 2008: 16). Significantly, the UK codes of practice were developed in consultation with service users, carers and social work professionals. The codes clarify the standards and values that service users can expect from a social worker. They are also the criteria for raising and investigating complaints about social workers. Breaching the codes can lead to suspension or removal from the register, thus interrupting or ending a social worker's career.

A regulated profession is associated with professionalism, confidence, integrity, trustworthiness and high standards. Importantly, this strengthens the social work voice in legal and multidisciplinary contexts. Regulation also confers a mark of state approval on social work as a valuable occupation (Orme and Rennie 2006). Regulation has its critics however: it can be seen to undermine professional autonomy, suggesting that social workers are untrustworthy, incompetent and require systems to monitor and control them (Banks 2004). Also, there is no universal agreement about what constitutes 'professional suitability': which creates dilemmas in deciding who should be excluded from the social care register.

Measuring professional suitability

When deciding on a person's suitability to join (or remain on) the social care register, care councils consider information about their character and conduct. However, the definition of *mis*conduct is open to interpretation. In Scotland it is explicitly defined in relation to the codes of practice (SSSC 2009), yet although these set out the standards expected in the workplace they do not specifically define misconduct in a broader sense. In the rest of the UK the conduct rules merely state that '*Misconduct* means conduct which calls into question the suitability of a Registrant to remain on the Register' (GSCC 2003: 6).

However, the absence of a precise definition is because the care council

> has adopted a largely principles-based conduct scheme rather than a more prescriptive rules-based scheme ... Principles-based schemes have their benefits but the greater their role in a regulatory scheme, the more difficult it is to predict its application.
>
> (Hayes 2008: 19)

In practice, 'case law' is developing from the deliberations of bodies such as the Care Standards Tribunal (CST) which rules on appeals against care council decisions in England and Wales. An early tribunal concluded that misconduct is 'about lack of integrity and how an individual is perceived by others' (CST 2006: 3 in McLaughlin 2007a: 250). Subsequently, 'integrity', in the sense of possessing openness and honest intentions, has continued to be important in determining whether a social worker's actions are considered to be misconduct (Wiles 2009).

Likewise, 'any action which undermines trust must call into question the suitability of an individual to work in social care services' (CST 2006: paragraph 18). However, deciding what kind of behaviour would jeopardize service users' trust in their social worker may not be straightforward. Even having a criminal record is not always considered to make someone unsuitable (CST 2007; SSSC 2008c); although serious offences, for example, those involving violence or cruelty, are likely to be carefully scrutinized (GSCC/Joint Universities Council Social Work Education Committee 2007).

The most commonly breached code of practice for social care workers is paragraph 5.8, which tells social workers that they must not 'behave in a way, in work or outside work, which would call into question your suitability to work in social [care] services' (GSCC 2002a; SSSC 2005).

About a third of misconduct allegations in England involve reports of social workers having sexual or other exploitative relationships with service users (GSCC 2008). Failure to maintain appropriate professional boundaries is also 'a recurring issue' in Scotland (SSSC 2008c: 13). Crossing such boundaries clearly contravenes professional and ethical principles (BASW 2002), and a recent survey by *Community Care* (Hayes 2008) confirms that the majority of social workers recognize this kind of conduct as completely unacceptable. However, only 53 per cent of respondents thought that what social workers did in their spare time should be subject to care councils' conduct processes; 25 per cent said it shouldn't, and 15 per cent were undecided. McLaughlin* (2007b: 1269) argues that code 5.8 is a worrying development which

> clearly extends the employer's control into areas hitherto considered outwith their remit. It also places the social worker under the scrutiny of colleagues, service users and members of the public, any of whom can report 'unsuitable' behaviour to the GSCC.

Writing soon after compulsory registration was introduced, Clark* (2006) noted code 5.8's implications for private life and argued that that a social worker's 'moral character' is just as important as their technical skills and adherence to professional principles. He suggests that 'welfare professionals have to be personally committed to values and ways of life that extend well beyond the scope of their contract of employment' (2006: 76). Perhaps, after all, a social worker *should* be the kind of person whose private life stands up to scrutiny.

Some practitioners are uneasy about this blurring of the boundary between private and professional life (CareSpace 2008). What kinds of behaviours are unacceptable? How should we view the social worker who gets drunk on a Saturday night, or who is arrested on a political demonstration? Code 5.8 seems very open-ended, and it raises questions about what it covers and where the lines are being drawn. It also raises concerns about social workers' human rights to a private life.

Human or perfect?

In one of the earliest appeals heard by the Care Standards Tribunal, the panel concluded that

> Working in social care, an individual is working with vulnerable clients ... This places on an individual a responsibility [to] behave appropriately and to be above reproach, to be ... [a] role model and not to let people down is a reasonable expectation of a professional.
>
> (CST 2006: paragraph 18)

High standards are being set here that apply both in and outside work, but are they achievable? Are they even desirable?

The authors explored social work students' perceptions of professional registration in England. A frequently expressed view was that the codes of practice were 'commonsense', embodying the kind of values that should routinely be held by social workers. One participant said

> There are aspects of my personal identity that I hope are in my professional identity in terms of the way I conduct myself with people ... I don't think that would be different in my personal and my professional identity.
>
> (Wiles 2010: 101)

However, students with previous criminal convictions (including those which would normally be considered 'spent') may face particular challenges in demonstrating their suitability for social work. One in five people in the UK have a criminal record – and this rises to one in three for men under thirty (Madoc-Jones *et al.* 2007). It is unsurprising, then, to discover that between 2003 and 2007 around 13 per cent of social workers and students who applied for registration in England declared a criminal conviction, although the majority of these offences were considered to be relatively minor (GSCC 2008: 9). Research suggests that social work students may be more likely than other students to have difficult personal histories, and these experiences may influence their choice of profession (Lafrance and Gray 2004; Sellers and Hunter 2005).

In the author's research, a view was expressed that when things go wrong, practitioners should have the opportunity to redeem their good name and professional status by being open about their mistakes, and seeking to overcome them:

> We're supposed to be a profession that gives everybody a second chance aren't we? Well that's my feeling. And we're human and we make mistakes.
> (Wiles 2008: 39)

Campbell, a disability activist and employer of personal social care assistants (currently not required to be registered), argues that 'Giving people second chances and fresh starts in life is an important part of being a social care employer'. She adds: 'I have employed people who would not have been registered in a million years ... My current driver has special needs, and one of my Personal Assistants has mental health issues' (Brindle 2008). This argues for maintaining some flexibility in assessing professional suitability. On the other hand, the guiding principle of social work regulation is protecting the interests of people who use services: who may be less powerful, less articulate and more vulnerable than those cited here. Their rights should not be compromised by the career needs of individuals.

Care councils' decisions

Although it is difficult to compare statistics across the UK due to differences in reporting, it is clear that to date only a minority of social workers have been suspended or removed from the register. In Scotland, for example, the care council reports that between 1 April 2003 and 31 March 2008, findings of misconduct were made against only 0.02 per cent of those registered (SSSC 2008c). This amounts to one social worker suspended and four removed from the register. During the same period in England, the GSCC registered 109,341 social workers, and subsequently removed or suspended seventeen, with a further sixteen being admonished (GSCC 2008: 17). A similar picture emerges for Wales and Northern Ireland (NISCC 2007; CCW 2008). When it comes to new applicants (including social work students and newly qualified workers) about one per cent were refused entry to the GSCC register between 2003 and 2007 (GSCC 2008: 10).

These low figures send a positive message to the public about the overall integrity of the workforce. At the same time, the GSCC (2008: 7) points out that although the number of social workers removed from the register is small, their 'potential to have an adverse effect on the lives of people who use services is considerable'. Without regulation, therefore, it is likely that some 'unsuitable' social workers would still be in direct contact with service users.

From the care councils' statistics it would seem that, despite real concerns about where the line should be drawn between private life and professional suitability, the fear of being labelled 'unsuitable' may be overstated. On the other hand, a significant number of social workers face a period of uncertainty while their case is examined.

Between 2003 and 2007, about 11 per cent of registration applications in England raised serious concerns (GSCC 2008: 10). Between 2003 and 2008, around 500 complaints against registered social workers were investigated

(2008: 13). Thirty-nine people were temporarily suspended from the register while the case was considered (GSCC 2008: 17).

Research about social work students' experience of the regulatory process (Madoc-Jones *et al.* 2007; Wiles 2010) suggests that undergoing a suitability process can be devastating and undermine a person's confidence. This has been exacerbated by unreasonable delays in the conduct system. Also, the care councils have been criticized for taking an unreasonably lengthy time investigating (Council for Healthcare Regulatory Excellence 2009).

It is not only allegations of misconduct which come under the care council's scrutiny. Serious concerns about competence can also call a social worker's registration into question. This highlights a weakness in the codes of practice – care councils have no jurisdiction over employers. Social workers can be sanctioned for poor practice, whereas incompetent employers cannot. This shortcoming may soon be remedied in England by a recommendation to introduce 'a clear national standard for the support social workers should expect from their employers in order to do their jobs effectively' (DCSF 2009b: 12).

The regulatory requirement to declare health conditions in England and Wales has been controversial. In 2007, a social worker won a disability discrimination case against the GSCC for questioning his trustworthiness in relation to non-disclosure of his HIV status (Lovell 2007). The Disability Rights Commission (2007: 5) has identified the requirement for 'physical and mental fitness' as a potential barrier to entering the social work profession.

Whatever the benefits of registration, both for service users and practitioners, implementation is fraught with dilemmas. The care councils have come in for some criticism, sometimes considered overzealous, sometimes too lenient (Ahmed 2007; Brindle 2007). In England, concerns have also been raised at government level. A review by the Council for Healthcare Regulatory Excellence (2009: 27) concluded that the GSCC's conduct work was 'not effective, efficient or well governed'. Shortly afterwards the Social Work Taskforce (DCSF 2009b: 41, 51) recommended a new 'licence to practise', to be regulated by the GSCC. The regulatory landscape appears to be on the brink of change: but it seems likely that care councils will always steer a challenging course between the expectations of different stakeholders in changing social, political and professional contexts.

Professional implications

This chapter has briefly outlined the development of social work registration, and some of the challenges still to be resolved. So what can social workers draw out for their own professional practice and development? Three messages seem to stand out.

First, it is important that social workers familiarize themselves with the relevant codes of practice and use them to guide their professional relationships with service users and carers. It is also important to understand the implications of breaching the codes, both for the service user and for the practitioner. It is worth heeding the advice of someone who has been through a suitability investigation:

> People should be aware of what they're getting into, and what the expectations are ... of being registered with the [care council] ... I think there's a lot of very experienced social workers who are registered and aren't really sure.
>
> (personal communication to the author 2009)

Second, the concept of integrity is central. While a person's criminal or disciplinary record is not a bar to professional suitability in every case, the qualities of integrity and insight are always taken into account. What seems important, therefore, is that social workers are prepared to be open and honest with employers and the care council about their behaviour, both in and out of work.

Finally, judgements about professional suitability are fluid and influenced by public, political and professional debates. Becoming familiar with the codes is not a once-and-for-all exercise, therefore, but a matter of remaining alert to changing policy and guidance.

Questions for reflection

Should everything social workers do in their own time be subject to care councils' conduct processes?

What behaviour do you consider to be unacceptable in relation to code 5.8, that is: not to behave in a way 'in work or outside work, which would call into your suitability to work in social care services'?

6 Diverse service users and diverse workers

The impact of globalization

Alun Morgan

This chapter helped me to value the different experiences faced by social workers who have lived and trained in other countries, and the significant impact this can have on their practice in the UK. I particularly enjoyed and learnt from the section, 'diverse staff'.

(Social worker, Early Intervention (Children and Families))

Introduction

A cornerstone in the values of social work is the willingness to celebrate diversity and embrace difference, a position central to the understanding of anti-discriminatory and inclusive practice. This diversity incorporates the many varying backgrounds, experiences, styles and beliefs of individuals and groups. Practising social work is, therefore, about working towards removing the physical and psychological barriers to the understanding and satisfying of diverse people's social needs. But diversity also incorporates complexity, which is increasingly becoming a hallmark of current social work practice. This chapter explores the contribution that globalization makes to this complexity, arguing that developing and sustaining a global critique may now have become an important baseline practice skill for working with increasingly diverse groups of service users and staff. For social workers, therefore, to 'think global' when 'acting-local' may no longer be just an optional-extra.

Globalization

The evidence of globalization appears to be everywhere. The interconnectedness and interdependence of countries, cultures and societies is increasingly self-evident, with goods, knowledge and services traded and exchanged internationally in ways unthinkable less than a generation ago. Globalization is usually understood in economic terms, relating to the reduction of trade barriers and the willingness of national governments and large international corporations to cooperate economically. It would appear generally that in more developed countries, increasing globalization usually results in a decrease in the expenditure on state welfare (Alston 2007; Kim 2009: 219). But beyond the economic sphere, as Galpin (2009: 70–1) indicates, globalization permeates military, legal, cultural and social life; with social globalization, for example, bringing with it 'new groups of service users with specific cultural needs. Legal globalization is an expansion of international law in the form of human rights that has the potential to directly influence social work practice and public sector provision'. Social care and social work, therefore, are likely to be influenced significantly by political and structural forces that range freely across national borders. Payne and Askeland*(2008: 6) argue, in relation to this, that it is important for social workers to achieve and value an understanding of international social work as part of their profession, suggesting 'Even if they are not international social workers themselves, their daily practice and the needs and problems that users of their services face will be affected by international social trends'. Chapter 7 discusses this further.

Neoliberalism and social work

Part of the critique required to contextualize the idea and the position of globalization is an understanding of the much used and perhaps the much misunderstood term 'neoliberalism'. In economic terms, to be liberal is to believe in the free (liberal) market and free trade, where the pursuit of profit is considered to be appropriately motivating, and in the best long-term interests of all social development in an increasingly globalized world. This liberal economic model was generally the norm in many developed and developing countries from the eighteenth century onwards. In the 1920s and 1930s, however, the Great (economic) Depression confirmed dramatically a crisis taking place in the progress of liberal economics. As a result, Western governments subsequently took on much more ownership of the national wealth and the responsibility for employment and social welfare, and social work became associated with the political movement for equality and social justice through state intervention and social protection (Jordan 2008: 440).

In the late 1970s, economic liberalism re-emerged and seemed re-invigorated, with familiar assertions of the presumed primacy of market-forces, financial deregulation, privatization, the cutting of public expenditure and the promotion of individual responsibility over the public good: the assertion in fact of 'new' neoliberalism. For social work, this general trend brought about service environments characterized by increased government regulation of social risk, with an emphasis on performance targets, using business and management models promoting value for money. In a strong critique of these developments, Ferguson *et al.** (2005: 2) argue that in Britain, 'the implications of this unquestioning acceptance of capitalist rationality for social work have been profound', suggesting in particular that the pursuit of value for money has been at the direct expense of social justice for the service users for whom social work organizations have a general duty of care. Lavalette and Ferguson (2007: 4) conversely articulate the radical social work approach 'which has stressed the need for social workers and service users to stand together and address the political and socio-economic conditions that negatively impact on our lives'. Radical social work is about understanding the position of the oppressed in the context of the economic and social structures they inhabit, recognizing that many problems can only be understood fully when such structural and political influences are taken into account. Originally, coming to prominence in the 1970s, it has had a renaissance in response to exposure of social work to the forces of the market.

The postmodern social worker

For some social workers in developed Western countries, a 'radical' analysis may seem valid, but hard to conceptualize in practice and even harder to make operational. Social workers in these countries are often deeply embedded in their service delivery systems, where despite a common presumption of services being needs-led and providing service user choice, in practice many services are far away from that ideal, often only falteringly responsive to service user diversity and, on occasions, regarded as negatively policing the boundaries of welfare (Humphries 2004a). In such settings 'choice' is either largely rhetorical, or only serves to further reinforce a market-driven service system, advantaging some but ghettoizing others (Jordan 2008: 449), through mechanisms such as personal budgets and the politics of tendering. Payne and Askeland (2008: 25) argue that the plight of social workers in such systems relates to the 'modernist' neoliberal nature of much of current social work practice, in that 'it [the modernist view] believes that structuring knowledge enables us to understand and manage a reality that we can understand without interpretation'. They give as an example the British Probation Service, rebranded in recent years as the National Offender Management Service where there is, they suggest, little expectation that the social reasons for criminality are used to formulate assessments and interventions, as they were in the early days of the service. Postmodern social workers, on the other hand, suggest Payne and Askeland appreciate that constant change in social work and in society is inevitable, especially change inherent in the processes and consequences of globalization. To be postmodern is to develop and value flexibility of thinking, and in direct practice to be clear about long-term objectives and values, concentrating on 'identifying and using skills to understand and respond to change in ways that help us to understand and exploit underlying flexibilities in our societies' (Payne and Askeland 2008: 5, Chapter 3).

Postmodern social workers in these terms take and value the holistic view, transferring cultural knowledge at all levels; they reject meta-narratives and universalizing explanations of social factors; they believe in contextualizing understandings and value critical reflection; they use communication technologies creatively and non-oppressively; and they are able and willing to work interchangeably with corporate, volunteer or state welfare organizations as required. Payne and Askeland further argue (2008: 106) that 'postmodernism creates flexibilities within globalizing societies that gives social work the political and social space to respond to the challenges of globalization'. In this respect, postmodern social work students evolve and later practice as 'updated nomads' (2008: 109), avoiding oversimplification, in their language, their understandings and in their interventions, and are able to work in flexible and sophisticated ways across barriers and borders.

Diverse service users

Globalization has undoubtedly generated diversity in the backgrounds of the service users that social workers encounter in their daily work. These may, for example, be represented by individuals or families seeking asylum, fleeing war, political persecution or economic collapse. Such movements of people have occurred throughout history, but the existence of global communications and relatively inexpensive global systems of travel have contributed significantly to the volume and actuality of global translocations exacerbated by globalizing influences. But it is not only the disadvantaged and dispossessed who migrate as a consequence of the forces of globalization. Danso (2009: 539) reports on the plight of many highly educated people encouraged by receiving countries to move from the underdeveloped South to the more developed North, where often, on arrival, they find structural barriers in the labour markets which deny them their expected access and employment commensurate with their training and expertise.

Alphonse *et al.* (2008), in reviewing globalization experiences in India, argue that globalization is also 'a local and household phenomenon that affects decisions related to family, education, employment, health practices and other civic and political roles', and that the pain experienced by all marginalized groups 'is intensified by the move to the individuated self as demanded by global forces ... framing structural problems within a personal context [away from the communal] and shifting the responsibility for problem solving on to the individual' (2008: 145).

For social workers engaged with increasingly international and diverse service user groups, Lyons *et al.** (2006: 2) consider 'loss' as one of the central theoretical constructions. They suggest that 'social professionals must have knowledge and skills in loss and grief in the cultural context', situating their responses in a carefully considered appreciation of individual circumstances, family history, cultural priorities and the forces that will have shaped and be sustaining their behaviour in reaction to the losses they have suffered. This is culturally competent practice, of course, but an appreciation of social, economic and political forces of globalization sets culturally competent social work assessments and responses in a broader and less oppressive framework. An awareness of transition theory is also relevant (Schlossberg *et al.* 1995) which explains how adults may react differently to transitions, depending on their individual situations, their social supports and the strategies they may have developed for coping with stress and change.

Diverse staff

Wellbourne *et al.* (2007: 27) report that in the UK in 2001–2, overseas-trained staff accounted for approximately 25 per cent of all new social work recruits. In addition, in the UK the GSCC 'letters of verification' for overseas staff working in 2003–4, comprised 20 per cent (Australia), 12 per cent (USA), 7.3 per cent (India), 5.4 per cent (Zimbawbe), 4.3 per cent (New Zealand) and also a number of others from Romania, Ghana, Nigeria, Poland and the Caribbean. Wellbourne *et al.* also observe that overseas-trained workers are not always prepared for the procedure-driven and highly regulated nature of much of the statutory work they undertake in the UK. All such recruits will have their own personal reasons for working abroad, and all will bring with them their cultural understandings and critiques of the causes and solutions for social problems.

In relation to this, Wellbourne *et al.* (2007: 32) comment that for Australian-trained social workers, 'their broad-based training which incorporates a diverse range of social work practices may be challenged by a more formally conceptualized standards-driven, relatively pragmatic approach to social work in the UK'. On the other hand, Saito and Johns (2009: 62), considering social work in Japan, comment: 'It is hard to find evidence of Japanese social work education making concerted and continuous efforts to enrich educational experience by reflecting cultural and ethnic diversity in its programmes ... Japan is relatively mono-ethnic. Ethnic issues outside Japan are deemed international problems'. So for Japanese social workers studying or practising in the UK, their particular cultural heritage could well pose very different but equally challenging issues.

Smith (2008: 372), with reference to South Africa, comments that while South Africa has achieved 'an impressive liberation from apartheid of the past thirteen years, extreme poverty, structural oppression, inequality and skewed power relations continue'; and in reference to social work, Smith remarks that 'South African social work practice with roots in capitalist, Western paradigms, faces a challenge of appropriateness and relevance [to the South African context], in terms of both training and practice' (2008: 381). And from Latin America, Reiter (2009: 157), talking of Brazil, observes that the distribution of income and wealth in that country is the most unequal in the world, where 'hand in hand with economic inequality goes a concentration of power among those who have been able to defend social and political privileges, rooted in colonial times and justified by European descent'. Both South African and Brazilian social workers, should they work in the UK, are therefore likely to have direct or indirect experience of people marginalized, stigmatized and excluded, in ways that social workers whose personal and professional experience is principally within politically stable Western democratic welfare states may find literally unimaginable.

Where does social work go from here?

William *et al.* (2009: 292) suggest that social work is inevitably political because 'in order to uphold humanistic values in a capitalist society, social workers must participate in social advocacy and promote reforms that will challenge the existing power balance, resource distribution and domination of the oppressed'. To be content only with the administrative and therapeutic agendas, with their emphasis on 'one-shot assessment and diagnosis' (2009: 295) in place of a deeper understanding, would be to ignore the likelihood that the 'articulation and realization of moral and political bases of social work practice need to be understood within their particular socio–politico–cultural context' (2009: 296). Like it or not, globalization is already here, and for the foreseeable future will have an increasingly significant influence on our personal and professional lives. Lyons *et al.* (2006: 186) argue that alongside such issues as human rights, inequality and poverty, 'a key word' in the current condition of globalization is 'interdependence'. This relates to an appreciation of the importance of economic and social interdependence, as well as interdependence in issues such as the sustainability and management of the environment. In this context the concept of interdependence is based on the premise that it is in everyone's best interests to work together, including promoting and responding to the needs of the marginalized and dispossessed.

Mohan (2005: 242) reminds us that 'the global human condition is far from satisfactory: about one billion children do not get drinking water let alone proper nutrition; 60 million people across the European Union live in poverty'; and although globalization forces may not have caused all such problems, the evidence suggests that neither does globalization respond to such needs particularly well. This is principally because globalization itself is inherently, if not essentially, neoliberal and it follows the money wherever it goes. It is important, though, that social workers do not romanticize the virtues of the 'local' when contrasting with the 'global', which may seem outside or beyond and thus more alien. As Munk (2005: 133) suggests, 'the local and the global cannot really be conceived as separate spheres of social life'. Valuing local communities, active citizenship, fraternity and working to develop and sustain the kind of networks that often thrive in marginalized communities, are important postmodern social work activities. But social workers must be aware that the influences of globalization will also continually permeate these local perspectives and carefully constructed solidarities, challenging and at time destroying their cohesion.

Many, if not most, social workers will continue to 'act local', but not to 'think global' when working with diverse service users and staff ...? Maybe that really *is* unthinkable?

Questions for reflection

What evidence of globalization can you see in aspects of your day-to-day work?

How does your knowledge of the constant change inherent in globalized societies, help you develop a greater understanding of the people with whom you work?

7 Professional identity and international social work

The view from afar

Sandy Fraser

This chapter ... helps to stimulate debate about the nature of social work across international boundaries and provides a valuable resource for further reading ... and provides accessibility to a complex issue.

(Principal Officer – Child and Family Services)

Empathy and professional identity

O wad some Power the giftie gie us
To see oursels as ithers see us!
It wad frae monie a blunder free us,
An' foolish notion:
What airs in dress an' gait wad lea'e us,
An' ev'n devotion!

(Burns 1994: 139, from 'To a Louse' 1785)

Oh would some Power (God) give us the gift of
Seeing ourselves as others see us
It would free us from many a blunder and foolish notion
What pretensions would we dispel, even (misplaced) devotion.

(Translated by Sandy Fraser)

You might think that an ability 'to see ourselves as others see us' would be fundamental to a social worker. This is because the job is not merely to articulate what services our agencies can provide to service users, but also to relate well to those we work with to achieve desired outcomes. Empathy has long been considered an essential aspect of social work practice (Wilson *et al.* 2008; Howe 2009). Empathy is often described as the ability to put oneself 'in another's shoes' (Trevithick 2005: 81) and thus see the service user's perspective. Likewise, inter-agency working requires a degree of inter-professional empathy (McLean 2007: 327). Effective negotiation means anticipating how we, as social workers, are perceived by allied professionals. In other words, following Burns to view our working world as another would see it, including how other professional disciplines view the part we play in their world.

Listening empathically to hear how we are perceived by others can surely prevent 'many a blunder and foolish notion'. Yet the insights of service users and allied professionals may offer, at times, an imperfect mirror to social work practice. In 'seeing ourselves as others see us' perhaps we might only reveal others' distortions of our intentions or actions or professional identity. Professional identity is precious because beyond specific *national* legislative powers and duties it is at the root of claims to legitimate professional discretion. If we do not know who and what we are, how can we provide a coherent service wherever we are geographically situated?

Professional identity and professional discretion

Professional identity is both powerful and problematic. Typically, professions have relied on a specific body of knowledge allowing and legitimating discretion to act (Burt and Worsley 2008: 28). For example, precise knowledge of the structure and functions of the eye allows optician discretion to prescribe a definite quality of lens. By contrast, social work's knowledge-base has always been diverse and often derivative of sociological and psychological disciplines. This, together with changing academic fashions and continuous extensive social, political and legal changes fundamentally challenges our ability to piece social work together as a meaningful whole.

On a day-to-day level our central role is to step into people's lives when expectations of familial or other support fall short for one reason or another. The social work role falls into the contested territory between *rights to services* in adversity and *freedoms from unwarranted interference* from an encroaching state (Chapter 2). So, inconsistent trends in what *constitutes legitimate knowledge* and legitimate *intervention* for social work can destabilize professional identity. Professional identity expands, contracts, fragments and congeals with different national or local emphases – with consequences for professional confidence and discretion. Nevertheless, behind all this challenge and change is there something that, like the human personality, seems to cohere over time and place?

Can part of the answer to these issues be found in how international 'others' see social work? Perhaps more understanding of professional identity can be gained by interrogating the ideas and practice of social work professionals who live and work outside of our immediate jurisdictions. They, like us, have an interest in holding a positive and assertive view of what social work is and can achieve, but in contexts quite different to our own. Social workers from other countries are therefore like us because they are social workers, but not like us because of where they live and work. We can reflect on ourselves as social workers through the *lens* of how other, internationally based social workers 'see' social work. Lyons *et al.** suggest that

> *all* social workers need to have some appreciation of international perspectives and feel better equipped for social work activities, which are increasingly likely to have cross-cultural and possibly cross-national dimensions.
>
> (2006: 2)

Globalization

No examination of international social work can avoid the concept of globalization (Chapter 6). Arguably, the twentieth-century internationalization of social work tended to be a one-way street where the West 'helped' in the economic and social 'development' of non-Western areas (Osei-Hwedie 1993; Al-Krenawi and Graham 2003). Looking back it seems clear that social work was 'exported' and often imposed, and social work played a minor role in demonstrating what it was to be a 'developed' society. Globalization has changed this dynamic. New if tentative rules are in place. Unilateral 'Western' versions of social work are harder to legitimately export. Moreover, in non-Western contexts there has been continuing resistance to neoliberal solutions to economic and social problems, and social workers have played their part in that process (Ferguson *et al.* 2005).

Midgely (1981) draws attention to twentieth-century professional imperialism in social work and started a dialogue supporting the view that 'social work in the industrial world had much to learn from [social work] colleagues in the developing world' (Midgley 2009: 34). He also notes progress towards appropriate bilateral international exchanges between academic and practice institutions but notes that examples of unilateralism remain. In particular he warns that because Western academic institutions carry more status, and because of electronic media and ICT, there will be increasing examples of inappropriate Western social work training being deployed in non-Western areas (Payne and Askeland 2008: 31). Nevertheless, Midgely still suggests that culturally appropriate and reciprocal exchanges should take place:

> The promotion of truly reciprocal exchanges in social work not only requires that the approaches exported from Western countries to the global south be culturally and developmentally appropriate, but that relevant innovations from the global south be imported into Western countries as well.
>
> (Midgley 2009: 42)

International exchange of personnel can, in this view, demonstrate a commitment to the value the acceptance of cultural diversity and an ability to learn from that diversity for social work practice. Such exchanges allow us 'a lens through which [we can] view local practice' (Lyons *et al.* 2006: 11). International exchanges are therefore useful because we all have an interest in comparing notes about how we do what we do, and how that constitutes 'social work'.

Increasingly there are trends towards a more globalized labour market for social workers. Thus, exchange of international perspectives may become less and less a matter for academics and international conference-goers and more about everyday exchanges between teammates as well as service users and their carers. For example, how does a South African trained social worker interpret their role in London compared to someone trained in the UK? How does a social worker trained in Chile interpret their role in New Britain, Connecticut compared with a locally trained social worker? And assuming that the flow of social work labour is not entirely one way, what impact would a South African social worker's practice in Dagenham (Essex UK) have in Polokwane (Limpopo Province, South Africa), or a Chilean social worker's practice in New Britain (Connecticut, USA) have in Santiago (Chile)?

Social work as local not global

Some have argued that social work is pre-eminently and definitively local, that there is more or less no such thing as international or global social work (Webb 2003). Others have argued that as a consequence of globalization social work is gaining a globalized character (Khan and Dominelli 2000; Penna *et al.* 2000; Ahmadi 2003). Ferguson *et al.* (2005) argue that, given the common problems of globalization and social work's commitment to social justice, social workers and service users can unite in common cause against the effects of globalization. Healy (2001: 98–103) has attempted an expansive, flexible definition of social work that accepts local diversity in the delivery of social work but which nevertheless fits an overarching global definition. Others, in line with Webb (2003), have emphasized the global importance of the local, that is the 'indigenous' versus a particular 'Western' oriented idea of social work (Gray *et al.* 2009). Gray *et al.* cite the various attempts to discuss and define social work on an international basis and further define international standards for social work as unhelpful:

> Cultural relevance is forcing us *to entertain the idea of multiple social works and social work knowledges*, rather than a universal profession with universal values. The latter amounts to a McDonald's-ization of social work, a one-size fits all approach that is paradoxical in a profession which values and extols diversity.
>
> (Gray *et al.* 2009: xxv–xxxvi, emphasis added)

The view from afar

There is danger here for the concept of professional identity. If we take Gray *et al.*'s view then social work may not have a real transferable 'core'. Any pretension to a set of knowledge supporting specific kinds of intervention is merely an aspect of a particular harmful globalizing ideology: 'the social work juggernaut' (Gray *et al.* 2009: xx). However, this struggle *for social work* between understanding the global and the local, given the diversity in the human condition, is *not* intellectually novel. Anthropology has historically taken this as its primary subject area:

> anthropology ... takes man as its object of study but differs from the other sciences of man in striving to understand that object in it most diverse manifestations.
>
> (Levi-Strauss 1987: 25)

Anthropology was thus *a view from afar*, examining diversity in order to reveal structural similarity within diversity. Anthropology has always struggled to understand the empirically verified diversity of the human condition. Two broad conceptions emerged to account for localized diversity concerning myth, ritual, kinship and social organization.

The first view accounted for diversity in terms of 'race'. The consequence was that the fragmentation of the human condition became intellectually legitimate and exemplified, in an extreme form, by Nazism and apartheid. There was not one human condition, rather there were many different and separate human conditions, each of which expressed themselves in particular and parallel ways. The second view asserted that behind, beyond or beneath local diversity there was inherent and comparable 'structure' within diversity. The human condition, though varied, could not be fundamentally fragmented.

Levi-Strauss viewed a variety of local cultures at various sites throughout the world 'from afar' while living and working in Paris as an academic, using empirical data collected by other anthropologists. Yet in principle *the view from afar* can be located at *any* point of geographical or cultural origin. The Straussian perspective did not seek to ignore, suppress or extinguish diverse local cultures by highlighting structural similarities between seemingly incongruous myths and kinship systems. Levi-Strauss saw it as emphatically important to collect examples of local diversity. Likewise, the search for structural similarity within the diversity of social work ideas and practices through discussion of the defining features of social work need not of necessity lead to the marginalization or suppression of indigenous social work practice by the so-called 'social work juggernaut'.

Reflective minds, at least since Socrates, have always thought about what defines something. Definitions thereby give us some sort of 'grip' in uncertain contexts and also help us to measure change in times of uncertainty. Even if globalization is not leading to 'international social work' as Webb and Gray seem to suggest, as an economic and social phenomenon it is changing the societies in which we live and work; and thus it contributes to the complexity of, and uncertainty in, local social work practice (Chapter 6). Attempting to define what we do in this context is likely to be helpful for professional identity rather than being some kind of secular sin.

Open and closed definitions of social work

Closed definitions of social work tend to suggest that particular knowledges should be linked with particular types of social or individual problems and thus be culturally exclusive. Open definitions of social work, by contrast, focus not on what knowledge is by definition necessary to a profession but rather on the particular *process* in which knowledge is employed. Therefore we are able to consider social work process as the primary *structure* through which our various knowledges and activities can be linked and which can define our role and professional identity within a given society. Social workers can work with individuals or collectives in an inclusive way in order to assess situations, reach agreed decisions on optimal outcomes, agree plans for how to achieve these, intervene to achieve them and evaluate whether agreed outcomes have been achieved. Importantly, social workers must also evaluate if 'social work' is the best way to achieve identified optimal outcomes. Sometimes 'social work' is inappropriate and another type of intervention is necessary.

Social work as others do it

Lyons *et al.*'s (2006) *International Perspectives on Social Work* is one of a growing field of publications concerned with introducing the international into the local (Lawrence *et al.* 2009; Gray and Webb 2010; Pugh and Cheers 2010). Increasingly, introductory textbooks provide a chapter on the subject. Often these chapters, like this one, are written at a general and invitational level rather than providing a series of case study materials. Perhaps this is because concrete examples incur a risk that particular examples used might not be helpful as a lens to view any one person's practice. However, in line with Lyons *et al.*, I would suggest that you attempt to access internationally based case studies, for example, The Open University 2008, to see if and how these confirm or disconfirm your own view of social work. Additionally, someone in your team may have been trained in another national context or grown up there – ask them about their experience of social work. Service users from international contexts may also have important information about social work in other countries. Exploring the IASSW/IFSW* websites (IASSW 2009) gives the opportunity to examine what these organizations say about your professional identity. It may even be possible to agree with your management the opportunity of international student and practitioner exchanges with the help of local Higher Education Institutions which award social work qualifications. This can open up ways and means of exploring and reflecting upon your professional identity using information from international contexts.

Conclusion

One source of developing a consistent professional social work identity can legitimately rely on the study of what constitutes social work practice in locations outside our nation specific borders. The *view of social work from afar* can be used both to challenge ourselves as individuals and how we practice. Just as importantly it can be used to challenge how our legislators and policy makers construe social work. If the local time and tides of events sometimes confuse us, then looking at what social workers elsewhere have to contend with can help us to re-establish a sense of confidence in our profession. Moreover, the effects of globalization impinge on our own social work organizations and practice. Therefore attention to social work beyond our national borders directly informs practice within our national borders. Looking at examples of international social work then is not something removed from local everyday experience but rather part and parcel of it.

Questions for reflection

What view of international social work do you have from your previous experience and training, and how does it affect your sense of professional identity?

In your own situation what information/material can you explore to 'open up' your own practice and understanding in this area?

Part II

Complex roles, responsibilities and relationships

Mick McCormick and Alun Morgan

Thompson has described social workers as being 'caught in the middle' (2009: 5) between care and control, navigating complex relationships between service users, peers, colleagues from other professions, employers and the public. Part II of this book considers the roles, responsibilities and relationships of social workers in practice and highlights some of the issues social workers encounter in this hard middle ground, as well as offering the reader some thoughts on how best to negotiate this territory.

The first four chapters of this section consider social work roles and responsibilities in a number of contexts. Seden (Chapter 8) begins with a look at the social work role in relation to managerial contexts, arguing that although social workers have both care and control functions they can be change agents, and that by 'doing being human' (Heller 2009) social workers can be catalysts for change. Dowling and Sextone (Chapter 9) pick up this theme as they discuss the social work role in relation to refugees and asylum seekers. They point out the hard place in which social workers can find themselves, between caring and supporting whilst at the same time having to adopt what can feel like uncaring roles in relation to 'failed' asylum seekers. They advocate the growth and development of international networks in an attempt to promote and maintain principles of social justice for this vulnerable group.

Cooper and Hester (Chapter 10) turn their attention to the social work role in the youth justice system, again exploring the care and control elements of the social work task, as well as considering work across social work boundaries (in this case, childcare and youth justice), firmly rooted in professional social work values. Dowling (Chapter 11) focuses on the social work role in an international context in relation to disabled children and suggests many useful ways in which social workers can engage with disabled children, their families and community networks. It is noteworthy, but perhaps of no surprise, that many of the themes and issues discussed by Dowling from an international perspective are reiterated by Aldgate (Chapter 19) from a UK perspective, who also reminds us of the importance of putting children first.

Payne refers to the 'constantly changing balance' (2006: 21) between the therapeutic, the social order and the transformational roles in social work practice – roles which are constantly present but which can cause role confusion and role conflict at times. These areas of conflict and confusion are considered by Matthews (Chapter 12), who discusses the challenges to social work identity in relation to the changing roles and responsibilities of the social worker in mental health practice. In highlighting the often statutory nature of social work practice in this area, she also recognizes that the 'softer' parts of the social work role (support, advocacy, partnership working) are critical to social work practice in this field.

Chapters 13–16 look more closely at the relationships social workers form with service users and multidisciplinary colleagues, highlighting some of the pressure points and dilemmas. Holland (Chapter 13) considers the skills social workers need to work effectively with older people, including the need for respect, empathy and understanding, as well as the more practical skills of negotiating and brokerage. Similarly, Dumbleton (Chapter 14) explores the social work role in relation to people with a learning disability and she, too, points to the dual role of developing nurturing and supportive relationships alongside more technical and bureaucratic roles of advocacy, assessment and risk management.

This range of roles and responsibilities is considered by McCormick (Chapter 15) in relation to safeguarding adults – where social workers have a central responsibility as well as a crucial role in engaging multi-agency colleagues in protecting and supporting this service user group. McPhail (Chapter 16) examines ways in which service users and carers can find a real voice in their relationship with social workers and points to ways in which social workers can facilitate this process. Sieminski (Chapter 17) talks about the aspirations and contradictions in the social work role with older people. While Holland (Chapter 13) argues for empathy and understanding as the cornerstones of good practice, Sieminski points out the dilemmas between this traditional social work role and the ways in which an increased emphasis on audit and management threatens to marginalize some of these primary social work skills.

Morgan's chapter (Chapter 18) on service users finding a 'voice' through ICT recognizes the value of new and emerging technologies and the potential benefits they can bring to a range of service user groups. Morgan argues that there is an appetite in social work for the increased use of ICTs to enhance practice and for incorporating service user voice, but he draws attention to the likelihood that people who use social work services are vulnerable to digital exclusion and exploitation. He urges practitioners to be open to ideas and be prepared to find creative applications and opportunities for maximizing the potential and minimizing the risks associated with ICT, with service users, in social work agencies and in their continuing professional social work education.

Aldgate (Chapter 19) ends Part II of this book with a look at child and family work, advocating the full and active participation of both children and their families at all stages of assessment, planning and intervention. Aldgate, like many of the authors in this section, recognizes the 'hard place' in which social workers find themselves, but argues that full engagement with service users (using basic social work skills like empathy, communication skills and advocacy, etc.) go some considerable way to squaring this circle, with positive outcomes for all involved.

8 The use of self and relationship

Swimming against the tide?

Janet Seden

This chapter provided me with an opportunity to reflect upon my own value base, my developmental needs and aided me to clarify my thoughts particularly around the importance of effective supervision both as a supervisor and a supervisee.

(Team manager – Intermediate Care Team)

Contexts

In *Counselling Skills in Social Work Practice* (2005) I wrote from the perspective that counselling, communication and relationship skills remain at the heart of social work practice. This theme is now embedded in the National Occupational Standards for training social workers (Topss 2003a). This chapter considers the 'use of self' and 'relationship-based' work in a climate where these concepts are debated because of the increasingly managerial contexts for social work practice which have been developing since the late 1990s (Harris and White 2009).

The development of policies and procedures which set targets linked to the increased used of new technologies have led to more proceduralism and to social workers spending more time at their desks than with service users. Despite this, service users and carers have consistently reported a preference for working with social workers who are knowledgeable and also show the ability to support, listen and relate in a humane way. This is seen clearly in the statement of the views of carers and service users which was published with the regulations for the new degree (Topss 2003b) and is supported by research findings across service user groups (Prior *et al.* 1999; Beresford *et al.** 2008).

In this chapter I argue for the professional use of self and relationship in social work practice. The space that social work occupies in society has always been contested, there have always been control as well as care functions. There remains an imperative to operate from the values that underpin professional identities and professional judgements, as social work is inherently a profession concerned with social justice (International Federation of Social Workers 2008). Social workers, as Hardiker and Barker (2007) have argued, are rarely 'arbitrary'. Practitioners endeavour to work in partnership with a range of other professionals and build relationships which enable everyone to carry out their roles to the best of their abilities, based on knowledge, skills and values.

However, social workers' relationships with the public have been hindered by the underfunding of well-intentioned legislation, leaving a widening gap between the rhetoric and reality of service provision; a belief from government that 'targets' create solutions and media misunderstanding of what social work in these contexts can realistically achieve. It is a challenge to individual social workers and their teams to remain resilient in this climate and to find time to use the values, knowledge and skills which are available to them to practise as effectively as they would like, in partnership with service users and carers. There remains a tension between the roles they carry out and their personal caring skills.

Contributions

It can be argued that in a time of financial crisis the social worker's only sure contribution to the well-being of others is the self, their personal qualities and their skills in relationship and advocacy. At the very least, assuming that they do have some capacity to offer supportive services and resources, the contribution social workers make when working with people in society remains based on the conscious use of self in a range of ways. Therefore this topic is a critical part of the social work literature and the discourse of qualifying training and post-qualification continuing professional development.

To be human, use the self and achieve change in partnership with service users requires practitioners to be constantly engaged with challenging some of the dominant stories that emanate from some commentators and the assumptions that exist in relation to the place of social work in society propagated by some sections of the media. To engage in social work at all is to expose yourself to a range of influences that may give you some very mixed messages about yourself and your role in society. Thus, the use of the self in some of the managerial climates that now surround practice is a challenge indeed, and one for which practitioners need good support from educators, colleagues and their employers otherwise they may become stressed, leave the profession or become cynical survivors of bureaucratic processes.

Self-awareness, that is the capacity to reflect on and analyse your impact on others and theirs on you, is something that is examined in qualifying training and should continue post-qualification as the challenges to personal styles of working continue and the complexities of practice situations increase over time. How do social work practitioners use themselves creatively in what Harris (2003) calls the 'social work business'? It can be argued that human dilemmas require human solutions (Seden and Katz 2003) and that humane practice does not compromise the use of authority or proper procedure. Key is that social workers critically examine the contribution they make in any situation (see Chapter 5 and Fook 2007). This includes continually developing self-awareness and skills in personal values, personal qualities and the capacity for professional relationship.

Personal change and the social work role

Most entrants to social work start from a desire to undertake a job where they 'make a difference', 'help people' or 'change society'. This is often a personal motivation, perhaps created through life experiences in childhood and adulthood. Personal qualities that individuals bring to the job are shaped by the diversity and richness of human experiences. However, in becoming a social worker each of us signs up to the requirement to use and adapt what we personally bring to the 'role' that is accorded to social work in society and now captured in the registration requirements of the GSCC (Chapter 5).

This brings new challenges to the sense of self, to the question of what personal attributes individuals creatively bring to the role and which of those have to be changed or adapted according to the requirements of the job. This challenge continues throughout a professional career as each practitioner adjusts to the demands of the workplace and responds to experiences with service users, from whom much is also learned. Sometimes this is painful and creates tensions and conflicts which only supervision and/or further development through training can support.

It is only human to feel frustrated by the blocks and barriers to achieving goals that you and a service user have identified, or to feel distressed when children's or adults' lives are clearly going badly or when vital resources are simply not available. When social workers, and other professionals, lose their ability to 'care', practice can become defensive (the practitioner covers theirs and the agency's back) rather than defensible (the practitioner can give a good account of the process of their practice). A balance can be difficult to achieve when working under pressure. It is, therefore, important to 'care' for yourself and to engage in continuing professional development with others to discuss these issues, especially where your view and that of your manager may conflict.

It is critical for service users that they experience facilitated change rather than a feeling of being 'processed through the system' which can be experienced as very dehumanizing. In the past, social workers have criticized medical professionals for seeing the 'condition' rather than the person, but it is likely that caring medical professionals might find the ways that some social workers 'categorize' service users equally worrying. As Harrison and Ruch write (2007: 40):

> The risk of a self-less approach is that the social work students and qualified practitioners resort to 'doing' social work instead of 'being' social workers.

This matters for service users and also for practitioners if they too are to remain whole people despite the constraints their environments put upon them.

Self and self-awareness

In the 1990s a 'competency training' approach to social work implied that what was necessary was to be able to 'do' the job. This view has contributed to a generation of social workers missing out on some key elements in their courses. While it is patently obvious that social workers need to be professionally competent in key skills – for example, writing reports, interviewing, completing forms, organizing the diary and organizing services – they also need other attributes. Underpinning their actions, a conscious self-awareness enables practitioners to be to be flexible, respond creatively to a crisis and appreciate that 'one size does not fit all'. When responding to service users' needs, such a practitioner must be ethical and, above all, be capable of making complex assessments. The capacity to be in a professional relationship with the service user enables the practitioner to keep each person and their significant others central to the social work process.

A preoccupation with self-awareness can be criticized when it appears that social workers are more preoccupied with their own inner responses than in their relationships with their clients. For example, Prynn (2008: 112) identifies that some of the casework approaches utilized between 1948 and 1972 could be criticized for being 'insufficiently aware of structural and cultural issues' and 'embedded in a culture of paternalism' which, therefore, concealed or perpetuated social injustices. However, she concludes that

> Critiques of casework and personal social services in the 1970s and 1980s from the political left and political right led to a diminution of the central role of relationship in social work. This is reflected in the current language and style of social work practice and in the increased prominence of the managerial function in supervision. If a study of the recent past in social work offers us pause for thought, it might lead to consideration of how twenty-first century social workers could offer a more relationship-based practice.
>
> (Prynn 2008: 112)

Paradoxically, psychological and counselling literature has retained an emphasis on the concept of the therapeutic relationship while developing more social and cultural awareness (Seden* 2005). It has consistently argued that self-awareness, when heightened and examined, enables the individual to be more sensitive and responsive to others. Higham (2006: 124–5) argues that values clarification and insights from psychological literature lead to a developing self-awareness which is 'an important trait in achieving moral competence and working effectively with others'.

Self-awareness helps the practitioner to clarify the moral and values basis of their interventions and to manage their own reactions so that they do not impede the way they behave in response to any situation. Knowing that something is difficult for you to handle for personal reasons enables you to either work to overcome it or to put in place strategies to handle it (be it fear of animals, dislike of hospitals, uncertainty around religions or something more significant from your own background). Jackson (2007) offers an insight into how understanding your own experiences and making sense of them can shape practice for the better. She says (2007: 181):

> I began to see that understanding one's own early attitude towards loss was important in shaping how we are able to hear and deal with the losses experienced by our service users as social workers, particularly because it can give us an insight into coping strategies and strengths of individuals.

The worst scenario is to be unexpectedly caught out by a personal reaction which derails you emotionally and clouds your responses and decision-making abilities. Knowing and facing your more significant limitations, such as little experience in communicating with children or people with dementia, is a driver to seek continuing professional development which is relevant to your needs. No one can emerge from qualifying training with experience and skills in everything – there will always be room for development. What is important is to emerge from qualifying training with an awareness of your own values, generic abilities, specialist expertise and personal strengths and limitations, plus an ability to continue to engage with learning and development opportunities.

Assumptions, ideologies and world views

Self-awareness is also important for the development and critical questioning of values. As Higham (2006: 125) puts it:

> Values clarification argues that by identifying personal prejudices and rigidly held, but poorly argued beliefs, the individual will adopt better informed, more reasonable values that are more tolerant of other people's differences.

In training, practitioners should have engaged with an examination of their assumptive world views (Chapter 4). For example, there are different views of social work and you will have been challenged to consider where your values originate from and where they may clash with those expected of a social worker in practice. You will have explored how these values influence your actions and impact on your practice. Your growing self-knowledge in relation to cultural awareness, differences of world view between social work and other professions and differences of cultural outlook within society are all part of an evolving growth of self-knowledge and knowledge of other perspectives.

This awareness is part of the 'role' of being a social worker, where often personal prejudices and assumptions have to be put on one side in order to respect the rights and preferences of others or the assumptions and philosophies carried by legislation and policy. There are also those times when a personal position or a service user's perspective will mean you challenge the assumptions carried by legislation or policy interpretation.

Social workers have often, alongside others, been at the front of challenging societal assumptions, through anti-oppressive and anti-discriminatory practice.

As Hardiker and Barker (2007: 40) argue, practitioners have to grapple with ideologies, by which they mean 'a set of ideas and beliefs which is systematic enough to convey an underlying attitude to society, shared by members of a social group'. They also point out that ideologies which are not examined impact on choices and decisions. Such ideologies may also be embedded within the legislation and procedures that practitioners have to follow. For example, social workers may often find that prevailing ideologies in society work to disadvantage some groups, for example, travelling families (Cemlyn 2008). Hardiker and Barker identify the need for practitioners to examine throughout their careers the extent to which the interests of one group are met at the expense of others. Social work in current contexts will need continuing examination in this respect, as Human Rights legislation has sharpened awareness of rights and conflicts of rights.

Emotions, feelings and handling pain

As argued earlier, social work cannot be just about 'rules and procedures' despite the pressures from some to make it so. Rules and procedures can guide and underpin but cannot be a substitute for professional judgement. It is also becoming evident that when social workers and their managers seek to avoid the pain and distress they encounter in individual cases, poor judgements is often the outcome. This has been very much the case in recent high profile childcare cases (Cm 5730 2003).

Social workers are present with individuals during some of the most traumatic and difficult situations in their lives: the identification of abuse at the hands of carers (by adults and children); a crisis such as bereavement; the loss of physical and/or mental health; a move to care or institution or from country to country. In situations like these, social workers need to be able to witness and support the pain of others, while at the same time not over identifying or projecting their own pain onto the other. As Brearley* (2007: 96) comments:

> Growing self-awareness enables the social worker to distinguish his personal material from what the client brings to the encounter and to pick up accurately the underlying communication.

Social workers in complex practice situations need this kind of advanced communication skill, as well as the support and back-up of colleagues and managers. Unfortunately, Prynn (2008) has identified the supervisory process in social work as very much a performance management process, with little space for practitioners to air their worries and concerns. As Harrison and Ruch (2007: 48) identify, 'It takes a self-aware, resilient and determined practitioner to challenge prevailing expectations and demand better support'.

However, despite managerial contexts and procedural practices there has always been a 'voice' for the necessity of person-centred and relationship-based practices and there is a resurgence of interest in the need for a relationship-based social work which does not repeat the mistakes of the past by ignoring social and cultural contexts and which operates in a way that still takes account of the constraints of the social work role. Emerging research literature (Beresford *et al.* 2008) continues to support such ideas.

Capabilities

In one sense, nothing has changed since the writings of Compton and Galaway (1989). Social workers' 'use of self' is a necessity which links to the simple fact that it is a profession which works with loss, disadvantage, violence and aggression in areas such as child protection, mental health, disability and ageing – where personal issues and strong feelings abound. It will, therefore, always be important to be able to manage your own and other peoples' emotions and to face personal difficulties without retreat into defensiveness or denial.

This is where the capacity for continuing critical reflexivity is absolutely essential (Chapter 5), as any situation might be similar but never quite the same as another. The social worker needs to be able to continue to develop appropriate responsiveness for the needs of each service user. Fook (2007: 374) has argued that 'critical reflective ability can be shown to improve practice responsiveness' and that it can also offer 'transformative possibilities' within the managerialist contexts and media attacks on social work. To face the challenges of change, practitioners can use critical, self-aware reflexivity to respond as creatively as possible. The danger is that in the drive for efficiency, economy and effectiveness these human survival skills or talents are lost or undervalued.

Social workers are engaged in both care and control functions for society but can work to achieve positive change with some of the most marginalized people in society. They can be 'catalysts' in the community of practice and the communities where they work. They can be change agents and through their awareness and critical reflection, can increase the rate of reaction in others and precipitate positive change in service users' situations. Through self-awareness and positive personal skills this can happen in any context and is part of the unique contribution which social workers make to those societies which offer them appropriate space for action.

Questions for reflection

Am I able to assess myself and my impact on others?

How do I recharge my batteries and keep a sense of realistic optimism about what I can achieve?

What support, supervision and training opportunities are available at work to maintain healthy critical reflexivity?

9 Refugees and asylum seekers

The social work role

Monica Dowling and Parissa Sextone

> This chapter added to my admittedly media filtered view of this topic and reinforced some traditional social work values such as the importance of anti-discriminatory practice within the context of the increasing denial of rights toward refugees and asylum seekers.
>
> (Inspector – Health and Social Care)

Introduction

The plight of refugees and asylum seekers is a historical and global issue which is often reduced to an economic problem by the laws and policies of individual countries. Because of this, social workers are often compromised in relation to their profession's responsibilities and duties in working with refugees and asylum seekers, including unaccompanied minors (Humphries 2004b). Asylum seekers, in contrast to refugees, are people who enter a country without legal documents or whose documents expire once they have arrived and who claim refugee status (Nash *et al.* 2006).

The legal contexts for practice

Legislation in the UK has steadily sought to deny refugees and asylum seekers social rights which the welfare state proclaims as universal. The 1993 Asylum and Immigration Appeals Act withdrew asylum seekers' access to social housing tenancies, the 1996 Act ended their right to social security benefits unless they had children, whilst the 1999 Act created a separate welfare regime for asylum seekers and their families with food vouchers at levels significantly less than the official poverty line. It also introduced compulsory dispersal which took people away from the informal support of their ethnic communities. The 2002 Act abandoned vouchers and dispersal in favour of warehousing in prison, whilst the Asylum Acts of 2004 and 2006 further tightened the monitoring of asylum seekers and accelerated detention and removal by the withdrawal of legal rights.

The government has identified a shift towards 'managed migration' in the context of growing shortages of, for example, social workers, dentists and teachers. In relation to race and ethnicity, 'legal' migrants have been mainly white people from the new member states of the EU, while those without documentation come from outside the EU and are ethnically distinct (Ginsburg 2009). Furthermore, the EU's 'fortress Europe' policy on asylum means that individual countries no longer have the same freedom to respond unilaterally to applications for asylum.

The contribution of research findings informing practice

Research in this country and overseas (Valtonen* 2001; Hessle* 2007) raises questions about the policies of governments, and welfare agencies, in the complex immigration and social welfare environments in which social workers operate. Where good social work practice exists, it does so despite negative circumstances. The common picture from research is one where workers feel guilty, resentful and frustrated because they do not have the legal knowledge or expertise to offer a good service and where service users are neglected and vulnerable (Hayes and Humphries 2004).

Humphries* (2004a) cites work by Duvell and Jordan (2000) who interviewed members of asylum teams in London and reported that staff often lacked preparation and training for work with refugees, while research in Greater Manchester found that although local authorities could claim a special grant for unaccompanied asylum-seeking children, young people were often not supported because the relationship between asylum teams and social work teams was not clear.

Jordan and Jordan (2000) also found that some social workers do not accept that social problems faced by asylum seekers are any of their business, while some local authorities avoided their responsibilities under community care and national assistance legislation. Team members were aware of and concerned about the trauma experienced by young refugees but had little knowledge of their immigration status or the legislation.

Poole and Adamson (2008) looked at the difficulties faced by the Roma community arriving in Govanhill, Glasgow without employment. They were unable to make any claims on public funds given the primary legislation developed by the Department of Work and Pensions and the Home Office (Home Office 2008). This limited their access to emergency payments from social work in times of 'destitution'. Such restrictive legislation created a tension between professional social work ethics and the principles of anti-discriminatory practice on the one hand, and the day-to-day realities of trying to work with excluded minority ethnic groups on the other. Furthermore, changes in the role carried out by social workers and others in acting as agents of the Home Office through taking steps to confirm immigration status, can result in aiding deportation.

Research with asylum seekers and refugees in North Glasgow (GoWell 2007) found they had difficulties in accessing health services because of problems including language and registration. The research also identified a range of health needs, many of which were unmet or required involvement of other support, for example, social services, health services and housing.

Hayes and Humphries (2004) point out the importance of anti-racist practice and the response of social work agencies. Save the Children's research (2003) found statutory agencies were not always aware of the extent and impact of racism experienced by refugees and asylum seekers. Black and minority ethnic groups are often diagnosed as having higher rates of mental disorder than the general population, and refugees and asylum seekers are especially disadvantaged (Chase *et al.* 2008; Browne 2009). Depression is frequently overlooked and these groups are less likely to be referred for psychological therapies (Chase *et al.* 2008). However, refugee rather than asylum seeker status is necessary to access community mental health teams.

Hayes and Humphries (2004) cite examples of good practice from housing providers, including the private sector whose workers were well informed and were providing support and advice which went beyond the provision of accommodation. Housing providers and support workers in this research were often the first to identify mental health problems and were instrumental in helping refugees and asylum seekers to register with a GP.

Research evidence from the UK and other countries indicates that social work with refugees and asylum seekers is developing into a new area of practice where information is sought from lawyers, medical practitioners, NGOs and the voluntary sector rather than social work practitioners working with other client groups (Valtonen 2001; Findlay *et al.* 2007).

Skills and knowledge for the complexities of practice

The realities of working with asylum seekers and refugees will vary from country to country and from time to time. The examples of practice discussed here are from the UK in 2009 and are used to highlight general issues and practices which are summarized in the conclusion.

Social workers tend to work with a small section of the refugee and asylum seeking population – either women and children in financial difficulties or children and young people in need of safeguarding (Bokhari* 2008). A key role of the duty and assessment social work team in a local authority is to assess an unaccompanied minor. The core assessment will classify them as a child in need and then will take them into care under Section 20 of the Children Act (2004), which allows the social worker to provide a comprehensive service including being entitled to Leaving Care services under the Leaving Care Act (2000). Social workers are specifically required to complete assessments that determine whether a young person is entitled to a service, and age disputes are a huge problem. While social services are required to do age assessments, the Home Office can dispute the assumed age. An assessment is required to build a picture of the unaccompanied minor over time, and there should be two social workers present for this type of skilled assessment which will include medical reports and dental records.

Social workers and others are increasingly required to integrate their role with the Home Office and their policy is clear in making it difficult for the individual to stay in the UK when there is no longer any support (Asylum and Immigration Act 2004). The aim of the immigration policy in these circumstances is to encourage the person to return to their home country.

If the asylum seeker is a child or young person who is assessed as a child in need and is taken into care, the social worker will need to work closely with them to establish whether they have a right to refugee status. Many young people who are refugees or asylum seekers may have a different cultural conception of the role of a social worker or do not understand the role of social services and the time it takes to work through the bureaucracy. The social worker will need to have the skill to explain what is possible from a professional perspective and the knowledge to clarify the workings of the benefit system so that the young person may experience the system with external support.

The social worker may have to find his or her own network of expertise outside the local authority if they are the only worker in the team providing this service to young people. However, the social worker's role in coordinating services is only part of the picture. It is also important to have listening and counselling skills for when the young person explains their experiences, and simply being there with the young person and giving them space is a fundamental part of the role and involves skills and knowledge that cannot be underestimated. The relationship a worker will develop with a young person or family who is seeking refugee status can be powerful and enabling. Failed asylum seekers are the most disadvantaged group in this population. Children who are permitted to stay temporarily can experience acute anxiety about their uncertain status and fear for their future (Chase *et al.* 2008; Hill and Hopkins* 2009). The social worker's role in this context may be primarily about getting to know the child so that he or she can decide how to balance a focus on the loss and trauma the child has suffered with an equally important focus on strength and durability.

Clearly, some local authorities will have more knowledge and experience of working with asylum seekers and refugees, mainly due to their locality. How seamless the service is for the service user will depend on how experienced the social worker and colleagues are and whether they have the right resources. Sensitivity is paramount when working with refugees. Support services that are anxious to help sometimes bombard new arrivals with advice and guidance and this help can be met with resistance as many people who are seeking asylum and refugee status are living in a state of uncertainty as they do not know how long they will be remaining. If an appeal is reached and refugee status is not granted, asylum teams have to remove families from National Asylum Support Service support, including accommodation. Social work teams are also expected to play a part in their deportation.

There have been some positive policy developments in the UK which will aid social workers in developing their practice with refugees and asylum seekers. The guidance for local authorities' assistance for young people leaving care after eighteen (Leaving Care Act 2000) now includes a specific reference to taking account of a young person's immigration status (Dennis 2007). This enables the local authority to fund education for the refugee leaving care until they are 21 years old, and refugees tend to make use of the provision with a high percentage going on to further education and university (Findlay *et al.* 2007). The Department for Children, Schools and Families (DCSF) has a revised framework for *Every Child Matters* where its five outcome statements apply to every child and young person 'whatever their background and circumstances' (DCSF 2008) and they acknowledge that asylum-seeking children are one of the practice areas of greatest need (Hill and Hopkins 2009).

However, every day in the UK people in the asylum system are condemned to sleeping on the streets or waiting years for a decision on their refugee status, they can be locked up in detention centres and eventually sent back home. The British system at times makes children take on the burdens of their traumatized parents and prevents parents from being the protectors they want to be to their children.

Walters (2009) suggests there are hundreds of families who could talk about their treatment in the UK but feel too frightened to speak out. In 2007, approximately 30,000 people came to the UK seeking asylum and 4,000 of these were children. Nothing is gained in terms of justice or efficiency by compounding the trauma of families who have already experienced persecution in their home countries by locking up families in detention centres.

Nevertheless, refugees and asylum seekers often talk about the individual acts of kindness that sustain them day to day, and social workers play their part in supporting and comforting these families. There are some social workers who provide an outstanding service in this field and the ripple effect on the lives of people, groups and societies has an everlasting positive impact.

Recommendations for practice

Healy (2001) has called this type of casework the 'international/domestic practice interface' where the complex problems that social workers encounter are often linked to the person involved having different countries of origin. She gives many examples of cases where social workers must cross national borders both symbolically and sometimes physically in order to arrive at acceptable solutions in dialogue with clients.

Hessle's (2007) approach is to suggest that transcultural and inclusive principles are key responsibilities for frontline workers when working with these vulnerable groups in society. She argues for understanding the worldwide agenda and getting help, support and expertise in dealing with these issues from international and professional networking and suggests that

> Social workers are at the frontline of solidarity with vulnerable groups in all societies and international exchange of knowledge is necessary for dealing with trans-cultural problems.
>
> (Hessle 2007: 240)

What is evident from research and the realities of practice is that social workers need to be knowledgeable and effective in their role with refugees and asylum seekers. Professional leadership, support and training both nationally and internationally in transcultural issues, immigration legislation, trauma counselling and support and inter-professional working is essential to prevent the demoralization of social workers working in this area.

Conclusion

This chapter has looked at how the social worker is at the heart of a punitive system for immigrants and asylum seekers. This can create conflict and tension for social workers if they feel they cannot support this vulnerable group in society in the ways they wish. More research is needed with good practice examples, on how barriers can be overcome and effective solutions can be achieved.

Lovelock *et al.* (2004) point out that social work research needs to grasp the moral and political realities as they question the 'what works agenda' and its implications for human rights and welfare principles in contemporary Britain. They suggest a continuing awareness of connections between policy and practice, the nature of anti-oppressive practice and the role of ethics, politics and strategies of alignment of social work with forces that contradict its expressed values.

The profession cannot avoid the moral and political aspects of its operation. It is time to progress networks with social workers from other countries working in similar situations and use the knowledge and support gained to assert the principle of social justice and defend social workers' professional practice in supporting vulnerable citizens.

Questions for reflection

What are the vulnerabilities and strengths of refugees and asylum seekers in the UK?

How can I develop my network of knowledge and expertise to ensure that I practise effectively and appropriately?

What practice approaches are helpful when social workers become involved with refugees and asylum seekers?

10 Youth justice

Children in trouble or children in need?

Barry Cooper and Richard Hester

> I liked the emphasis towards giving social workers 'permission' to challenge the systems within which they work; to take a 'constructively critical approach to policy' ... and the discussion/critique on the 'old and new ways of working'.
>
> (Group manager – Children's Services)

Introduction

In this chapter we argue that social workers who are members of youth justice services have to see the children and young people with whom they work as being both 'in need' as well as being 'in trouble'. Part of the complexity of the social work role in any setting arises from social workers being expected to work effectively across the boundaries of many social and organizational systems. Practice that crosses the complexities of youth justice and childcare services, however, offers particular scope for the social worker to focus upon the welfare needs of individual young people. Where necessary, a youth justice social worker (YJSW) should prioritize and advocate for the needs of children and young people to be recognized within the demands of the criminal justice system. This requires confident, critical practice. We illustrate in this chapter some of the contexts, contributions and capabilities of social work within the complexities of the youth justice practice context.

Contexts for practice

The possible conflict between the justice and welfare aims of practice is not only symbolized in the title of this chapter but can actually be found carved in the portals of London's Old Bailey: 'Punish the Wrongdoer and Defend the Children of the Poor'. However, as Pitts (1988) has pointed out many times, the wrongdoer and the child of the poor are sometimes the same person. Social workers are expected to weigh and balance the potential for competing needs and rights between individuals, their families and the wider community.

It is, therefore, vital that YJSWs develop a coherent approach to professional values about young people who offend, and are able to both acknowledge the effects upon their families and their victims whilst enhancing interventions that can meet their needs as developing young people. This balance between 'welfare and justice imperatives' (Hendrick 2006) can be traced back to the beginning of the twentieth century with the introduction of children's legislation and the establishment of juvenile courts, through the Children Act 1908. A combination of trying to meet the needs of ill-treated children through relationships and activities while simultaneously applying criminal sanctions to offending behaviours can be found, in varying mixtures, in subsequent legislation. The Children and Young Person's Act of 1933 (Section 44) specified the duty of magistrates to consider the welfare of the child when passing sentence and, as Hendrick (2003) argues, brought together neglected children, young offenders and young victims in a common purpose, where the primary aim was intended to be reformative rather than punitive. This emphasis upon welfare became more pronounced in the Children and Young Person's Act of 1969 with provisions for social work interventions and care proceedings to address 'delinquent behaviour'. The balance of responsibility in this legislation between an individual young person and their social environment became tilted much more in favour of the latter. However, many of the Sections of the 1969 Act failed to be implemented, for example, the raising of the age of criminal responsibility to 14, due to a change in government just months after Royal Assent was granted, a development which in effect lessened the swing to welfarism. Indeed, some of the measures that were implemented in the 1969 Act had an opposite effect to improving the welfare of children; for example, the introduction of the Section 7(7) Care Order which gave courts powers to make care orders on the grounds of the commission of a criminal offence, and resulted in an increase in the incarceration of children (Thorpe 1980). Later, and linked to the public's reaction to the death of James Bulger in 1993 and the subsequent struggle for power preceding the 1997 General Election, the pendulum swung once again, this time towards an altogether more punitive mood.

Youth justice, therefore, occupies a tricky position at the boundary of the welfare and justice systems, and the requirements of both need to be satisfied in order to deliver effective practice. The 1998 Crime and Disorder Act (Section 37) defined the purpose of the youth justice system simply as 'to prevent offending by children and young persons'. Whereas the Criminal Justice and Immigration Act 2008 is more specific, in stating that for the purpose of sentencing, the court must have regard to: (a) the principal aim of the youth justice system (which is to prevent offending or re-offending); (b) the welfare of the offender; and (c) the purposes of sentencing (defined as essentially punishment, reform and rehabilitation, the protection of the public and reparation). Thus, the practice of all those working in the system should be driven by, or if not driven at least related in some way to these objectives. In other words, if the welfare of the child became somehow lost or underemphasized in the 1998 Act, it returned in 2008 as one of the guiding principles. This principle arguably derives from the influence of the United Nation Convention on the Rights of the Child (UNCRC 1989), which was ratified by the UK government in 1991. This devolved area of public policy (see, for example, Welsh Assembly Government 2004) has been responded to in different ways in the UK. For example, in England the public profile of professional responses to child protection in the wake of the Victoria Climbié tragedy (Cm 5730 2003), resulted in the far-reaching changes of the *Every Child Matters* agenda (DfES 2004a, b).

The current context of multidisciplinary youth justice (YJ) teams, established in 1998, provides an opportunity for the two agendas of 'welfare' and 'justice' to be constructively promoted as complimentary activities. The YJ teams have a working membership that span the professions and disciplines such as probation, police, social work, education, housing, substance misuse, youth work and a variety of seconded specialists. YJSWs have an opportunity to play a central role as multidisciplinary 'boundary-spanners' in these hybrid teams, as part of their primary focus upon the young person. The next section explores their contribution.

Contributions of youth justice social workers

Social work in the UK balances a professional tradition of a personalized approach to the rights of individuals (GSCC 2002a) with the increasing emphasis upon the networking acumen needed for effective multi-agency case coordination. Social workers within integrated YJ teams are therefore well placed to meet the demands of the *Every Child Matters* agenda for integrated responses to problems, while maintaining the young person as their primary focus of concern. This is, of course, a difficult balancing act. In YJ teams the primary organizational remit is, as we have seen, 'the prevention of offending'. To this end the expectations of control through power and authority is an explicit part of the role. Nonetheless, within this overall brief, we argue that the critical YJSW must retain some scope for the social work practice arts of negotiation and advocacy, as core skills within professional systems and with young people themselves (Williamson 2001).

In carrying out this balancing act of offending prevention whilst meeting the welfare needs of individuals, the YJSW can be seen as a negotiator and advocate across both personal and organizational boundaries (Steadman 1992). Part of this negotiation and advocacy involves changing the way that others may come to habitually view things. The following quote from a social worker in a voluntary drugs service for young people illustrates how and why the contribution of 'changing perspectives' is important:

> I thought actually, do you know what, the more you do something the more complacent you can get, so maybe it's alright to challenge,

> because if [social workers] are true to their registration they should take challenges and throw some back. I think that's most of what my job comes back to, because a lot of young people are quite easily written off, especially when you say they're seeing us for a drug or alcohol problem, and its challenging people's perception of them as a young person or their background or their upbringing, and challenging them to see things differently.
>
> Excerpt from a research interview (Cooper and Nix 2009)

The 'challenge to complacency' should be a major aspect of what social workers contribute to practice settings that are increasingly multidisciplinary. For example, challenging stereotypical views about young people, particularly if they have developed a problem with the use of drugs or alcohol. It is certainly part of what this drugs service social worker understood to be a defining feature of their role. Moreover, in terms of professional registration, challenging prejudice and oppression is one of the defining features of a social work identity. This very positive approach is rooted in a 'strengths perspective' of good practice in social work (Saleebey 2006) and is in accordance with the broad requirements for professional registration set out in the Code of Practice for Social Workers (GSCC 2002a). However, the balancing of apparently conflicting expectations from within and outside of professional systems demands more than just a positive attitude.

Jones *et al.* (2008) argue that 'best practice' in social work encompasses complex activities that take a realistic but positively critical approach to both the potential and the constraints of social work across the many boundaries of complex practice. These boundary-spanning activities can be understood at both a system level and at an individual level. Senior and Loades (2008) make the case for skilled organizational practice being an essential part of a social worker's contribution, and this seems particularly relevant to the multidisciplinary settings of YJ teams and services. A 'cross-systems' approach to what is done well in organizational settings also translates into practice situations with individuals, through a focus upon the interpersonal struggles for power and meaning with service users. Cooper (2008a, b) argues that this underpins the detailed, constructive processes of working relationships through negotiation and assessment, where what is at issue is the extent to which public interventions have to be made into private lives.

The youth justice requirement to meet the demands for justice as well as the needs of welfare is not new for social workers. It is a variant upon the well established conundrum of 'care and control' (Satyamurti 1979). The critical debates, particularly in the early years following the establishment of social work services within local authorities in the 1970s, are often about how social workers can exercise both care *and* control of the children and families with whom they work. In a critical examination of welfare professionals Ingleby (1985: 101) argues that:

> the provision of care has become increasingly a matter of socializing people, so that it becomes difficult to think of 'help' as separable from 'control' ... I shall suggest that this is because of a fundamental ambiguity in the politics of intervention.

One way in which this care/control ambiguity could be resolved in a YJ setting is to see 'welfare' as a high level holistic need that subsumes 'being in trouble'. In other words, one obvious need for all young people is to be able to *not* offend or re-offend. Meeting this need to 'desist' from offending is also dependant upon wider and more fundamental personal, socio-emotional and development needs being met. Therefore the contribution of the YJSW has to be upon a young person-centred approach of hope and solution-focused planning for the future, rather than a reactive problem focus upon the past (Smale 1977; De Shazer 1988; Myers 2007). The next section examines the capabilities needed for social workers to maintain a critical best practice focus upon the uniqueness of young people and their particular 'lifeworld' needs within the YJ system.

Capabilities of youth justice workers

The expertise required of a YJSW relies on the complex interplay between different ways of knowing about and understanding practice. This can be expressed through a duality of practice or knowledge. Kubiak and Hester (2009) point out the differences between *idiographic* practice that attempts to understand the unique characteristic of each young person; compared to *nomothetic* practice that is informed by an understanding of the more generalizable explanations of youth crime. This corresponds well to Nellis' (2001) duality of 'overarching' and 'underpinning' knowledge. Nellis suggests that the effective practitioner needs to know not just the day-to-day 'trade' of a profession, for example, the systems that operate and how things get done, but also the overarching knowledge that make sense of professional expertise and values. In the same way, YJSW practice cannot rely entirely on competences (based on, for example, how to complete a standard assessment form), but they must seek to explore ideas and theoretical explanations through an enquiring or critical stance towards complex situations. Making professional decisions requires the capability for informed discretion that reflects upon both the particularities of individual lives and circumstances, alongside the results of wider research and policy development.

An integrated professional understanding of how and why something works, as well as what doesn't in youth justice, requires grounding within the knowledge of where youth justice has come from. Practitioners need to be conscious of the youth justice system's roots in social work practice, an inheritance that can sometimes be forgotten. To illustrate this point one of the authors (Hester 2008) once asked a group of youth justice students to describe the difference between the way in which youth justice was organized before 2000, and the way in which it was organized in 2004. The responses were interesting and perhaps rather extreme. For one group, the period before New Labour's 1998 Crime and Disorder Act marked a time of inefficiency and confusion where the 'victims of crime' were placed firmly in the background, with the post-2000 period being seen as a time of renaissance with a flourishing restorative ideology and preventative interventions. For the other group, youth justice practice was felt to be in serious decline, dominated by 'tick box performance management' that got in the way of the real work of engaging with young people, thereby creating intense pressure on the workforce with the ultimate result being a reduction in the *quality* of the relationship between workers and young people.

This is interesting not only as it reflects what might be characterized as the 'old' and 'new' ways of working in youth justice but because it also illustrates the potential amnesia for what was achieved in youth justice practice before the onset of New Public Management in the 1980s. This was characterized by an emphasis upon increased market orientation, or business perspectives, with the widespread application of government targets and performance indicators which in youth justice can be argued to have led to an 'actuarial' approach to crime control (Feeley and Simon 1994). This approach can lead practitioners to dispense with deeper concerns about understanding the origins of offences from a young person's perspective, (Taylor *et al.** 2010) in favour of more standardized processes of 'risk minimization' in key parts of the practitioner's role, such as in assessment and intervention planning.

Examples of these increasingly systematized approaches to practice can be seen in the introduction of a Scaled Approach (Youth Justice Board 2009) based upon the Risk Factor Prevention Paradigm (Case 2007; Kemshall 2007) and the Risk Need and Responsivity (RNR) model (McNeill *et al.* 2005). The staple of youth justice practice has now become the identification of risk and protective factors, and the tailoring of programmes of intervention to match these. The intensity of intervention is defined and prescribed by an assessment of the intensity of risk of re-offending, the risk of serious harm to others, and the risk to self (vulnerability). The nature of any subsequent intervention is based on the nature of the 'risk factors' or 'criminogenic needs'. Much of this identification of both need and risk is based, in part at least, to an actuarial approach to offending, which can obscure the need for more personalized responses to practice that place the individual young person at the heart of the process. We argue, however, for a more fundamental distinction between professional practice framed and driven by systems of accounting and audit (an actuarial driven system), to be set alongside practices that are responsive to the diverse needs of personal lives through what can be known as 'lifeworld' approaches.

Cooper* (2010) draws upon the critical theory of Habermas (1986) to make just this distinction, arguing that professional social workers have unique expectations placed upon them. They are expected to operate across and span the boundaries of different and often conflicting institutional systems and structures, as well as across unique and varied diversities of cultures and individual lives. Habermas characterizes this fundamental constitution of the social domain as 'system and lifeworld', and the public–private intermeshing of the two can give rise to profound uncertainties and ambiguities. Similarly, the balance between accountability to YJ actuarial system demands as illustrated earlier, while attempting to discharge professional responsibility to meet the needs of vulnerable young people, is a constant tension, calling for highly skilled practice contributions in YJ services. The Habermasian notion of a 'lifeworld' places a renewed emphasis upon personal and interpersonal perspectives and priorities and helps to highlight the importance of the third part of the RNR model which is responsivity and engagement with young people. We argue here that for practice to be effective, YJSWs need to take a constructively critical approach to the policy and 'standards' frameworks in which they operate as a way to transform complexities into personalized practice solutions. The contexts of youth justice and of social work are increasingly of systematized accountability and audit, but the contributions and necessary capabilities of critical practitioners require individual sensitivities and advocacy within a firm base of professional values. Working across the boundaries of professional services that intervene into private lives requires the assertive use of authority and the expertise of continuing professional development based on a commitment to children's rights.

Questions for reflection

Is it possible to achieve a fair balance between welfare and justice for young people?

Does your practice with children and young people incorporate a 'challenge to complacency'?

11 Children with disabilities

International perspectives for developing practice

Monica Dowling

> I thought this chapter was enlightening, identifying the knowledge, skills, core values and ethics that are required to support practice with children with disabilities and their families. It also identifies the importance of research and how informative this can be to one's own practice.
>
> (Social worker – Fostering Agency)

Introduction

> Children with disabilities and their families constantly experience barriers to the enjoyment of their basic human rights and to their inclusion in society. Their abilities are overlooked, their capacities are underestimated and their needs are given low priority. Yet, the barriers they face are often as a result of the environment in which they live rather than a result of their impairment.
>
> (UNICEF 2007: iv)

This chapter poses the question: How can social workers and other professionals help children with disabilities and their families overcome barriers and support their inclusion in activities and opportunities that other families take for granted?

The principal themes which will be discussed in relation to this question are working with parents and children with disabilities to discover and define disability, working with parents and children with disabilities when a child needs to be protected from harm or abuse, and working with parents and children to build community-based services.

Research examples quoted here are from The Open University and UNICEF sponsored qualitative study of 140 parents, disabled children and providers in Bulgaria and Bosnia and Herzegovina. While they relate to a particular set of circumstances, the professional practices illustrated here offer insights which can be applied to the context of other disabled children's lives and family situations. This research also demonstrates that community-based services which are led by families, children and young people can be developed by countries with different levels of service provision.

Discovering and defining disability

Because of the stigma associated with disability in some countries and cultures, families may be reluctant to report that their child has a disability. In countries where diagnosis is more advanced and the likelihood of survival is greater or where state benefits are available to support the child, there is a greater incentive to register a child's disability, thus contributing to a higher recorded prevalence of disability. Disabilities are also not always discovered in very young children and some children acquire impairments through accidents or illness.

How a disability is discovered and defined will vary from time to time and place to place, however, there are complex issues surrounding discovery and definition that need to be examined. For a practitioner to have a good knowledge about different types of disability is important in parents' eyes, but so is understanding the child's disability from the parent and child's perspective. Bailey *et al.* (2006) have a 'top down' approach to practitioners sharing information about a child's disability. In an evaluation of US programmes working with families of young children with disabilities, they suggest that successful family outcomes are measured by how well the parents understand the information provided by the professional and share it with others, advocate for services and respond effectively to the child's needs. However, such an approach does not allow for an interactive dynamic between parent and professional and it can be argued that a more child-focused approach is also needed.

Such an approach is suggested by Howe* (2006) who notes the importance of sensitive interactive communication with families and cites the example of communicating with a blind child – where parents will need to learn to develop their sense of touch, sound and movement rather than be rewarded by visual facial communication through smiles and facial gestures:

> Parents need to be helped to get inside their child, to think about how she experiences the world and the sense she is likely to make of this.
>
> (Lewis 2003: 306)

An understanding of families' social context and the impact of practitioner intervention is also relevant. For example, from Canada, Goddard *et al.* (2000) suggest that professionals need to be aware of the invasiveness of intended help and the lack of appreciation of the parents' personal context:

> Once you have a child with a disability, it's almost like it's not your child, it belongs to the system ... I already had a child and nobody came into my life. I had this child and within three months I had probably visits from four different professions – the health unit, child development centres, infant development on and on ... I never had so many people in my life and you felt like this child did not belong to you.
>
> (Goddard *et al.* 2000: 282)

What also appears important in relation to overcoming barriers for parents in discovering and defining disability is peer group support (UNICEF 2005; Dowling 2006). Mahoney and Wiggers (2007) suggest social workers can be instrumental in supporting and developing such groups and in involving parents in early intervention. 'One of the major barriers is that the majority of professionals in this field do not come from a theoretical and experiential background that emphasizes the role of parents in child development services' (2007: 14).

Therefore, training in parent- and child-focused communication for health care professionals, social workers and civil servants is needed, which would include more accessible information provided by children, parents and professionals within government and within voluntary projects, dissemination of information through health and social work centres and children and parents' organizations.

Protecting a child with disabilities from harm

Most social workers would support the social model of disability and are aware of the existence of barriers, inequalities and unequal opportunities for children with disabilities and their families. They would view this model equally as important as the medical model of disability which seeks to define, quantify and objectively test and then improve and sometimes cure different impairments. Dowling and Dolan* (2001) proposed that social organization disables not just the family member with impairment, but the whole family unit. They argue that by applying the social model to the family unit rather than just to the individual child, new ways for creating policies and practices can be developed for children with disabilities. This perspective fits well with the previous discussion concerning the involvement of families in the planning and implementation of early intervention initiatives. However, if domestic violence and/or abuse of the child with disabilities is occurring within the family it is more difficult to apply such a model. Parents of other children with disabilities can encourage and support the individual family to seek help (Dowling 2006) but the complexity of the situation is that, on the one hand, the difficulties the family as a unit is facing need to be addressed, while on the other hand the child with disabilities has a right to be protected from harm.

Baldry *et al.** (2006) suggest that internationally, the occurrence of domestic and other forms of violence in families affecting children with disabilities is poorly understood. Studies suggest that the rates of abuse for children with disabilities are much higher than for children without disabilities, but importantly, available international studies do not distinguish between abuse in residential settings by carers and others unknown to the child or young person and abuse within the family (Sullivan and Knutson 2000).

The costs of looking after a child with disabilities – giving up work to look after the child, the costs of travel to appointments, treatment, special food and medical equipment and medication – have meant hardship for many families. If families are also experiencing domestic violence, this may increase their sense of social exclusion at being 'different' and non-offending members of the family may be prevented from going out. These combined effects are likely to result in the non-offending carer of the child with disabilities being unable to leave. If the child has complex needs, it may be impossible to provide adequate care outside the family home. It has further been suggested that child protection and safeguarding teams do not have the knowledge of disabilities that is needed to complement their interventions (Morris 1999; Aarons and Powell 2003).

The combination of disability and child protection issues makes for a vulnerable population of children and creates dilemmas for professionals working with families with a child with a disability. A number of recommendations are suggested below to aid professionals where there is suspected violence and/or abuse to the child:

- It is important not to make assumptions about the level of impairment that the child is supposed to have. Many children in situations of domestic violence will be aware of threatened and actual violence in the home.
- Practice is enhanced when professionals work together with and alongside families to construct solutions which families can live with and own.
- Understanding the many different methods of communicating with children with disabilities is essential to give children the opportunity to create some control over their situation.
- For many children with disabilities relating to a stranger can be stressful and exacerbate difficult behaviours – it is important to seek advice on how to interact or talk to a child.
- Knowledge about local services – for example, short-term respite care, intensive family support or accessible women's refuges – can be essential when determining a child's safeguarding needs.
- Coordinated cross-agency arrangements are invaluable and can determine, for example, the legal position regarding the non-offending carer and child's rights to stay in already modified accommodation.

Lundeby and Tossebro (2008) point out that in Norway the family structure in raising a child with a disability is similar to other families. Whether this is a positive finding for parents' relationships, or whether having a child with a disability may produce a stronger feeling of obligation to stay together, is not known. They also point out that the Norwegian welfare state system allows both parents to work while caring for their child with a disability, which can help maintain positive relationships within couples.

Supporting families and building community-based services

Changing an institutional system to a community-based system is not a task that social workers can deal with alone, but when policies support that approach they can intervene to implement community-based support systems. Additionally, their contribution in ensuring that parents and children have been consulted and have been heard can be of fundamental importance in changing policy and practice. For example, it is important that parents and children are involved in defining criteria both in the development of community-based projects and the evaluation of the outputs and impact of projects and interventions. However, even when providers create what they see as a positive transition from institutional care, it does not necessarily lead to a better quality of life for the young person or child with disabilities.

For example, in Bulgaria social workers' focused intervention and development work with residents could have helped transform one Bulgarian institution (Example 1) into a centre that offered day care, foster care, respite care, leisure and educational opportunities for disabled children and young people and group support for parents and providers (UNICEF 2005).

Example 1: Changes to institutional care – Bulgaria

> The staff in the residential institution demonstrated an eagerness to modify their work towards community style living. They are building smaller houses in the nearby village with the idea that this form of accommodation is more suited to the needs of their residents. However the children and young people living in them hardly have any contact with the village residents and they still have their classes, meals and attend events in the main buildings of the institution. This well intentioned change is producing institutionalization in the community. Disabled children are still denied a voice and choice of where they live. Even though the new houses are well equipped, living in a remote village with elderly locals and heavy supervision from institutional staff has not brought mainstream socialization, inclusive education or employment.
>
> (Bećirević *et al.* 2010)

Example 2 shows another community-based approach that *has* involved social workers in multidisciplinary work with NGOs and health professionals and defectologists (medical professionals in Eastern Europe who are qualified in disability practices).

Example 2: Good practice – day centre – Bosnia and Herzegovina

> The day centre for children with multiple disabilities 'Koraci Nade' (Steps of Hope) is recognized for its ways of working. It was opened in 1994 with support from Oxfam and it has developed into an important community resource for children and parents. For several years the centre was financed by various international organizations and NGOs and now half of the financing comes from the Ministry for Social Policy and the rest from various fundraising activities. This centre emphasizes

> inclusion, with activities aimed at the promotion of children's rights, rehabilitation and socialization, and the encouragement of disabled children into mainstream schools. It also provides education for parents in order to equip them for their role. The centre works closely with the Faculty of Defectology in Tuzla which organizes some of the practical teaching and provides student volunteers for the centre employment.
>
> (Bećirević *et al.* 2010)

Developing community-based services, which are led by families and young people with disabilities, is a policy that can be applied to a variety of countries with different levels of service provision. The following further two examples develop this theme.

A group of parents with children with disabilities in Newham, London were elected to the local council and began the process of radically changing mainstream schools so that all children, whatever their needs, could learn together. They changed the percentage of children assessed as having special educational needs and attending mainstream schools from seven per cent in 1986 to 79 per cent in 2001. An independent report noted that having to make better provision for all pupils had resulted in a marked improvement in school examination results throughout the Borough (UNICEF 2007).

In Mexico, PROJIMO (Programme of Rehabilitation Organized by Disabled Youth of Western Mexico) has promoted many community-based health and rehabilitation initiatives, including the Children's Wheelchair project which produces over one hundred low-cost customized wheelchairs a year from the Sierra Madre mountains (UNICEF 2007).

Foster care, independent living, personal assistance, respite care and outreach services can be developed and organized by local NGOs in cooperation with social workers. Successful local grassroots initiatives with parents and NGOs need to be identified and supported by social workers, national governments and international donors (Holland 2008).

Conclusion

This discussion of the role of professionals in delivering services for children with disabilities in different parts of the world shows the criticality of the three principal themes in relation to working with parents and children outlined in the introduction. While services in some countries are embryonic, there is no room for complacency in the so-called developed world. Many of the issues raised remain unresolved for families in the UK and elsewhere. For the newly qualified practitioner, consultations with children with disabilities and their parents on what services they need and how these services could be achieved is essential. As well as close liaison with the family after the child's diagnosis, professionals' time is also well utilized by developing and supporting peer groups in the community that could help and advise children and young people and their parents.

There are some clear messages from the research included here. Parents and children in the community are still far from adequately supported and served. At the same time, in many countries institutionalization is still the only option for disabled children. Improving community services and de-institutionalization are dependent on recommendations for action in a number of key policy areas (UNICEF 2005, 2007). Further research on domestic violence and child abuse in relation to children with disabilities is essential.

Best practice is associated with rights and the recognition that children and parents can be supported to exercise choice and control over services (United Nations 2006). The important message to take away from this chapter is that good working partnerships with parents, young people and children with disabilities are fundamental, accompanied by an active approach to skills development and building capacity in communities.

Questions for reflection

In what ways do I and my employing agency ensure that children with disabilities are heard and protected?

How can I use research findings to support and develop my work with children with disabilities and their families?

12 The changing role of social workers in developing contexts for mental health professionals

Sarah Matthews

It is always good to read something which stimulates questions, this chapter achieves that well. It will open eyes to the positive effects of social work as a profession.

(Independent social worker)

Context: new ways of working

For mental health professionals the first decade of the twenty-first century has been dominated by a shift to 'new ways of working' (Department of Health 2007), as increasingly mental health roles and tasks are viewed in terms of competence and capability rather than just being assigned as the specific integrated activity of one profession. Simultaneously, the decade has seen a reform of mental health legislation in England, Wales and Scotland, including ongoing consultation on possible reform in Northern Ireland. These legislative changes have led to different outcomes in relation to people considered eligible to perform compulsory mental health assessments, and in the case of England and Wales, has opened up this function to a range of other non-social work professionals. This chapter discusses the challenges which sharing a formerly exclusive professional identity with others may bring to compulsory mental health social work. It also considers the impact of this developing context for mental health professionals in general.

Compulsory mental health assessment refers to the process whereby a mental health professional is required to determine if the criteria for detention as set out in mental health legislation are met, and if so whether an application for detention should be made (Department of Health 2008: 33). The decision maker is required to judge, given all the circumstances including the person's social situation and the availability of other appropriate services, whether such detention is the least restrictive way in which that person may receive treatment (Department of Health 2008: 5). The recommendation to include other non-medical professionals as being eligible to conduct compulsory mental health assessments in England and Wales was first suggested in 1999 by the Expert Committee appointed to advise on the need to review mental health legislation in these countries (Department of Health 1999: 48). Subsequent amendments to mental health legislation, culminating in the Mental Health Act 2007, eventually introduced the legal framework for the Approved Mental Health Professional (AMHP). This role replaced the Approved Social Worker (ASW) in England and Wales, and opened up the task of compulsory mental health assessment to other non-medical mental health professionals, bringing with it a formal change of name. The consultation on reform of mental health legislation in Scotland, on the other hand, recommended retention of the role as exclusive to social workers. The Scottish committee deemed that social work was the only profession to combine independence from the health service with training and experience of working within a statutory framework (Scottish Executive 2001). In Northern Ireland a similar review by the Department of Health, Social Services and Public Safety (2007) is following Scotland's lead and recommending the retention of a sole function for ASWs. For England and Wales, therefore, it is relevant and timely to consider what challenges these developments will bring to compulsory mental health social work and what impact, if any, they will have in the wider context of mental health practice?

Contributions: independence of role, of assessment and of decision making

One of the main consequences of the creation of AMHPs in England and Wales may be that the former relative independence of the assessment role itself will be in danger of being eroded. Opening up the assessment role to other professionals, who are likely to have similar professional backgrounds to the medical profession, may, by default, blur former boundaries based on professional independence, resulting in collusion; but there is little evidence to conclude whether such erosion has so far taken place. Instead, the Code of Practice 2008, which accompanies the Mental Health Act 2007, provides seemingly full backing to retaining independence as key, arguing that: 'although AMHPs act on behalf of a Local Social Service Authority (LSSA) they cannot be told by the LSSA or anyone else whether or not to make an application for compulsory admission. They must exercise their own judgment, based on social and medical evidence, when deciding whether to apply for a patient to be detained under the Act' (Department of Health 2008: 36). Herein is an emerging challenge. AMHPs are still to be approved by local authorities in England and Wales, but they do not now need to be employed by them as formerly they were required to be. This may result in a lessening of allegiance and, in turn, a decreasing motivation for local authorities to carry out the formal approval process in a robust manner. This potential trend, however, has not yet been identified and so far seems not to be established.

The 1983 Mental Health Act in England and Wales was considered at the time of its inception to be a major step forward in recognizing an individual's right to an independent mental health assessment (Jones 1993). Independence in this context applies primarily to the central decision-making function about compulsory detention as being free from medical influence. Independence is seen as the underpinning principle of compulsory mental health assessments and is one of the main arguments made by BASW and the Approved Social Worker Interest Group to the expert committees in England, Wales, Scotland, and now in Northern Ireland, in favour of retaining compulsory mental health assessments as an exclusively social work function. For the Scottish committee this was central, arguing 'it would not be appropriate for the independent role of the Mental Health Officer to be performed by someone employed within the health services' (Scottish Executive 2001: 89). For the English committee, while they agreed that independence is key, they did not agree that this should be 'exclusive' to ASWs (Department of Health 1999: 48).

Independence in decision making does, however, remain a central tenet in what is currently the new role of the AMHP in England and Wales. Guidance contained in the AMHP regulations introduced in 2008 describes matters which should be taken into account to determine competence of AMHPs, including being able to make 'properly informed independent decisions' (National Institute for Mental Health in England 2008: 5). But will this guidance be enough? The crux of this challenge would seem to centre on training, as suggested in the phrase 'trained with equivalent rigour' (Department of Health 1999: 48). 'Relevant training' needs to allow all those wishing to undertake the AMHP role to achieve the standard of competence which the former training for ASWs based on social work approaches and methods afforded, and which has been recognized by the expert committee and subsequent guidance as being of a high standard (Department of Health 1999; National Institute for Mental Health in England 2008). Any professional outside of social work will need to understand and be assessed against key competences, on a par with those which were formerly used to approve ASWs, and which, over many years, have been considered effective. Initial indications are that AMHP training in England and Wales is intentionally being grounded in the social work model. For example, in the guidance developed for the selection and training of potential AMHP applicants is included the statement, that 'all candidates need to work to demonstrate what are in effect, social work values and practice' (National Institute for Mental Health in England 2008: 30). This is probably a cause for celebration, as it appears to be a clear acceptance of what social work can contribute. Moreover, regulation of new AMHP training is to remain within the remit of the GSCC, the regulatory body for all social work training pre- and post-qualification. Appropriate, rigorous training in all competences will be crucial to the success of the AMHP and hopefully should allay fears which have been expressed by some, that the Approved Professional making the final decision to apply for compulsory hospital admission may be examining the case for detention through 'non-social work eyes' (Rapaport* 2006: 38). The need to be approved as social work competent in the role enriches compulsory mental health social work and provides an excellent opportunity for social work's particular contribution to achieve appropriate recognition.

Contribution: a social perspective and least restrictive alternative

The Code of Practice which accompanies the reformed legislation in England and Wales recognizes that AMHPs need to bring 'a social perspective to bear on their decision' (Department of Health 2008: 36). A principal theoretical critique applied by the social work profession is the social perspective, and for mental health social work, this perspective 'demands a much deeper engagement with the many layers of feeling and meaning, concerning a person and their social experience' (Tew* 2005: 16). In other words, the perspective that social work brings challenges the perhaps familiar medical model, which in essence views mental distress more as a symptom of an illness to be treated without necessarily fully taking into account the possible impact which difficult social circumstances may have upon a person's mental health and emotional well-being. The introduction of the ASW role in compulsory mental health assessments in 1983 was viewed as evidence of a move to ensure that all such assessments should be socially informed. Early findings of investigation into the work undertaken by ASWs described the importance of 'social factors, both in the form of social disadvantage such as race and gender and the social process of assessment in understanding [mental health] sections as a consistent theme' (Sheppard 1993: 232). It is important for this practice and qualitative approach not to be lost, and to retain the element of the social contribution is crucial to social work. But the process of approval to be an AMHP may in fact prove to be a valuable opportunity for the social dimension in assessment to be re-asserted and manifest itself once again.

There has been little research conducted into the effectiveness of the Approved Social Worker. Much of what little research does exist, however, has focused on the limited number of social workers undertaking the role (Huxley *et al.* 2005), or on the impact of assessment on the individual service user (Hatfield 2008). It is likely, therefore, that evidence of the particular contribution needs are now to be detailed and promoted, providing space for social work to articulate its contribution to compulsory mental health work, which until now has not always been coherently presented. The guidance for the selection and training of AMHPs makes a helpful contribution in this regard, where it identifies a different emphasis in competence for professions other than social work. Alongside developing a social perspective it suggests three other important elements: developing an understanding and ability to apply anti-discriminatory and anti-oppressive practice; developing an understanding of legislation and its requirements on services; and finally, developing advanced reflection and critical analysis skills (National Institute for Mental Health in England 2008: 31). None of this will be new to any social work educator.

However, it is important to note that independent decision making, while crucial, is not necessarily the main task in the AMHP role; rather it is the judgment as to whether treatment in hospital is the least restrictive alternative (Department of Health 2008: 5). This key contribution, though laudable, has been challenged. Reflecting on the origins of the ASW, Prior (1992) for example, argues that 'professionalizing' the role of social workers in mental health legislation was in effect setting up compulsory mental health social work to fail. Having a professional decision to make about a least restrictive alternative is 'based on the assumption that there is an alternative model of care and treatment' (Prior 1992: 107). It may be though that this is a dilemma which social work can now also share with the other professionals? The ASW role, Prior argues, not only has this inherent contradiction, but it has also had the outcome of focusing specialized training only on a small part of the mental health workforce. It may be then that the opening up of the role in England and Wales to the broader based AMHP cohort is an opportunity to share the particular skills, knowledge and value base of social work? The exclusivity of the role may have been an attempt to gain credibility for the social work profession based in legislation, but it could correspondingly have the detrimental effect of ignoring the remaining mental health workforce and, therefore, ultimately not acknowledging the treatment and support context of the very people who use mental health services. Should the focus and priority for social work, therefore, be less inward looking as it may have become through the ASW role? The challenge undoubtedly is to have an overall well trained workforce while retaining the social perspective and promoting highly developed skills in making judgements about least restrictive alternatives. But to maintain an exclusive single-profession function as a way of protecting professional role and status could unwittingly be to the detriment of those whom the profession espouses to empower. It may be, therefore, that opening up roles and functions may be a timely and significant factor in new ways of working, providing important challenges for the whole workforce, not just exclusively for social work.

Capabilities: future developments

The focus in this chapter so far has been the introduction of the AMHP. The 2007 Mental Health Act, however, also signalled changes relating to other professional roles, including the replacement of the Responsible Medical Officer with the 'Responsible Clinician'; and the introduction of the 'Approved Clinician'. As with the AMHP role, the roles of Responsible Clinician and Approved Clinician have also been opened up to other non-medical professionals. There are significant implications in these changes and a positive challenge for all professionals including social workers. These new roles present an opportunity to carry out functions which have hitherto been ring-fenced as primarily medical and there are therefore potentially new opportunities to develop wider capabilities. This is a cultural shift for all mental health professionals, and it is a time in which the contribution of social work could be more fully recognized and thrive.

Those eligible to act as Approved Clinicians may now be drawn from professionals working alongside medical staff, including psychologists, nurses, occupational therapists and social workers. A Responsible Clinician replaces the Responsible Medical Officer and an Approved Clinician is given overall responsibility for a patient's or service user's case, and the Approved Clinician will undertake the majority of the functions previously performed by the Responsible Medical Officer. This responsibility in effect divides into four possible areas of work: where the patient is detained; where a patient is subject to a Community Treatment Order; where a patient is subject to Guardianship; and finally, consideration in the context of other legislation, including the Human Rights Act 1998, the Mental Capacity Act 2005 and the Equality Act 2006. The latter incorporates duties bound by public authorities, and as such are ideal settings for the social work profession in contrast to the medical profession. Guidance on the role and competences expected of Approved Clinicians was published in November 2008 (National Institute for Mental Health in England 2008). It is clear from this guidance that processes for the selection and approval of Approved Clinicians are not yet that robust, in contrast to the guidance developed for AMHPs built upon the former processes relating to ASWs. This lack of robustness for Approved Clinicians instead of being feared as a weakness, could arguably be an excellent opportunity for other professionals to influence the measures against which Approved Clinicians are approved. The opening up of the former medical professional role may paradoxically be an opportunity for the social model of mental health to thrive where previously the traditional medical model has so often dominated and prevailed.

Approval of Approved Clinicians is the remit of an Approval Panel and is a statutory duty. The published guidance suggests that Approval Panels may also wish to ensure that appropriate training is available and to audit the quality of this training and the calibre of candidates (National Institute for Mental Health in England 2008: 19). This directive appears though to have limitations, appearing to make it only optional for SHAs to ensure that robust training and approval processes are in place. This also appears to be borne out in practice. Initially, training for Approved Clinicians was built upon training provided for those wishing to be approved as Section 12 doctors under the Mental Health Act 1983, and was managed variously within each SHA area. A report commissioned to investigate early implementers of both AMHP and Approved Clinician roles (National Mental Health Development Unit 2009) made it clear though from an early analysis that approval processes and procedures for Approved Clinicians were in their infancy, noting that while publication of the guidelines for approval will undoubtedly make more straightforward the training and approval, processes seemed absent in some SHAs (National Mental Health Development Unit 2009: 16). Herein perhaps are opportunities for training not just to match the standard elsewhere, such as for AMHPs, but it may also be where new approval criteria will incorporate those competences which refer to and have embedded in them the social perspective as a crucial paradigm for effective and empowering assessment.

Conclusion

Policy and legislative changes to compulsory mental health work in the first decade of the twenty-first century have led to a cultural shift in the ways in which mental health professionals operate. The introduction of the Approved Mental Health Professional in England and Wales was initially met with significant and perhaps understandable concerns that opening up the role previously undertaken exclusively by social workers to professionals outside of social work could erode both the contribution which social work had made thus far, and in turn maybe negatively impact upon social work as a profession.

So far there is very little evidence to suggest that this will be the case; rather, there is maybe even an emerging recognition that demonstrating effective social work competence is central to any robust approval process and as such, the AMHP role underpins and positively represents the overall social work contribution. The opening up of roles has not just been limited to AMHPs however. The introduction of the Approved Clinician and the possibility for a wider range of individual professionals being appointed as Responsible Clinicians provides a major opportunity for those other than medical professionals to be recognized as being competent in such roles. The key for these developments will be the influence which other professions eventually have on the training and subsequent approval processes, and for those duties which are bound by public authorities this is an obvious function and potentially exciting future challenge.

Questions for reflection

How much of a threat to social work as a profession are the emerging new roles in mental health?

To what extent are these new roles an opportunity for social work to strengthen its perspective?

If I am considering taking on these emerging roles how does this affect my own professional identity?

13 With respect to old age

Caroline Holland

> I like the reference to the personal experiences of older people which helped me to feel as though the author had grounded their knowledge in these. It was helpful to be reminded that social workers assist in shaping social attitudes towards older people and, therefore, I have a role to play in this.
>
> (Social worker – Children and Families Team)

Introduction

What do older people want from social workers? This chapter considers what it means to be an older person in the twenty-first century and the increasing contribution that social workers can make to the well-being of older people, their supporters and dependents. The chapter argues that respect for the older individual and the avoidance of making inappropriate assumptions based entirely on the category of 'age' is key to good practice. Assumptions about people's needs based on age alone have the potential to be misleading, oppressive and sometimes dangerous. Not everyone working in social care can be an expert on ageing, but interactions with older people happen across the range of social care and support: for example, older people may be primary carers of children or vulnerable younger adults, or of other older people. This means that a basic understanding of the variability of old age is helpful for the practice of all professionals in health and social care.

Context for practice

Global long-term trends in population ageing are driven by two main factors, both with implications for social work practice. The first is increasing longevity: more people are able to live longer because of developments in health, welfare and medical technology. The second trend is declining birth rates: this means that over time the proportion of older to younger people has shifted, with an impact on the ability of younger generations to provide informal support for elders.

But when is 'old'? Between and within global national jurisdictions there are differences in the thresholds by which people are regarded as being 'older', for example, there are variations in the age of eligibility for retirement pensions, access to concessions or eligibility for senior housing. In addition to formal definitions there are cultural and individual variations in the perception of ageing that make simple age-based definitions less relevant to how individuals experience their own ageing process. Because people are not all the same, individuals may vary in their own consciousness of ageing and experience of being treated as aged, and this relates to many other parts of their life, such as health, wealth, education, pension rights and socialization (Gilleard and Higgs 2005). For some people discrimination on the grounds of age is experienced in a context of earlier and/or current discrimination based on ethnicity, sexual orientation or disability (Ward and Bytheway 2008). People may, therefore, be defined or consider themselves to be 'old' across a wide age range stretching from the mid-fifties to over one hundred. Older populations are also highly varied in terms of culture, attitudes and expectations, so that people who have experienced lifelong poverty and deprivation may experience a very different old age to many of the affluent and well educated post-war 'baby boomers' who are arguably part of the rise of the 'individualized consumer citizen' (Rees Jones *et al.* 2008). It is important for professionals working with older people to understand the contexts of ageing, and to have a good sense of the kinds of support that are available, and appropriate, in particular circumstances.

Understanding ageing

Looking at the whole person enables social workers to consider different aspects of ageing – physical/biological, cognitive/psychological and social/cultural – and how these aspects work together to affect individuals and families. As knowledge about ageing increases, there is a wealth of writing and research available including work by and with older people and practitioners. Social workers can bring to their practice a view of later life that demonstrates an understanding of diversity and the practice challenges involved and which avoids focusing exclusively on the pathology of ageing. This means regarding ageing as one aspect of the individual's complexity, not their defining characteristic.

Health

Studies with older people repeatedly show that many are concerned to a greater or lesser degree about actual or potential loss of good health and what that means for their independence (e.g. Bowling and Gabriel 2007). But there is no simple correlation between age and health because people vary so much in their genetic and social inheritance, in the impact of their past and current lifestyle and health behaviour and in the general environment within which they live.

Older people also worry about the consequences of losing cognitive ability as they age, especially if they have experienced dementia in a relative (Corner and Bond 2004). The prevalence of dementia increases in populations with increasing age, doubling for every five-year increase in age after sixty-five so that around one-third of people aged over ninety-five have some form of dementia. Most people with dementia are cared for in the community by family and friends, with or without formal care services. In many cases the primary carer will be a spouse or a child who may themselves be 'older' and have their own need for social work support.

As with the population in general, older people may also experience mental illnesses, but these have tended to be less clearly identified and at times inadequately treated, arguably sometimes because of assumptions about the effects of ageing. For example, depression has been described as the most common mental health problem in old age, but it has often gone undiagnosed for a number of reasons including older people themselves being reluctant to seek help, the association of depression with physical health problems and the side effects of medications, or the common occurrence of trigger factors such as loneliness, bereavement or other losses (e.g. of sight or hearing, or of a person's own home when entering a care home).

Wealth

As with the rest of the population, older people are found at all levels of income distribution, from billionaires to those in extreme poverty. Many older people in wealthy and middle-income countries have assets, including capital in housing, occupational pensions and savings, as a buffer against the loss of earned income after retirement, and these may well be taken into account when assessing eligibility for state benefits or assistance. However, many more older people rely on pensions provided by the state, and in the UK this especially applies to people aged over seventy-five and older single women, many of whom have not had the opportunity to acquire occupational or private pensions (Office for National Statistics 2009). Consequently there is huge variation in the wealth of older people, but in general terms later life tends to be associated with restricted income, with all that entails.

One persistent source of anxiety in this situation is the high cost relative to income of difficult to avoid expenditure on basics such as food, energy bills, housing costs and council tax/domestic rates (Office for National Statistics 2009). 'Fuel poverty' is the term used to describe the situation where people need to spend more than ten per cent of their available income to keep adequately warm, and it is estimated that this applies to one in three older households in the UK.

The costs of care can also present problems to older people – partly because of the relationship between great old age, disability and low income; partly because entitlement to care services and the actuality of getting access to them can be confusing and subject to change; and partly because of a reluctance to set out on a path that they may see as leading to loss of autonomy.

Social lives

Social networks and relationships are of huge importance to older people and the absence of fulfilling relationships has severe consequences for happiness and well-being (Victor *et al.* 2008). In the UK older people live within networks of family and friends (Phillipson *et al.* 1998; DWP 2005), however, in countries with a strong recent tradition of nuclear family living, many old people live alone. In the UK, almost 90 per cent of older people live in independent accommodation (i.e. not communal establishments), of whom around one-third live alone. While this does not necessarily imply isolation, many older people in this situation will experience periods of loneliness, especially in the evenings and at other times when they do not have much human contact. Yet some will still state a preference to live independently alone rather than alternatives such as living with their children or in a residential care home (Peace *et al.* 2006), demonstrating how important the idea of independence can be.

One of the problems of ageing is the potential for a gradual accumulation of losses, as social roles (work, leisure) become surrendered, old friends and contemporaries die, and with increasing age the likelihood of chronic illnesses and disabilities increases (Pitt 1998). Combine these circumstances with financial hardship and an unwillingness to appear not to be coping, and it is easy to see how some older people slip into isolation.

Social workers also need to be alert to the possibility of elder abuse in all kinds of settings and circumstances. The UK charity Action on Elder Abuse (AEA) describes how abuse may take many forms – physical, psychological, sexual, financial or neglect: it may happen in care homes, hospitals and family homes. It can be intentional or unintentional, and sometimes it is carried out by stressed carers. The physical and emotional signs of abuse are often there to be seen, but when an older person is isolated or afraid of the effects of disclosure it takes great sensitivity to uncover the facts. AEA recommends a careful, listening approach and treating the older person as an adult with opinions that must be taken into account.

Diversity

In addition to a variation in the health, and in the material and social assets available to individual older people, it is important to recognize other aspects of diversity that may affect the services that older people need, as distinct from what they may be offered. For example, older people vary in their experience of and approach to sexuality and intimate relationships. There is often a tendency for people to assume that older people are essentially asexual, with expressions of sexual desire characterized as 'radical'

(Jones 2002). Such assumptions resulted, for example, in the acceptance of older couples becoming separated in care institutions.

Furthermore, older people with a non-heterosexual orientation have tended to be hidden, or subject to even more discrimination in services (Jones and Ward 2009). Non-heterosexuals, especially those who have not been 'out' about their relationships, can face particular problems of non-recognition and isolation in old age, for example, following the death of a long-term partner. People of all ages make choices about what to disclose of themselves to others, and when to do so. Many older people with lesbian, gay, bisexual or transgender identities have lived through profoundly discriminatory times, even in countries where such discrimination is now illegal, and social workers need to be sensitive to the possibility that older people's privately held intimate relationships will affect their preferences in services.

Older people within ethnic minority groups may also have unexplored service preferences. While patterns of migration historically have varied, social workers often find themselves dealing with the effects of successive waves of migration and resettlement. Older members of minority ethnic groups may be native born, long-settled or recently arrived. They may speak the local language as a first or second language, or not at all. Cultural and language barriers can result in misunderstandings about the situation in which older members of minority communities live. Things that people think they know about other cultures – for example, that family will provide adequate care for older members – may not be examined or revisited.

However, social workers' professional understanding of the complexities of family life and variation within, as well as between, minority groups can and should play a crucial role in helping individual older members of minority groups towards the best possible quality of life. Social workers' familiarity with day-to-day issues of diversity, equality and ethical treatment are also beneficial to older people where other aspects of their identity or lifestyle do not conform to generally held expectations of old age. Older travellers and people living alternative lifestyles, those with alcohol/drug/gambling problems, ex-prisoners and homeless older people challenge stereotypes of ageing and may particularly need skilled social workers to hear and understand their needs and to advocate on their behalf.

Respect in practice

> Age does not limit the capacity to love; neither does it diminish the expectation to receive dignity and respect.
>
> (China National Committee on Ageing 2008)

The Research on Age Discrimination (RoAD) project (Bytheway* *et al.* 2007) looked at instances of 'everyday' discrimination, and identified a complex of cumulative practices which for some older people added up to a grinding diminution of their sense of value. The project involved older researchers as fieldworkers to commission and analyse diaries from other older people. A fieldworker described one woman's such experiences:

> She has a strong feeling that, as an older person, 'the world isn't for you'. A theme running through ... is how, on account of her age, she feels treated as someone to whom the normal rules of courtesy, human fellow-feeling or even the law no longer apply. You get ignored in queues for service, pushed off the pavement, people push past you in queues – and no one will lift a finger to help.
>
> (RoAD fieldworker, Bytheway *et al.* 2007: 90)

Turning the tide on such social attitudes is a long-term and complex project, but it is one in which the role of health and social care professionals should be progressive and not entrenched. Good practice respects people as individuals and aims to deliver according to their needs. 'It is clear from the evidence ... that people value respectful delivery of services over task-oriented care and, getting to know people for what they are is therefore an essential aspect of person-centred health and social care practice' (SCIE 2009).

The role of the social worker

The social worker's ability to skilfully negotiate and mediate may be essential in helping many older people and their supporters to navigate their way around complexities of service provision and levels of entitlement. These same skills are essential in advocacy on behalf of older people, where social workers can find themselves negotiating between the older person, their family and formal carers, and a whole range of other professionals in health and social care. Efficient joint working between different services and between public and private provision is often very difficult to achieve in practice, making a social worker's ability to work with other professionals at a personal level all the more valuable to the well-being of older service users.

Some older people come to request help for the first time very late in life – for example, if a care responsibility becomes thrust upon them, or becomes more than they can handle. Social workers should acknowledge any feelings they may express of frustration, humiliation or anger, and work with them in a non-condescending way. Where an older person is emotionally vulnerable, an unsympathetic or ineffective encounter with one social worker may discourage further requests for help. It is crucial that the social worker both respects the integrity of the person before them, looking beyond 'the mask of age', and uses his or her professional skills to negotiate in often challenging situations.

A knowledgeable social worker can also play a crucial role in directing people to sources of information, advocacy and support. For example, recent research in the UK (Holland and Katz 2010) suggests that while many older people know something about residential care homes and 'sheltered' or supported housing, there tends to be much less understanding about alternatives such as adaptations to current housing, assistive technologies or other kinds of supportive housing provision.

Conclusion

There are specific areas related to ageing, including dementia, risk management and end-of-life that represent challenges to social work practice, particularly where there are managerial pressures around budgets and assessments (Ray *et al.** 2008), making it more than ever important for social workers to focus on the individual older person and the context of her or his life and not be distracted by the processes of case management. Social workers trained to look at all the elements of a 'case' and think analytically, provided they give people the attention they need, can sometimes find solutions where others have seen only an intractable problem. This is particularly the case when dealing with older people because the 'fog' of old age can obscure underlying causes and effects unrelated to age. It is, therefore, of the utmost importance that social workers do not fall unwittingly into the trap of age discrimination. Older people rely on their social workers to work creatively and with respect.

Questions for reflection

How do you feel about the prospect of your own ageing? Does your attitude to this have an effect on how you see older people?

How well do you know the older people that you work with, as individuals with a lifetime of experience, attitudes and assumptions?

14 The well-being of people with learning disabilities

Sue Dumbleton

The focus on Scotland was interesting and informative. It considers how the transformation of social care might affect the social work role in this care group. The quotes provide useful insight into what is valued by service users.
(Professional Head of Social Care (Mental Health))

Introduction

This chapter examines the current role and potential contribution of social work to the lives of people who have learning disabilities. It concentrates on social work with adults, though this is not to deny the significant contribution of social work to the lives of children with learning disabilities (Chapter 11). It looks at contemporary principles of practice such as service user involvement and self-directed support. This chapter is located in policy and practice in Scotland (Scottish Executive 2000; Scottish Executive 2006b) and elsewhere. It is beyond the scope of this chapter to provide detailed discussion about the legislation which impacts upon the lives of people with learning disabilities, which in any case varies from country to country. Further, although it is not customary to write about current ways of working with people with learning disabilities without some reference to the history of learning disability services, this chapter does not deal with past practices in any depth. Histories of learning disability abound, including testimonies of people with learning disabilities themselves (see, for example, Atkinson *et al.* 1997; Ingham 2002; Atkinson *et al.* 2005). This chapter does, however, include service user and carer contributions through discussion of the issues raised.

It is difficult to reach consensus on the meaning of the term 'learning disability' as definitions vary according to time, place and culture. Recognizing these ambiguities in definition is not a new phenomenon, nor one confined to Scotland or the UK (Valentine 1956; Purdie and Ellis 2005). The Scottish Executive document *The Same As You?* proposes a definition which will be used for the purposes of this chapter:

> People with leaning disabilities have a significant, lifelong condition that started before adulthood, that affected their development and which means that they need help to:
>
> Understand information;
> Learn skills; and
> Cope independently.
>
> (Scottish Executive 2000: 3)

While not without its complexities, it reflects some previous legal definitions. For example, The Mental Deficiency Act and Lunacy (Scotland) Act (1913) states that:

> Mental defectiveness means a condition of arrested or incomplete development of mind existing before the age of eighteen years, whether arising from inherent causes or induced by disease or injury.

It seems that, in some respects, the identification of people who are today recognized as having a learning disability has not changed greatly.

What do social workers do in their work with people who have learning disabilities? Given that a person who has a learning disability is a person first (British Institute of Learning Disabilities 2004), the easy answer is that the role of the social worker in relation to someone who has a learning disability is the same as it is with anyone. Given government estimates (Scottish Executive 2000) of more than one in fifty of the population with learning disability, or between one and two per cent of the UK population (British Institute of Learning Disabilities 2004), it is almost certain that social workers will come into contact with service users who have a learning disability or to know someone in their family, community or neighbourhood who has a learning disability. This is particularly the case for criminal justice social workers as people who have a learning disability are disproportionately represented in the prison population (Loucks and Talbot 2007). Nevertheless, many frontline social workers state that they lack the knowledge required to work effectively with people who have a learning disability and their families (Scottish Executive 2000), and consequently as they have limited opportunities to practise with people who have a learning disability they lack the context in which to develop 'practice wisdom' (Trevithick 2008: 1231).

In adult social care social workers are primarily care managers or, for service users who have less complex needs, care coordinators. Care management is a sophisticated task which involves assessment, planning and implementation, review and monitoring of a care plan, responding to often rapidly changing needs and managing risk. Care management attempts to target limited resources on those people judged to be in greatest need, including greatest need of protection. The *tasks* of care management should not be separated from the *process* of care management. Care management is dynamic; it should involve the people who use services at all stages, taking into account their views, preferences and aspirations. It should be based on core social work values and approaches such as respect, minimum intervention, empowerment, anti-oppressive and anti-discriminatory practice and build on the service user's personal strengths and natural supports.

It would be hard to argue with any of these propositions. Contemporary public and professional values, policy and legislation all state that people who have a learning disability must be consulted about the services which they use, about the assessments they receive for such services and about the implementation and review of support. Standards for social work education (for example, Scottish Executive 2003) and professional codes of practice (for example, GSCC 2004; SSSC 2005) require social workers to practise in ways which demonstrate these values. Harder to consider is whether there remains a *unique* role for social work in an era of service user involvement, commissioning of services, the contribution of the third sector, multidisciplinary teams and a wider social services workforce.

Practice contexts

What is the role of social workers in the lives of people who have a learning disability? This begs the question of the role of social workers in general. There is a wide literature on the role of social work in the UK and in other countries (for example, Margolin 1997; Douglas and Philpot 1998; Humphries 2004b; Blewett *et al.* 2007; Prynn 2008), but again a definition from the current Scottish literature will suffice:

> the social worker's task is to work alongside people to help them build resilience, maintain hope and optimism and develop their strengths and abilities ... Social workers also have a role as agents of social control ... In this role they have statutory powers to act to protect individuals and communities.
>
> (Scottish Executive 2006b: 26–7)

In short, the role of social workers is as it has been for decades – to provide care and control.

Social workers work with social problems. In twenty-first-century Scotland social workers address the social problem of learning disability largely through assessment, commissioning and overseeing services. The social problem of learning disability is one of many centuries standing. In all societies there are people who are identified as unable to operate competently within social norms (Mittler 1979). Furthermore, they are usually identified as being deficient in something which is highly valued within these social norms. Late twentieth- and early twenty-first-century knowledge-based Western economies value learning, particularly lifelong learning. As Dumbleton (1998: 152) notes:

> learning has become code for adaptability within rapidly changing economic, social and vocational circumstances ... it is not surprising to find that the terminology [learning disability] not only reflects the social significance of learning, but continues to marginalize by identifying a group of people by their failure to possess the most socially desirable attribute of the age.

If people who have learning disabilities did not exhibit the characteristics of requiring help to understand information, learn skills and cope independently, then it is unlikely that they would come to the attention of social workers. Exhibiting these characteristics is by no means a guarantee of receiving a social work service, for while some people with a learning disability do receive a social work service, 'by far the most support is provided by parents, brothers and sisters and other relatives' (Scottish Executive 2000: 7). According to Johnston (2008), receiving such support, especially in the family home, is a key determinant for a person with a learning disability *not* receiving a social work service.

The Scottish Executive definition of the role of the social worker is framed in twenty-first-century Western European social norms. Legislation, including legislation related to people who have a learning disability, is similarly framed within these social norms, and since we 'cannot separate social work from society' (Cree 2002: 275) it follows that social work with people who have a learning disability is also framed within these same social norms. The principles which underpin legislation and policy in relation to people who have a learning disability in twenty-first-century Scotland (and elsewhere), are that these people have the same human rights and needs as anyone else and are entitled to be included in society by, for example, living in ordinary homes rather than hospitals or hostels. In 2006 people who have a learning disability said that what matters most to them is

> getting their own home, having friends and being able to go out more. They also want to make sure they stay in contact with family and they keep the support that is essential to their independence. They enjoy socializing more than anything else and next to that, sport. They hope for new experiences.
>
> (Curtice 2006: 5)

Clearly, the role of a social worker cannot simply be to ensure that people get what they want. Sometimes people have to be prevented from getting what they want, if this places them at risk, or be protected from others who might exploit or abuse them. However, MacIntyre* (2008: 64) notes that the drive to provide increasingly flexible and individualized services in order to enable people with learning disabilities to access appropriate education and employment opportunities as well as health services.

In reality, though, people with learning disabilities experience bullying, harassment, poverty, social exclusion and physical or mental ill health in far greater measure relative to the general population (Enable 1999; Stalker *et al.* 1999; Emerson 2007; MacIntyre 2008; Parckar 2008).

The involvement of people who use social work services and their carers in developing direct services and education programmes is a contemporary policy imperative (Levin 2004; Duncan 2007) and has occurred to a greater or lesser extent with people who have learning disabilities in the UK and internationally. Two further policy developments which have potentially significant influences on the lives of people who have a learning disability are self-directed support and individual budgets. Self-directed support 'is used instead of, or in addition to, support services that the local authority might otherwise have provided' (Scottish Executive 2007: 2). An individual budget is a sum of money which is for 'the person's [who is involved in a self-direct support] sole use to arrange for their support needs' (Scottish Executive 2007: 90). Given the definition of a person who has a learning disability as someone who finds it difficult to understand information, learn skills and cope independently (Scottish Executive 2000) is it possible for an individual who has a learning disability to manage his or her affairs in this way? Directing one's own support is a challenge for most users of social services, and also for providers of services (Spiers 2008). Ways in which such challenges can be met, at least for the user of services, are through centres for Independent Living or organizations which can support the practical aspects of self-directed support, such as becoming an employer or running a payroll – organizations independent of social work services usually run by and for disabled people rather than by social workers.

What role does this then leave for social work? The functions of assessment, commissioning and overview of services are all undertaken by social workers. These functions are major components of the tasks and process of care management. But these tasks and processes can also be undertaken by others – not least the users of services themselves. For example, many social workers who work with people who have learning disabilities are located within multidisciplinary teams where the functions of care management are shared with nurses or occupational therapists (Slevin *et al.* 2008). Direct provision of services, for example, housing support, day care or supported employment tends to be commissioned by social workers rather than provided directly from within social work's own resources.

Uniquely in the UK, Scotland has adopted a system of local area coordination (LAC) in relation to people who have learning disabilities. Originating in Australia, the introduction of LAC was one of the recommendations of the review of learning disability services (Scottish Executive 2000). LAC is described as an 'innovative, person-centred way to support people with learning disabilities and their families to build a "good life"' (Stalker *et al.* 2008: 216). LAC has a strong value base and is committed to working in person-centred ways to promote social inclusion. In this respect it is difficult to distinguish between LAC and social work. One difference between care management and LAC is that LAC is supposed to be a universal service which individuals and families (the term preferred to 'service users and carers' by LACs) can access without assessment.

The role of LAC is to challenge barriers and build community and individual capacity to support the social inclusion of people with learning disabilities (Scottish Government 2008b). Its independence from care management is emphasized (Scottish Government 2008b), although shared aspirations are acknowledged. LAC does not bring with it a budget for individual services – rather it attempts to broker ways of realizing the goals which individuals have identified. But the development of LAC has been patchy and uneven across Scotland. Problems exist with its role and status and, crucially, with funding. In some areas it is both welcome and effective; in others less so and in some it does not exist at all (Stalker *et al.* 2007). Despite its vision of being a universal service, access to LAC is limited by factors such as geography and local priorities.

Conclusion

Social workers have clear legal powers and duties in the effective implementation of legislation such as the Adult Support and Protection (Scotland) Act 2007, the Adults with Incapacity (Scotland) Act 2000 and The Mental Health (Care and Treatment) (Scotland) Act 2003 or equivalent legislation in other parts of the UK. These pieces of legislation, along with many others, will impact upon people who have a learning disability. Many social workers are skilled care managers whose interventions enhance the quality of the lives of people who have learning disabilities. Many social workers are well versed in and committed to working in partnership – with service users, with carers and with other professionals, thus ensuring creative commissioning of resources and coordinated provision of services. Many service users report high levels of satisfaction with their social workers (Davidson and King 2005). It is incontestable that a role exists for social work and that social work makes a valuable contribution to the lives of people who have learning disabilities.

But is there a *unique* role for social work – and does it matter if there isn't? Or is it more important that people who have a learning disability have opportunities to grow and develop, to achieve full citizenship, to contribute to their communities, to realize their ambitions and to be protected? Leaving aside the (vitally important) dimension of adult protection where, as the law is currently framed, the role of the social worker, Mental Health Officer or the Approved Mental Health Practitioner is central (though even here, as MacKay notes, there is scope for people not professionally qualified as social workers to act in some aspects of the law (MacKay 2008)) there are many others – groups of workers, service users and carers – whose knowledge and practice have a positive effect in the lives of people who have a learning disability.

For social workers this should not be cause for pessimism. Trevithick (2008: 1221) notes that

> service users and carers greatly value the human qualities of warmth, interest, concern, acceptance and the 'interpersonal skills' that social workers bring to their work.

While these qualities are not the sole province of social workers they have been recognized as central to effective social work practice and the focus of post-qualifying development (SSSC 2008a). Knowledge about learning disability, or any aspect of social work, is not confined to social workers – and indeed is often exceeded by that gained by users and carers (Trevithick 2008). So what? Social workers' knowledge, skills and values can support effective interventions with people who have learning disabilities. Generic social work skills can be as effective in work with a person who has a learning disability as with any other user of social work services. Rather than feel disempowered or disabled by the knowledge, skills and values which others contribute to work with people who have a learning disability, social workers should feel confident in what they do, be prepared to articulate and justify their practice, demonstrate their accountability for their decisions, operate on the best available evidence and knowledge, recognize the humanity of the people with whom they are working, respect and promote (as far as possible) their independence and wishes and assess and manage risk in their lives. They should, in other words, be social workers.

Questions for reflection

How can social workers contribute to effective multidisciplinary work and promote good practice in their work with people who have a learning disability?

How can social workers use their communication skills, knowledge and values to find out what people who have a learning disability want?

15 Policies and practice with 'vulnerable' adults

Mick McCormick

> This chapter increased my understanding about social work with vulnerable adults and the importance of collaborative/partnership/inter-agency working when working to safeguard vulnerable adults.
>
> (Social worker – Children and Families Team)

Contexts

The term 'vulnerable adult' is being used more often in adult services work (Brammer 2010) and there is an increasing range of legislation in place to help and support adults who may be vulnerable and/or at risk (Mental Health Act 1983, Mental Capacity Act 2005, Carers (Equal Opportunities) Act 2004 and Health and Social Care Act 2008). This chapter examines the concept of the vulnerable adult and considers the contributions and capabilities needed by social workers who work with adult service users.

The first comprehensive guidance on safeguarding adults was published in 2000. *No Secrets: guidance on developing and implementing multi-agency policies and procedures to protect vulnerable adults from abuse* incorporated the concept of 'vulnerable adult' to establish who are the adults on whose behalf additional assistance may be required. The definition of vulnerable incorporated two elements identifying a person over the age of eighteen:

> who is in need of community care services by reason of mental or other disability, age or illness; and
>
> who is or may be unable to take care of him or herself, or unable to protect him or herself against significant harm or exploitation.
>
> (Department of Health 2000a: 8–9)

This suggests that any potential user of social services is entitled to assistance in relation to abuse which will cause them to be vulnerable, while those people who also lack capacity to make their own decisions to take protective steps on their own behalf will warrant more proactive intervention to ensure their best interests are safeguarded. This definition reflects both an eligibility element and a judgement about capacity.

This is a broad definition which incorporates the groups of people specified separately in legislation, namely service users who are vulnerable through age, or who have a physical disability, a mental disorder or a learning disability. The definition is not uncontested, however, and in the context of adult protection the Association of Directors of Social Services (ADSS) considers that the use of the term 'vulnerable adult' is contentious. It prefers 'safeguarding' rather than 'protecting':

> those [adults] who were 'unable to protect themselves from significant harm' were referred to as 'vulnerable adults'. Whilst the phrase 'vulnerable adults' names the high prevalence of abuse experienced by the group, there is a recognition that this definition is contentious. One reason is that the label can be misunderstood, because it seems to locate the cause of abuse with the victim, rather than placing responsibility with the actions or omissions of others.
>
> (ADSS 2005: 4)

Law and policy can separate out individual characteristics of adults and lead to the creation of organizational teams which reflect this. However, the reality encountered in everyday social work and social care practice is less clear cut. For example, some older people will also have a physical disability which may or may not be associated with age; someone with a mental health problem may also be dependent on substances; older people may have mental health problems which may be associated with ageing; and someone with a learning disability may also have a physical disability.

There are, therefore, a great many difficulties inherent in the use of strict categories focusing on different characteristics, and social workers will in practice have to work across a range of legislation and policy in providing good quality services to adults in need and any social services department adopting strict eligibility criteria may screen out people who are in many ways as vulnerable or more vulnerable than others. It is also the case that some service users may be deemed ineligible because they do not fit the profile of a 'vulnerable adult' – they may pose a risk to others as well as to themselves and this can cause conflict and exclusion. 'Vulnerable adults' could also include those perceived to be 'difficult', as well as others with a long history of violence and adults with chaotic lifestyles:

> Even if these are rarely glimpsed beneath a veneer of bravado and addiction such that others may struggle to empathize with them … The goal has to be that vulnerable people, as citizens, are properly assured of their rights and safety whether they live in supported settings or independently in their own homes and communities.
>
> (Brown 2009 in Adams *et al.* 2008: 313)

Contributions from social workers

From early 2000 it was clear that social services departments would be required to take the lead in coordinating local safeguarding arrangements (Department of Health 2000a). This did not mean, however, that other agencies did not have a role. Rather, they would be brought together by a single multi-agency protocol for service delivery under the leadership of social services. Multi-agency working, though, requires collaboration at different levels – ranging from senior management to the creation and positive utilization of strong alliances between practitioners directly involved with individual service users. This has proved, as argued in Chapter 1 in relation to children's services, both a valuable aspiration of practice and a complex reality to achieve.

But working with vulnerable adults is not a clearly delineated process with one problem and one solution. Payne* (2006) describes a case in which a social work colleague was working with many interpersonal and practical problems, dealing with a range of agencies. The tasks undertaken by the social worker were varied and included a number of complex assessments and reports. This 'jack-of-all-trades' (Payne 2006: 162) role for social workers will not come as a surprise to social workers and managers. A further example of this role for which social work would seem well placed is cited by McCormick (2009), who points out the close relationship between mental distress and material and social deprivation, arguing that the policies aimed at promoting mental health should be primarily economic and social rather than medical and curative, so that mental health services (including social workers as part of the multidisciplinary team) can offer people more opportunities to get their lives back and to focus less on medication and symptom control. Hugman, too, considers that

> Social work is a whole that is made up of micro and macro perspectives on social need, of the pursuit of social change and social harmony and stability, and of the way in which all of these elements interconnect in achieving human well-being. Portrayals of social work that say it is only this or only that are cases of mistaken identity. No one part can be privileged without distorting or so misrepresenting the complex whole.
>
> (Hugman 2009: 13)

While it would seem to be the norm in the UK for social workers to respond to 'the borderline, non-standard elements of people's lives that cross organizational boundaries and impinge on the main focus of the agency's work and other professionals' interests' (Payne 2006: 162), research by the Thomas Coram Unit found that social workers in England were in charge of case management and direct contact with families, whereas in many European countries these responsibilities were split between several highly trained professionals. They asked if it is, 'reasonable to expect social workers in England to do a job that is shared among members of multi-professional graduate teams in other European countries?' (Boddy and Statham 2009).

Partnership working

Working in partnership is crucial in providing quality services to vulnerable adults. Thompson* (2009) points out that working in partnership is an important social work value which involves collaboration with others involved in the situation in order to maximize the resources available and the opportunities for making progress. Thompson lists the steps that social workers can take to ensure that their own work enshrines the value of partnership:

- Keep the channels of communication open.
- Make sure you consult with the relevant people when forming your view of the situation.
- Work with people – do not do things to them or for them unless required by the specific circumstances of the case.
- Do not rely on untested stereotypes or assumptions.
- Remember the responsibility for resolving the situation is shared.

(Thompson 2009: 161)

Throughout this book many references have been made to the unique contribution that social work and social workers make in the provision of health and social care services. Seden and McCormick (Chapter 24) also point to the work of Beresford (2007) who identifies both personal and professional qualities which service users appreciate in social workers and social work practice. These messages are echoed in the first level social work practice learning course for The Open University BA in social work (England, Wales and Scotland). In the course materials are audio recordings of service users talking about what they want from social workers. For example, they say:

> Listen to what people with learning disabilities have to say, they are the important ones, they're the ones with the voice that has to be heard, so you need to listen to them, what the people with learning disabilities say. 'Listen to us now.'
>
> Social workers can't go into a situation and impose ideas that they might have about what would be good for an individual. If we want to provide good individual support, it really is about listening, and not just listening on a superficial level, but really paying attention to what people are saying, and following through on that. Not just a tokenistic listening, but following through on what the service user is asking for.
>
> (The Open University 2006)

What is also clear from readings in this book and elsewhere (Payne 2006; Cree and Myers 2008; Morris 2008), is that the ability to work interprofessionally is widely regarded as essential to effective social work practice and is central to the complex practice encountered in working with vulnerable adults. So, too, is the ability to work collaboratively and to be an effective member of the multidisciplinary team.

Recently, major government policy has focused on integrating services as a way of successfully achieving collaboration. The development of health and social care trusts following the Health Act 1999 provided a rationale for the development of workers whose skills crossed traditional professional boundaries. The formation of Children's Trusts following the Children Act 2004 also contributed to the general policy of integration as a way of improving services and bridging perceived gaps in provision. But collaboration between services is not the only way to improve outcomes. A key component of successful working together involves the relationships formed between individual practitioners at the level of direct practice. These are crucial to achieve successful collaboration. However, as Morris (2008: 173) points out, 'for many multi-agency settings the experience of developing multi-agency working can be seen to be one of territorial debates and difficulties'.

This issue is highlighted by Orr (2009) who describes the work of social workers working as Approved Mental Health Practitioners. In describing their relationship with psychiatrists, she observes that

> The smallest fissures in cooperative relationships soon turn into dangerous chasms of unpredictability and risk.
>
> (Orr 2009: 5)

The complexity of the collaborative task is also recognized by Barr* (1998), who argues that there is a particular set of skills, knowledge and dispositions needed by practitioners as a part of their professional competence. One competence identified by Barr is collaborate competence, defined as

> Dimensions of competence which every profession needs to collaborate within its own ranks, with other professions, with non-professionals, within organizations, between organizations, with patients and their carers, with volunteers and with community groups.
>
> Barr (1998: 184)

The constituent elements of this competence are helpfully articulated in some detail and incorporate important aspects of professional education and development, including communication, networking ability, partnership working, and leadership skills. They also include other qualities of professionalism that are central to successful inter-professional working, such as values, vision and leadership. All of these are important for effective and competent practice with vulnerable adults, as well as for the maintenance and development of successful multi-agency and inter-professional working and for producing competent practitioners. It is also clear that the importance of respect, tolerance, communication, empathy, networking and the willingness to learn from and to teach others, apply equally as much to work with service users as they do to personal and professional relationships with colleagues.

Conclusion

There are many laws which inform social workers in their roles and practice, as well as a vast quantity of accompanying codes of practice, regulations and guidance. Safeguarding involves action at several stages in the cycle of vulnerability, and partnership with and the participation of service users, carers and colleagues in decision making should always be present. In addition, the principle of minimum intervention necessary to safeguard and promote the welfare of the service users should be at the heart of practice. Finally, the wishes of service users should be included insofar as they can be ascertained, and a variety of forms of communication should be used to identify and clarify their perspectives. The views of service users and their carers should always be taken into account where it is practical and reasonable to do so because, with support, most vulnerable adults can and will make good decisions for themselves.

Questions for reflection

In a multi-agency context, how do I demonstrate collaborative competence?

How do I demonstrate working in partnership with service users and colleagues?

In what ways can I maintain my social work identity in a multi-agency environment?

16 Untangling the web of service user involvement in social services work

Mo McPhail

This chapter adds an important dimension of political analysis to the topic of service user involvement and widens understanding of the thinking underpinning service user involvement. The voices of service users provide a positive challenge to current practice.

(Practice Learning and Development Manager)

Introduction

> Once they have qualified, social workers do not need us for 'feedback' in the same way as student social workers do. The power has shifted; they spend less time with you and are harder to get hold of.
>
> (Comments from service users September 2008)

These comments were voiced by three young people involved as service user representatives in a voluntary sector residential and 'through care' project for children and young people in Scotland. This seems to be an obvious statement of fact, that qualified social workers have less time, but it is also a statement of a sense of betrayal of trust and feeling used. How can social workers best support service users, such as these young people to be involved in the design and development of services which are relevant to their individual and collective needs? This is a potentially confusing and complex area of professional practice – scattered with different perspectives, types of involvement at individual, agency and national levels, employed by a variety of professionals and service user organizations. This chapter attempts to untangle the web of approaches and levels of user involvement and suggests a set of skills and capabilities required for effective involvement which goes beyond stated good intentions. Although set in a Scottish context, this chapter is intended to speak to newly qualified professionals involved across the spectrum of care in the UK and the wider European context whilst acknowledging the diversity of cultural traditions and influences on this work.

Reflections on experience

Sarah, Simon and Naseem (names have been changed to protect the identity of the young people) have been involved as service users in various roles at an individual care planning and agency level, on social work education programmes and as workshop contributors at a university stakeholder event. To give a flavour of their contribution, they reflect on their own experience of involvement with social workers. Although specific to each of their particular contexts, their comments below raise issues which resonate across service user settings and service groups:

- It is important that young people can see their feedback has an impact. It is very disheartening if you give feedback and don't see anything come from it.
- We want to be respected, not patronized, to be able to express our opinions and to talk about what is important to us. We want to be treated with honesty and not spoken to in social work jargon.
- Nothing is worse than social workers wading in with questions and ticking boxes rather than getting to know you as a person.
- Naseem is exasperated by the inexorable interest in her Asian cultural background rather than in her as a total person. Ethnicity is only part of her story, she stresses. She holds a sneaking suspicion that student workers may pounce on her as an example to 'demonstrate their ethnically sensitive and anti-discriminatory practice, to "get that box ticked"'.

In order to begin to untangle the role and impact of involvement of young people such as these, and the skills required to support their effective involvement, it is necessary to locate this debate in the wider context.

Different levels and approaches, contributions by service users and professionals

Service user and carer involvement has been on and off the social services agenda since the late 1960s (Brae 2000; Warren 2007). Despite a multitude of government policy statements and research publications it remains a controversial arena. Newly qualified social services workers may have had some experience of service user and carer involvement during their professional training, though this is likely to be patchy and piecemeal across professional programmes. The situation in practice is no less complex with a variety of approaches and levels of commitment to this agenda from individuals, managers, agencies, professions and at local and national government level. Some key approaches are identified and interrogated in relation to their underlying assumptions. The corresponding skills and capabilities required by staff and service users are discussed.

The locus of user involvement: individual, collective, strategic management and operational in policy making was acknowledged in a European commissioned report on Guidelines for Good Practice in User Involvement in 2004 (CDCS* 2004). This report aspires to be an integrated, holistic approach designed for use by all European member countries to promote the establishment of rights and responsibilities of user involvement. This includes ensuring access to relevant and effective service provision of significant quantity and quality. Users are portrayed as both recipients of and active contributors to shaping the design and delivery of services, located in a wider network of care. In a Europe-wide study, Evers (in Matthias 2006) outlines a range of perspectives: *welfarism*, *consumerism*, *professionalism*, *managerialism* and *participationism*. He argues that understanding these different approaches and their underlying assumptions about welfare provision is pivotal to appreciate the intended purposes of service user involvement and consequent evaluation of its effectiveness. Whilst this summary does not fully portray the complexities and overlaps within and between each approach, it aims to give a flavour of the main differences and underlying assumptions. In practice there is usually a mix and coexistence of a number of these approaches.

Welfarism is defined as a universal system of welfare, characterized by corporate governance and predicated upon professional expertise which may also include a basic charter of user rights or entitlements. Meaningful feedback at this level would involve children and young people's involvement in the development, implementation and regular review of charters against agreed standards, both at individual, agency and national level. It includes representation on various committees of the organization. The young people previously identified speak of their positive experience of involvement in the development and on-going review of a charter of rights and in representation of their unit on the management group of the agency. The skills required of workers to promote and support this activity include information giving, training and supporting young people to develop skills in representing views of their own and of others and in developing various 'committee and meetings skills'. The development of a Children's Charter (Scottish Executive 2004) in Scotland is further evidence of a social rights orientation. The organizations *Save the Children* and *Who Cares?* worked in partnership to engage and support young people in this nationwide consultation, which lends significant credibility to the process. To ensure this is relatively effective, on-going review and development of the charter and the experience of involvement in management are required.

Consumerism is characterized by market approaches to social care, where maximization of consumer choice is a sacred objective. This approach has been subject to heavy criticism (Beresford and Croft 1993, 2003; Harris 2003; Ferguson 2007; Warren 2007). It is indeed challenging to conceptualize children and young people 'looked after' or 'accommodated' by the local authority as consumers with a real sense of power and choice over their care options. In one sense they may be treated as if they were consumers in decisions about services. The failure to address the impact of social inequality and the fact that competitive tendering may be more in the interest of the provider than the service user are serious criticisms of this approach. A further consideration is the requirement to ensure that the legal rights of young people are fully protected in the increasingly market-led environment of social services provision. This would entail access to legal and advocacy skills.

Professionalism, by contrast, has an ethos which is much more about public service and upholding professional codes of conduct which regulate professional relationships with service users (SSSC 2005). Additionally, standards of care that young people and their carers should be able to expect are reflected in the Care Standards for Accommodated Children and Young People (Scottish Commission for the Regulation of Care 2003). Each child or young person and their carer/s receive a copy of this at their point of entry into the care system. Sarah, Simon and Naseem and their carers would be able to make representation to the SSSC if the workers involved in their care were not upholding professional standards of behaviour or care standards were found wanting. Hodgson (2002) evaluates this approach in a study where young people were involved in reviewing the impact of the National Care Standards in Scotland. Issues of genuine and authentic engagement with young people have been highlighted. Hodgson (2002: 55) has described conditions for effective participation as

> access to those in power; access to relevant information; access to a range of different options; support from a trusted person and means for effective appeal or complaint.

Skills and capabilities required of workers are to ensure that the conditions for effective participation are created and sustained. Significant negative factors identified by the young people are under-staffing of units and staff attitudes.

An up-to-date version of professionalism, according to Evers (2006), includes development of information and skills with service users to enable co-production of services. An example of this at an individual level is the active involvement of young people in their own care plans; at an agency level this would mean an enhanced level of participation in managing the agency. This approach is evident in the UK care councils, which regulate professional social work/care education and the wider national professional bodies. Gee and McPhail* (2008) document a process where young people have been involved in producing video materials in social work education at Dundee University in a way that takes account of their interests and talents. *Getting It Right For Every Child* (Scottish Executive 2005) is a further example where young people have worked side by side with policy makers to influence a potentially far-reaching Scotland-wide policy for children. Skills required of workers are of the empowering type, to explore approaches to involvement which are attractive to young people and draw on and develop their existing skills base. A limiting factor in such involvement is the capacity and resources of both young people and professionals to undertake the time-consuming co-work and necessary training. A further critique of this approach is that it is open to either paternalism or an empowering approach, dependent on the values base and orientations of the professionals involved.

Managerialism draws more explicitly on the world of private business incorporating target setting and management of complaints, service effectiveness and efficiency. According to Evers (2006) this can produce a conflict between economic concerns of the agency, professional issues and social justice considerations. Ironically, this context of user involvement can open up some new involvement opportunities in quality assurance and enhancement of service provision. There may be other benefits drawn from the commercial world such as online websites on the *Who Cares?* website or involvement in online consultation and evaluation (Brady 2006). Townson and Chapman (2003: 28) point out that a pressing concern about the managerial approach to user involvement is that it is a 'management'-led process, rather than 'person-led', with 'fundamental difference in origin, process and aim'. Skills involved here include a need to keep a strong focus on the user agenda rather than the management agenda in assuring and enhancing service quality.

Participationism is characterized by direct, practical support for involvement of service users, such as promoting and supporting social network building and self-help user groups. It is a less individualistic approach with a strong element of collective responsibility, defined by Beresford and Croft (1993, 2003) as a *democratic model* and is characterized by a commitment to users as citizens with rights and entitlements and service user-led approaches. The emphasis is on local activity and addressing diverse local needs but also can include involvement in national and international democratic processes. The Children's Parliament in Scotland (Scottish Executive 2005) is a further example of an attempt to locate children and young people's involvement at the site of national level policy making, supported by the Children's Commissioner for Scotland and voluntary organizations well versed in participation of young people. Such an approach requires development of the political skills of lobbying and campaigning at government level for both users and professionals, with an eye to ensuring participation of children and young people who are often the most marginalized and excluded. However, the limitations of such an approach are that it is dependent to a large extent on the availability of dedicated time, energy and resource, which for some young people in care will be problematic. Indeed, some children's services workers may be equally hard pressed and resource light.

A coexistence model is suggested by Evers (2006: 274), where service users are citizens with entitlement; as consumers to be empowered and protected, and ... as co-producers who take up their civic roles and their concerns as members of communities in cooperating with service managers and professionals or by building their own services.

The coexistence model corresponds somewhat with the relatively recent concept of *personalization* in the social services context in the UK (Leadbeater 2005; Scottish Executive 2006a; Ferguson 2007), which has rapidly become a central organizing principle. This concept is enticingly presented as an approach which can overcome the limitations of paternalism and consumerism and has a 'feel good' quality about it. In a critique of personalization, Ferguson (2007) challenges the concept as ambiguous, failing to address such issues as the sense of powerlessness of many service users, poverty, inequality and other forms of structural disadvantage. Instead, Ferguson advocates developing and strengthening alliances between service users and social workers on a collective basis, citing examples of innovative practice such as Independent Living Centres and the social model of disability.

Citizen leadership model

At a national and strategic level in Scotland a User and Carer Panel, supported by the Scottish Consortium for Learning Disability, has worked stoically for a number of years developing and refining the concept of Citizen Leadership. The quest is to offer training and support to service users to develop their capacity as co-producers of services at both strategic and agency levels of influence. This is an integral part of *Changing Lives,* the report of the *21st Century Review of Social Work* in Scotland (Scottish Executive 2006b). A pertinent issue here is the connection with a wider constituency of service users and carers to explore ways in which trained and supported citizen leaders are able to connect with other service users and carers, and in particular those in the most disadvantaged and disempowered sections of society. One idea has been the development of citizen's forums and network-building activities to ensure that the voices of service groups not often heard are represented and that the terms and conditions of service users' involvement are properly addressed.

With particular reference to working with young people as service user representatives, the SCIE position paper (SCIE* 2006) stresses the value of the development of a culture of user involvement as a shared objective between service users, practitioners and operational and strategic management. Other participation skills suggested here are skills to ensure access to appropriate training and support for young people and knowledge of the benefits system so that young people are properly rewarded for their involvement without a negative impact on their benefit entitlements.

Capabilities – service user involvement practice: the warp and weave

It is recognized that newly qualified social workers may have experience of involvement of service users during their professional education and in their previous work experience. A particular challenge for future social workers is to maintain and develop involvement with service users and carers, to develop responsive and innovative social services in a more demanding environment as qualified workers. The case argued here is that the approach to user involvement adopted by social workers and their employing agency impacts on the purpose, process and outcomes, and to some extent defines the skills and capabilities required of both social worker and service user. The existence of a mix of coexisting approaches may also be experienced in practice as problematic. Postle and Beresford (2007) note the difficulties experienced by workers trying to implement approaches based on citizenship in an environment dominated by managerial pressures.

Skills and capabilities identified here (often equally applicable to both social workers and service users) reflect these different perspectives, which are the warp and weave of user involvement at individual, agency and national policy level. In summary, they include: accessing relevant information; developing, implementing and reviewing charters and service standards; support to access those in power in organizations; choice of support of trusted individuals; skills in representing views of self and others, and meeting skills; development of creative and user-friendly participation methods; eliciting expertise from child-centred organizations; development of self advocacy, lobbying and campaigning skills; and skills in widening participation to ensure the most marginalized groups are included.

A range of guidelines for good practice in involving service users exist, including the European Guidelines for Good Practice in User Involvement in 2006, various SCIE position papers and reports and the Scottish Institute for Excellence in Social Work Education Good Practice Guidelines (Beresford and Croft 2003; Ager *et al.* 2006). Two overarching skills/qualities were highlighted in a two-year project of user involvement in social work education in Scotland (Scottish Institute for Excellence in Social Work Education 2003), drawn from the work of Shemmings and Shemmings (1995). These are:

- the development of 'demonstrable trust' between service users and workers; and
- a reflexive use of power by all involved in the partnership.

Among the confusing morass of messages and approaches in involving users and carers in social work, these skills prevail. If service user involvement is to go beyond stated good intentions (McPhail 2008), social work practitioners must attend to issues of power and development of trust, as Ferguson (2008a: 75) notes:

> Power is very often the elephant in the corner – seldom mentioned but its presence and operation is blindingly obvious to the service users present, despite the rhetoric of partnership.

Questions for reflection

In your current social work or social care workplace, which approach or approaches to service user involvement, if any, is dominant? Is there a mix or coexistence of different approaches?

What support and training is available for both staff and services users to promote good practice in involving service users?

17 Person-centred approaches to social work with older people

Aspirations and contradictions

Sandy Sieminski

> I liked that the author recognized that service users don't always fit into what policy makers strive for in regards to independent living. I also appreciated the author highlighting the dependence versus independence social framework towards the end of the chapter.
>
> (Social worker – Children and Families Team)

Introduction

Lawrence *et al.* (2009) report that in internationally developed countries there have been moves to provide care in the community, with the majority of people aged over sixty-five increasingly living on their own or with family rather than in institutional care. Social workers can potentially make a significant contribution to the work of inter-professional teams seeking to assess and meet the needs of older people. This chapter considers the role of the social worker in relation to person-centred approaches to the assessment of need and to the planning of care, within the general current health and social care policy context emphasizing choice and independence.

This policy direction appears to be in tune with what older people want. Tanner (2009: 108) suggests that a central concern for older people is the ability to 'keep going' by sustaining their perception and experience of independence. This may be achieved by maintaining the aspects which preserve their experiences of quality of life in the face of the various difficulties they may encounter. Tanner's review of research literature on older peoples' perceptions of quality of life reveals that this is often related to a number of recurring themes, including the significance of social relationships, social role and activities, health, a positive psychological outlook, home and neighbourhood, financial circumstances and independence. She reports that overall older people value low-level support which enables them to continue living in the community in their own homes, to be able to get out and maintain their social networks and to feel safe in their neighbourhoods. Holloway and Lymbery (2007) also acknowledge that older people have these aspirations regarding maintaining their quality of life, noting:

> The global trend towards community and home-based solutions seem to be generally what people want, delivered in ways which are flexible enough to allow them to shape their own package of care. The emphasis on making the service user central to the process of determining needs and appropriate services of care is a key theme in twenty-first century health and social care systems.
>
> (Holloway and Lymbery 2007: 377)

New Labour entered government in the UK in 1997 and presented its 'modernization' agenda for public services. Although this incorporated some continuity between the health and social care policies of the previous Conservative administration, there was to be no disbanding of market economy for welfare, however, and Labour outlined a new strategy for achieving 'quality' in service provision. A central aim of modernization was to provide 'high quality' and responsive services, addressing consumer demand through the principles of 'person-centeredness', partnership working, integration and the delivery of 'joined-up' services.

Person-centred assessment

In the UK, a mechanism for achieving a holistic multi-agency approach to assessment of needs has been a single or unified assessment framework, incorporating the perspectives of a range of professionals working with the older person concerned. The values of person-centred care and the promotion of independence are intended to be embedded in this process, with the older person's needs and wishes being prioritized. Assessment provides an opportunity for incorporating the perspectives of service users, family members and informal support networks. Lymbery (2006) suggests that the role of the social worker within collaborative working is not always clearly defined. But he notes that social workers have much to contribute to the work undertaken by multi-professional teams (see also Chapters 1 and 15). He argues social workers' skills and knowledge, acquired through their education and training, provide them with an appreciation of family and community contexts which enable them to undertake holistic assessments. This, combined with a professional commitment to anti-oppressive practice and empowerment, well equips social workers to adopt the principles of person-centred practice.

Person-centred planning

A person-centred approach to the planning of care has become a significant feature within UK policy. It was formally introduced in England in 2001 with the Valuing People Strategy (Department of Health 2001b) for people with learning disabilities. Staker and Campbell (1998) argue that person-centred planning is grounded in a rights-based approach, incorporating principles of independence, choice and inclusion. Practitioners working in this way are encouraged to focus on the abilities and aspirations of service users rather than upon their deficits and needs. Magito-McLaughlin *et al.* (2002) suggest that if person-centred planning is to be reality it is vital that assessments incorporate the breadth of each person's background, experience and personal attributes. They argue that this contextualizing information is essential for the design of individual support programmes.

Despite the emphasis placed on adopting a person-centred approach to assessment and the planning of care, a number of factors have been identified which threaten its full-scale implementation. For example, the research of Foster *et al.* (2006) reveals the restricted nature of assessment practice of some social workers. They found that frameworks and topics providing the focus for assessment are significantly shaped by the practitioner's personal assumptions and perceptions, influenced in turn by organizational priorities and the broader service environment. This has led to certain subjects being excluded from discussion, often inhibiting and preventing person-centred assessment in practical terms. The difficulty of different discourses being employed in the assessment process was also identified in an earlier study by Baldock and Hadlow (2002) reviewing the assessment of older people who were 'housebound', which again seemed to inhibit a person-centred approach. In a more recent study, Tanner (2009: 112) notes:

> The underpinning constructs and language used by practitioners were fundamentally different from those used by older people. Whereas practitioners engaged in 'needs-talk', characterized by a focus on resources, abilities and disabilities, older people used 'self-talk', concerned with themselves, their feelings and relationships.

According to Tanner (2009), another obstacle to a 'whole-person' approach is the emphasis on fragmented and restricted roles within social work and social care delivery. The fact that care management is often seen as a 'series of separate tasks' means that service users may not experience social work intervention as a 'seamless' process, because different professionals may take separate responsibilities for assessment, for the coordination of care, and for any subsequent review. This can lead to social workers only forming relatively superficial relationships with service users, possibly restricting the exploration of important and sensitive areas such as life history, mental well-being and an evaluation of the person's social and emotional needs.

Furthermore, within the process of care management there is often an emphasis placed on the social workers' role as manager of care services which can restrict the opportunities for the utilization of the professional and personal skills they will have acquired and developed in working with people. Tanner distinguishes these two approaches to the professional role as first, the 'technical rational' (which amounts to a mechanistic role concerned with arranging the delivery of services), and second, that of 'professional artistry', incorporating judgement, moral dimensions and intuition, associated with forming relationships with service users. She argues that without this second dimension the opportunities to promote well-being are likely to be significantly restricted.

Sanderson (2003) suggests that one organizational strategy to enable members of staff to adopt the person-centred approach is through the creation of person-centred teams. She argues that the characteristics of a person-centred team are that each member:

- sees the team's purpose as supporting people to achieve the lifestyle they want and contributing to their community;
- highly values personal commitment and relationships with the people it supports;
- reviews itself, not the people it supports;
- invests in community connections;
- continually tries new ideas and evaluates whether they improve the support it is providing to achieve the team's purpose.

(Sanderson 2003: 20)

Supporting the devlopment of such a team in practice, she suggests, also requires person-centred leadership. Sanderson defines the characteristics of effective person-centred team leaders as people who:

- see themselves as coaches who bring out the best in people;
- create an environment where team members can identify and solve problems on their own, delegating real power and responsibility;
- demonstrate and articulate the values of the organization;
- look for ways to use staff's interests and strength directly supporting people;
- share decision making;
- have a clear vision and direction;
- encourage personal involvement with the people being supported.

(Sanderson 2003: 20)

Personalization

The concept of personalization was central to New Labour's strategy to reform the public sector, embedded within which were principles of person-centredness for the delivery of health and social care. Carr and Dittrich cite the Prime Minister's Strategy Report *Building on Progress: Public Services* (2007) definition of personalization as

> The process by which services are tailored to the needs and preferences of citizens. The overall vision is that the state should empower citizens to shape their own lives and the services they receive.
>
> (Carr and Dittrich 2008: 33)

Personalization policy was shaped by service user groups, lobbyists, policy analysts, government 'think-tanks' and researchers. A significant contributor to the development of the concept was Leadbeater (2004) through his influential Demos report, *Personalization through Participation*, where he argues for increasing service user participation in the design and delivery of services. Within this vision, the role of the state is presented as being one of enabling rather than being the principal or exclusive provider of social care. In such a context the state creates the environment in which people are enabled and encouraged to take decisions about their lives in new and empowering ways. Leadbeater sees this as providing a preferred bottom-up rather than a top-down approach to social care.

Instruments to deliver the personalization agenda include direct payments and individual budgets, allowing people to receive cash in lieu of directly provided services. Such innovative schemes have a longer history in countries such as Australia, Canada and the USA, than in the UK. In England and Wales though, direct payments were initially introduced by the Conservative Government through the 1996 Community Care (Direct Payments) Act, following successful lobbying by a range of service user groups. This legislation initially excluded those aged over sixty-five from eligibility for direct payments.

In 2000 the Labour administration extended the policy to include older people over 65, parents of disabled children and carers and young disabled people aged between sixteen and nineteen. The 2001 Health and Social Care Act for England and Wales required local authorities to offer direct payments to all those eligible for community care services if they consented and were able to manage their payments. The Scottish Executive also supported direct payments as one means of 'self-directed support' to enable people to achieve independent living (Scottish Executive 2007). The commitment to this strategy is reflected in the allocation of a development grant of £530,000 in 2002 to Direct Payments in Scotland to facilitate the creation of user-led support organizations to provide training, build confidence and to promote awareness of the policy (Glasby and Littlechild 2009: 39). In 2003 direct payments were embedded within the Social Services Performance Assessment Framework Indicators for England and Wales.

According to Leadbeater *et al.* (2008), in implementing the personalization agenda social workers will have to adapt their practices so that they are able to act as:

- Advisers: helping clients to self-assess their needs and plan for their future care.
- Navigators: helping clients find their way to the service they want.
- Brokers: helping clients assemble the right ingredients for their care package from a variety of sources.
- Service providers: deploying therapeutic and counselling skills directly with clients.

- Risk assessors and auditors: especially in complex cases and with vulnerable people deemed to be a risk to themselves or other people.
- Designers of social care systems as a whole: to help draw together formal, informal, voluntary and private sector providers.

(Leadbeater *et al.* 2008: 61)

These authors suggest that such adaptations to the social work role will potentially enable practitioners to engage more effectively in person-centred practice. However, this does not acknowledge the influence of the professional contexts in which practitioners work. Social workers usually operate within the organizational domain of new public management, which emphasizes increased accountability within prescribed service-delivery targets. The impact of constraints generated by such requirements and the potential for adopting a person-centred approach to social work are considered next.

Personalization in practice

An important element in the delivery of personalization has been the availability of direct payments. The findings from research considering the impact of direct payments for older people, however, are mixed. Several studies identify the benefits for older people, while other research has highlighted the difficulties associated with this approach to social care. Clarke *et al.* (2004) explored the impact of policy in three local authorities. They found that people often choose direct payments to have more choice and control over the services they received, or alternatively because it was the only mechanism which enabled them to receive the services they require. They also found evidence that some older people consider direct payments to have positive benefits for their physical health and sense of well-being. Clarke *et al.* also found that older people from black and minority ethnic communities valued the possibility of using direct payments to employ a personal assistant who spoke their own language and understood their cultural needs. Glasby and Littlechild (2009) acknowledge that potentially direct payments can provide an effective means of meeting the needs of people from black and minority ethnic communities. However, they also note the research findings by SCIE (Stuart 2006), suggesting that black and minority ethnic groups are under represented as recipients of direct payments and that service users may face a number of barriers accessing direct payments, such as:

- assessment processes not taking account of black and minority ethnic service users' backgrounds and requirements;
- service users' being unaware of how to access or use information on direct payments;
- difficulty in recruiting personal assistants;
- shortage of appropriate advocacy and support services;

- variable levels of commitment to direct payments among local authorities.

(Cited in Glasby and Littlechild 2009: 68)

A partial explanation for these shortcomings in policy implementation is provided by Clarke *et al.* (2004), linked particularly to the fact that providing direct payments was not part of a care manager's usual way of working at the time of their research. They found mixed responses among care managers, with some being enthusiastic about this new way of working while others expressed the view that they believed many older people were too frail to manage direct payments for themselves.

Resource issues inevitably have an impact on implementation of personalization in practice. Clarke *et al.* (2004), for example, reveal that some care managers had concerns about workload issues and over-restrictive eligibility criteria. Tanner (2009) suggests the way in which eligibility criteria are applied is one of the principal obstacles to adopting a 'whole-person' approach to work with older people. She notes that although local authorities have a duty to assess need for community care services under the 1990 NHS and Community Care Act, access to assessment is often restricted by the practitioners', service users' and carers' awareness of eligibility criteria, although eligibility criteria are supposed to be applied only to the delivery of services rather than at the preliminary stage of assessment.

The *Fair Access to Care Services* guidance on assessment (Department of Health 2003) requires decisions regarding the basis for eligibility to be based principally on assessed risks to independence. These risks may be defined as low, moderate, substantial and critical. Tanner (2009) reports that between 2007 and 2008, 73 per cent of local authorities were planning to restrict access to services by providing them only to those assessed as within the critical or substantial bands. She suggests that this in itself limits the potential benefits of assessment to identify wider support options. Therefore, as Holloway and Lymbery (2007) contend, eligibility criteria threaten the ability of service staff to engage in preventive work which, if successful, would have the potential to enable older people to avoid future dependence on health and social care services.

Lord and Hutchinson (2003) examined individualized funding schemes in Australia, Canada and the USA. They concluded that individualized funding in itself does not necessarily lead to improvements in service users' lives, arguing that to be effective, such schemes need to be embedded in community capacity and network building. Scourfield (2007) notes that movement in this direction is likely to result in the demand for an enlarged role for the local state authorities through supporting community development, a prospect that was almost certainly not envisaged by New Labour in their vision of the implementation of the personalization agenda.

Some aspects of the personalization agenda have been criticized. Ferguson (2007) and Scourfield (2007), for example, suggest that by focusing on the central organizing principles of independence and choice there is a danger that this message correspondingly creates a stigmatizing perception of welfare dependency. Ferguson (2007) argues that what is absent from the personalization policy discourse is the consideration of the impact of poverty and inequality which service users experience. Because of this he contends service users may not match Ulrich Beck's description of 'choosing, deciding, shaping human beings who aspire to be the author of their life' (Ferguson 2007: 396). Scourfield (2007) reminds us that welfare provision has always been developed to protect those who are dependent and to ensure that they are treated with dignity and respect, suggesting that it is unlikely that all welfare liability can appropriately be devolved ultimately to individuals.

Conclusion

Social work practice in the context of new public management presents challenges for practitioners seeking to adopt person-centred approaches in their work with older people. The emphasis on audit and increased accountability threatens to compromise relationship building, the intrinsic aspect of the traditional social work role in assessing and planning care. There are strategies which can be adopted to counter this potential deficit, such as inter-professional education, ensuring that the principles of person planning are more firmly incorporated into practice, and the creation and development of person-centred teams. There is also a need to challenge the negative connotations currently associated with dependency (Chapter 13) and to recognize that some service users may never be able to achieve the levels of independence that policy makers expect. It is, therefore, essential that social workers consider how forms of community and network capacity can be developed more fully to support the needs and requirements of older people in an effective person-centred way.

Questions for reflection

To what extent does the team that you work in have the characteristics of a person-centred team?

What changes would need to be made to make your team more person-centred?

18 People who use services

Finding a voice through ICT

Alun Morgan

> This chapter ... initiates 'outside the box' thinking – posing questions of surveillance and social control. It identifies disadvantages and potential risk factors as areas for social work across all client groups. It has widened my thinking around ICT and reinforced the responsibility I have regarding my practice.
>
> (Social worker – Community Mental Health Team)

Introduction

Every once in a while a phenomenon emerges that seems to have universal application and appeal, accelerating the pace of social and community development – for example, the invention of the wheel and the development of writing and printing. In living memory the emergence and proliferation of Information and Communication Technologies (ICTs) appears to be a phenomenon that represents one of these infrequent developmental leaps, and if history proves this to be the case then we are participants in a significant event occurring in a short period of historical time. It is, therefore, reasonable to argue that social workers should not ignore how they might identify and maximize the opportunities that these technologies and developments offer to them as professionals and to the people who use their services.

Rafferty and Steyaert (2009) report that social workers are already responding positively and actively to ICT but that 'the use of technology for social progress will not happen appropriately and ethically without social workers working with others to mould technology developments and applications to their own and service users' needs' (2009: 590). This chapter explores how people who use social care services may find and have an enhanced recognition of their 'voice' in the social care system through exposure to and engagement with ICTs. It is also about how social workers may contribute positively in this process.

ICTs and the social work context

Information Technology (IT) refers to the use of electronic computers and computer software to store, process and securely retrieve information. ICTs, on the other hand, represent an enhancement beyond IT alone. In ICT, IT is combined with telecommunications, using telephones, networks, television, radio, other computers and any other device for transmitting and communicating information.

The Social Work Taskforce in 2009, established by the UK government to review and make recommendations for reform of the social work profession in England and Wales, made it clear that 'fit-for-purpose computer technology is a prerequisite for an accountable, modern Workforce' (DCSF 2009b: 19). This reflects the reality of many practice settings where social workers deal with large amounts of information, much of it sensitive and confidential; as well as concerns about the opportunities for managerial or government monitoring or surveillance of staff performance through ICT systems. Social workers have also reported (DCSF 2009b) that time spent inputting data is excessive and that the usability and reliability of some major social work software applications can, on occasions, be seriously flawed. Social workers encounter ICT information systems supporting their practice and administration and they also use ICTs for their learning and study. In their direct work they may see ICTs used to assist people with independent living and they will also work with many people who are socially and materially excluded – for whom access to ICTs, let alone finding a voice through ICT, seems either a distant dream, or may be a positive irrelevance. There are also issues about obtaining the technical support and having the adjustments to appliances that some service users will require to access and use such technologies effectively. However, for communities marginalized by poverty or culture there are possibilities for empowerment.

Exploring how people in marginalized communities may be able to find a voice through engagement with ICT, Tacchi and Kiran (2008) researched aspects of making technological change socially effective and culturally empowering in South Asian settings, often in poor rural areas. Their research found that rather than promoting information about ICT use for its own sake, it was better that the voices of the local people were allowed to emerge more naturally and in this way to be communicated organically, enabling people to identify more effectively their own ICT needs and aspirations. Such processes may provide useful models for social workers engaging with marginalized individuals and communities in the UK, supporting the introduction of ICT but starting with and building upon local motivations and needs, bearing in mind that most schemes and projects require start-up funding and can also incur ongoing costs for equipment and support.

The pace of change for ICT applications is rapid. However, the principles upon which ICTs are embraced and deployed emerge and evolve more slowly. For example, Parton (2008) highlights a concern that social workers – through the use of ICTs – may be concentrating more on the informational aspects of their work rather than on the traditional relational aspects. Parton describes this process as 'the shift from a narrative to a database way of thinking' (Parton 2008: 253). Parton accepts the inevitability of the increased speed of decision making inherent in and perhaps demanded by the use of ICT systems. He argues, however, that it is essential that the social and relational aspects of social work are not displaced or lost and that social workers must retain the value of theorizing and reflectively making sense of the situations they encounter. These processes inevitably take time and are not always linear in their progression.

ICT applications

The availability of faster and more reliable online networks and a seemingly inexhaustible desire for user-generated online content has led to a substantial increase in the use of online social networking. Two major current examples in this regard at the time of writing are Facebook and Twitter, but new social networking applications emerge and disappear with great regularity. The Department for Communities and Local Government in the UK reported in 2008 (DCLG 2008a: 7) that 'online social networks can provide a lifeline to those who are isolated and disengaged from family, friends and communities'. In addition, if Leadbeater (2009) is correct in his analysis that supportive relationships provide the key to tackling social ills, then online methods – if they help some individuals to forge and sustain important relationships in their lives – are probably worth social workers supporting, along with other more traditional opportunities for direct social interaction.

Kang (2009) reports an example where some of the digital opportunities provided by the internet are maximized in some parts of the London-based Chinese community, a group numerically and geographically marginalized and far from home. Kang found that rather than the internet contributing to individuals and groups becoming detached from geographical space, the use of high-speed internet connections allowed cultural and temporal practices through social networking, video and audio to be reproduced and in many cases in this community often becoming culturally parallel with those in their native China. For this group, Kang (2009: 326) observed that 'the boundary between home and abroad is challenged and the power dynamics of the majority and minority surrounding urban land-use are destabilized'. This is an interesting example of a community-led interpretation of people finding their internal and virtual community voice, perhaps leading to increased resilience in their external real worlds.

For children, the internet offers almost unlimited opportunities for education, self-expression and civic participation: indeed, for finding and expressing their voice. But children are vulnerable online and it is likely that vulnerable children, those most likely to be encountered professionally by social workers, are particularly exposed in online worlds where identities and motivations can so easily be disguised and misappropriated. Staksrud and Livingstone (2009) highlight some of these online risks for children as: giving out personal information; seeing pornography; seeing violent or hateful content; being bullied, harassed, or stalked; receiving unwanted sexual comments or meeting an online contact offline. They argue that children's ability to cope with online risks often vary across types of risk, cultures, gender and age. Although the experience of successful risk taking is a critical component in resilience-building, parents need 'a closer understanding of their child's perception of online risks and appropriate coping strategies' (Staksrud and Livingstone 2009: 383). They suggest that parents should help children to appreciate and manage the parameters and consequences of the risks they encounter online. A risk-free internet, however, is almost certainly unachievable and parents of vulnerable children often have many distractions or impaired capacities and limited resources to address such complex matters. For social workers, therefore, it is likely that it will be essential to take an active and on-going interest in the strategies and nature of online risk-management for children and also for other potentially vulnerable individuals, as much as it would be the case to appraise themselves of any other significant risk factor in the lives and in the environments of the people with whom they have professional contact.

In reviewing the research literature on Ageing and Technology, Blaschke *et al.* (2009: 642) observe that 'appropriate social work practice in the digital age requires knowing what tools are available and their documented effectiveness and limitations'. They conclude, however, that as the population as a whole ages then a larger proportion of older adults will reach this life stage with increasingly stronger technology skills and different perspectives on the value and limitations of technology in their lives. ICT and Assistive Technology (AT) tools currently available for older people can include applications to assist with safety in the home, to help with physical health and applications to relieve some of the burdens on care givers. Specific examples may be automated smart-home devices for heating or cooking, the remote exchange of health data such as blood pressure levels – often known generically as types of 'telecare' services (Poole 2006) – or online support groups for care-givers. A study by Barrett (2008) noted that a large majority of older adult respondents indicated they would be willing to give up some of their privacy if a technology tool would help them stay in their own home. Hardey and Loader (2009) observe that the increasing user-generated content in ICT applications used by older people and their carers is contributing to their influencing and shaping services, rather than what historically has been more a role of being a passive recipient with limited influence or choice. In the United States, McMillan *et al.* (2008) report that for 'senior citizens' trends such as these are already well established and 68 per cent of younger senior citizens are said to be using the internet, of whom 70 per cent are regularly going online for health related information.

One ubiquitous global ICT device with substantial penetration in almost all societies is the mobile phone – a highly versatile technology used by all social classes and income groups. Mobile phones liberate individuals from being tied to a place to communicate and in this regard they represent a unique development in human communication. The mobile phone is potentially democratizing, enabling permeable communication across barriers that may previously have been much more firmly policed, perhaps by rigid parents, abusive partners or other unwanted agents of control. Mobile phones also allow individuals to manage their social resources in entirely new ways. Geser (2004) observes that mobile phones allow people on the move to remain embedded in their social networks, adding though that they can contribute to the weakening of communities because they can promote extra-community interaction. On the other hand, he argues that mobile phones do make significant contributions for individuals in extending and improving their social networks. Social workers should not underestimate the value and potentially liberating impact of the mobile phone to people who use their services – as well as the obvious practical utility of such devices to them as professionals in their day-to-day work.

The digital divide

Mobile phones are self-evidently used widely, and community applications of ICTs such as commercial internet cafes, community telecentres for ICT access and training, or public libraries with internet access are visible and increasingly commonplace. It is important, however, that social workers are aware of the debate and the lived realities of those who fare less well in the race for information and connectedness: people who experience, and probably suffer, digital exclusion. For people who use services it is possible that in the process of finding their voice through ICT, social workers can have a role in working to remove or ameliorate some of the barriers to digital inclusion, barriers such as difficulties with access, problems with motivation to use ICT, and limited opportunities to improve ICT skills and confidence. Government research in 2008 argued that 'digital equality matters because it can help to mitigate some of the deep social inequalities derived from low incomes, poor health, limited skills or disabilities' (DCLG 2008b: 5). The lack of engagement with ICTs is known to be strongly linked to high levels of material deprivation (Longley and Singleton 2009). In addition, Dutton *et al.* (2009: 5), in their report on internet usage in Britain, suggest that it is at a 'tipping' point, where the social shaping and implications of the internet are becoming more apparent. This, they suggest, is in areas of: information, news, learning and entertainment; communication and social networking; and in work and in everyday life chances and civic participation. Therefore the implications for those at the socially excluded end of the digital divide are probably becoming increasingly significant and potentially more concerning.

With the increasing reliance on text-based internet applications, it will also be necessary for social workers to remain vigilant to the needs of people who are not fluent in English or who may be illiterate. There will also be people who are strongly resistant to the use of ICT, typically those described by Helsper (2009) as 'conscientious objectors' to the use of the internet, believing that we all got along perfectly well before computers and that computers are too impersonal, only serving to reinforce social isolation and electronic dependency. Of course, internet connectedness and computer use alone do not guarantee that people using services will automatically find a voice, and some consider with alarm whether only the more mundane or banal elements of ICT will prevail: 'will socially vulnerable citizens be amusing themselves to death?' (Steyaert and Gould 2009: 752). But social workers must always be alert to creative ICT applications and solutions and seek opportunities to educate and develop wherever possible – always bearing in mind the wishes of those who choose not to be digitally included. Morgan and Fraser (2009) report on the use of audio-computer-assisted self-interviewing (A-CASI) by childcare agencies in the UK as a way of recording the views of children in the care of local authorities. They found considerable enthusiasm from young people and from service mangers for the principles and processes of collecting feedback data electronically, but correspondingly they reported very limited use of the data collected for the subsequent evaluation and improvement of service delivery. It is often the case that access and exposure to information is not sufficient in itself. ICT is a means to an end in social work and social care. Those ends and objectives will almost always have been socially constructed. Nevertheless, they should be driven by the principles and values of professional practice.

Conclusion

Most social workers work with people who are vulnerable, socially disadvantaged or who are temporarily or permanently incapacitated from participating equally in society. It is by no means inevitable, but it is perhaps more than likely that social workers provide professional services to individuals, families and to communities, who have significantly fewer opportunities to access and exploit the advantages of ICTs, or to protect themselves from its disadvantages. Increasingly, however, personal, educational and civic participation is mediated through electronic systems and devices, a trend that is set to continue. Social workers, therefore, must engage fully with this complex area, recognizing where ICT poverty is leading to exclusion or exploitation and as with any other resource in society, negotiate, mediate and take steps to achieve inclusion and promote opportunity wherever possible. This is one of social work's urgent modern challenges: to embrace ICT, warts and all. This may not be easy and success may come fleetingly at times. But who said social work is easy?

Questions for reflection

Are the service users you work with digitally excluded? Is this a significant problem for them, or is it likely to be in the foreseeable future?

Is ICT used too frequently for surveillance and social control and why should social workers be concerned about this issue?

19 Child and family focused work in children's services

Jane Aldgate

> This chapter ... stresses the importance of proactive and preventative social work in equal measure. It offers good explanations of the assessment process and why this is important – but goes further and offers an excellent rationale for engagement of children and families in this.
>
> (Independent social worker – Child Protection)

Introduction

Practitioners take on many roles when working with children and families. Whatever their role, working directly with children and their families is a cornerstone of good practice and there is a substantial body of research that shows how participation in decision making by children and families relates to good outcomes for both child and family (Department of Health 2001a). There is also a good deal of evidence about what both children and families find helpful in the attitudes and actions of social workers (Department of Health 2001a; Rose 2006). Government initiatives, such as the frameworks across the UK for the assessment of children and families, have emphasized the value of practice that respects the rights of individuals, builds on strengths and promotes resilience (Daniel *et al.** 1999; Department of Health *et al.* 2000; Scottish Government* 2008a). This chapter considers the rationale behind effective direct work, drawing on a rights perspective. It then briefly describes some of the key features of assessment, planning and decision making, which are core parts of the social work role. It discusses information sharing, often an area of practice crucial to children's well-being but one which can exclude children and families. Finally, it summarizes the essential components of direct work with children.

Why involve children?

There are three main reasons why children should be involved in decisions that affect their lives. First, children have a right to be involved, spelt out in Section 12 of the UN Convention on the Rights of the Child and the UK primary legislation relating to the care and upbringing of children: Children

Act 1989, Children (Scotland) Act 1995, Northern Ireland Children Order 1995, as well as the Human Rights Act 1998.

Second, children can provide a competent commentary on their own lives (Rose 2006 and Chapter 12). Children bring their own perspective on what they see as important for their well-being. Children can also provide commentaries on how policies and practice should be developed to help them (Scottish Executive 2004, 2006a; Aldgate and McIntosh 2006a, b). Involving children in finding solutions to their problems can also help build resilience (Daniel *et al.* 1999). The concept of resilience is fundamental to children's well-being and is used in assessments by practitioners from many agencies. Resilience occurs where children living in difficult conditions do better developmentally than might be expected (Daniel *et al.* 1999; Gilligan 2000). Many of the children who need social work help are experiencing difficult conditions which may relate to their health, their progress at school or what is happening in their family or community. Building up their resilience gives children a better chance to overcome adversity and reach their best developmental outcomes.

Third, there is a therapeutic element in involving children. They need help to make sense of events and relationships that have brought them to the attention of social workers (Aldgate and Seden 2006). If children are not helped at times of stress, this may be detrimental to their emotional development (Fahlberg 1984; Aldgate and Simmonds 1992). Everyone coming in to contact with a particular child can play their part in this process by the way they communicate and interact with the young person. Children's views of practitioners suggest that they value most:

- reliability, keeping promises
- practical help
- the ability to give support
- time to listen and respond
- seeing children's lives in the round, not just the problems.

(Department of Health 2001a: 93)

Working with children will be more effective if the child's family can also be involved, because parents and carers are always significant in children's lives, even if children have been maltreated by them (Brandon *et al.* 1999) or are separated from them (Owusu-Bempah 2007).

Including parents and carers

Parents can also contribute to children's well-being in their own right. Parents and carers are 'experts' on their children in the sense they know more about them than anyone else. Practitioners cannot reach a full understanding of children's circumstances and needs or help families to find the best support for themselves without recognizing the knowledge and important role families have in contributing to their children's well-being (Family and Parenting Institute 2007).

Partnership, power and inclusion

It is easy to pay lip service to working 'in partnership' with parents and other family members but rather harder to achieve effective participation. Partnership working begins with the appropriate attitudes. Practitioners should treat all parents and carers with dignity and respect, acknowledging that the practitioner's role is to support and help families. Even if families refuse to cooperate initially, practitioners should not give up but keep trying to involve them as much as possible. So often a culture of defensive practice has developed, led by gate-keeping and shortage of resources rather than by a desire to see what can be done to help. Sometimes, a small amount of help, or even the offer of help, can support families to find their own solutions. Often a little effective intervention early on can forestall more complex difficulties developing. This is why preventive social work is so important.

Though partnership is always desirable, where children are 'in need' or 'at risk of significant harm', the power balance between the professional and the child and family will be unequal with practitioners holding the ultimate sanction of being able to remove a child. Practitioners should still take steps to help families recognize their participation is essential in these cases. If families feel that they have contributed fully to any assessment or planning process, they are more likely to be fully committed to putting plans into action (Department of Health 2001a). Above all, research has shown that, even in cases of compulsion, there can be better outcomes for children if parents are fully involved (Brandon *et al.* 1999; Department of Health 2001a). In complex situations where practitioners are going to have long-term involvement with a child and the family it is particularly important to build relationships with the child's parents from the beginning – relationships which enable the parents to contribute to the best of their abilities (Thoburn *et al.* 2000).

Assessing and planning help

Often before social workers can help children and families, they need to have a clear idea of the strengths and pressures children and families are experiencing. Across the UK, governments have developed assessment frameworks and practice models which are underpinned by knowledge of children's development and ecology (Department of Health *et al.* 2000; Scottish Government 2008a). These frameworks and models emphasize both involving children in assessment and keeping them at the centre of any services. Scotland's *Getting it Right for Every Child*, for example, promotes a network of help around the child. Central to the Scottish approach are eight indicators of well-being, which provide a common language across agencies and for children and families. Ideally, all children should be safe, healthy, active, nurtured, achieving, respected, responsible and included. These well-being indicators can be used to identify concerns, plan and take action (Scottish Government 2008a).

The aim of assessment is to understand what is happening in the child's ecology and to gather and analyse information as a foundation for planning and action (Horwath* 2009a). An open process which actively involves children and families has many advantages. Children and families can come to understand their needs and the services that might be helpful to promote a child's well-being. In Scotland, the *Getting it Right for Every Child* programme emphasizes that assessment should be proportionate – not every child needs a full assessment of every aspect of his or her life – and should not prevent help being put in place immediately while more information is being gathered. This approach reassures families that they are being taken seriously (Scottish Government 2008a). It is a principle which could usefully be applied within assessment in any setting.

Alongside the generic understanding of a child's world, there are many tools that can help an understanding of specific aspects of a child's or family's behaviour. In England, the Department of Health has published a book of questionnaires and scales to accompany the Assessment Framework (see Department of Health 2000c; Department of Health *et al.* 2000). These include measures of parenting hassles and children's emotional well-being.

Where children are likely to be at risk of harm from neglect or maltreatment, alongside the more holistic assessment of children's needs, practitioners may wish to use specialist risk assessment tools, such as those developed by Jones *et al.* (2006), which includes lists of factors to be weighed in assessing possible recurrence of harm.

Involving children and young people in assessment and planning

The principles of good communication between children, families and practitioners apply in all circumstances where they come together. Children need help to participate effectively in this aspect of decision making. They need information in advance about how decisions are made and by whom, as well as encouragement and support to attend meetings and speak up when necessary, or have someone to speak for them. Practitioners should help children express their views and make resources available to enable them to prepare or record these in ways that make children's views as influential as the opinions of practitioners. This means giving some thought to the age, and stage, of development and ability of an individual child and with other practitioners, for example, play workers or psychologists, ensuring that a child is in a position to communicate his or her views as clearly as possible.

Before decisions are taken, practitioners should take time to explain what is being planned in ways that children can understand. Young people should be given copies of reports about themselves. When decisions and plans are made, the social worker should talk with the child to make sure that he or she properly understands what will happen next and why. This kind of support to help children participate properly in assessment, planning and decision making can be provided in different ways and by different people, separately or in combination. They may include peer support from young people who have had similar experiences.

Information sharing and seeking consent

During the process of an assessment, it will probably be necessary for the social work practitioner to share information, especially if a multi-agency planning process is needed. Sharing information with a multi-agency team, each of whom has expertise in relation to certain aspects of a child's development and needs, is a critical part of the assessment of risk and need. Included in the challenges in this area of working practice are the issues of consent and confidentiality. Practitioners should discuss sharing information with parents from the earliest point of contact to secure the best services and help for the child and family. Most social work agencies will have protocols for sharing information. Children have a right to see information about themselves, if seeing this information is not damaging to them or others. Where a child has a disability it should not be assumed that child does not have capacity to consent to information sharing and practitioners must make a professional judgement as to the child's capacity to understand and participate, using relevant forms of communication.

Using family-centred approaches to planning and decision making

Parents may be fearful that practitioners will see them as failing parents and could use their power to remove their children. They want the practitioners they meet to be open and honest with them and treat them with respect and dignity, even in the most difficult circumstances. Parents want practitioners to give clear explanations about what is happening (Family and Parenting Institute 2007). Practitioners have a responsibility to develop communications skills and be sensitive to families' understanding without being patronizing or inappropriately talking in technical language. One of the key things parents ask for is to be kept informed (Department of Health 2001a). Practitioners should, at all times, select methods and approaches that adhere to the principles of working in a way that is child and family centred.

There are many ways of developing family-centred approaches to assessment and planning and intervention, such as family group conferencing, an approach that emphasizes strengths and resilience. The child's and family's wishes and feelings are a central consideration and it can serve to build trust and partnerships between family members and professionals

(Barnardo's *et al.* 2002). So, the way in which practitioners gather information from families is as important as the information itself. Parents have told researchers that the two key elements of enhancing their partnership are clarity about expectations and their rights and having a clear idea of what services might be available to them (Department of Health 2001a).

Helping children join in

Even very young children can clearly express views about themselves and their world to adults who are willing to take time to listen to them, do not give up easily and have skills in communicating with children (Rose 2006). Achieving real involvement means that practitioners spend time with, talk to and get to know children and build relationships so that children feel confident about approaching them and asking for help. As Gilligan (2000) suggests, every detail of communication with children counts and helps to build a positive working relationship with them.

It is especially important to help children handle uncertainty while plans are being made. Children can clearly spell out how they feel or what they would like to happen, if they are given time and opportunity to express themselves (Aldgate and McIntosh 2006a, b). Some disabled children may need to use alternatives to speech or writing.

Children also have clear expectations that they want professionals to be reliable, listen, give them time, see their whole lives not just the problems and act as advocates (Department of Health 2001a; Scottish Government 2006a). It is particularly important at turning points in their lives that children are enabled to express their wishes and feelings, make sense of their circumstances and contribute to decisions that affect them.

Working with children at risk of harm

Communicating with children who are at risk of harm needs social workers to develop additional skills. Jones has written an excellent description of the principles of practice with children at risk (Jones 2006). In cases where there are allegations of child maltreatment, research has suggested that sensitivity in early contact, even in circumstances where compulsory measures are taken, can result in positive working relationships at a later stage (Jones and Ramchandani 1999). Summing up working with children, there are five essential components in direct work with children: seeing, observing, talking, doing and engaging (Department of Health *et al.* 2000).

Conclusion

The challenges for practitioners after qualification are to continue to develop those skills which enable them to deliver the best practice they can in line with the research findings that tell them what children and their families find most helpful and within the legal and practice guidance provided for their agencies. They need underpinning knowledge of an ecological model of child development, the theory and principles of working effectively with children and families and a range of skills and tools to translate theory into practice. They must acknowledge children's rights and strive to build up strengths and resilience. Above all, children and families should get the help they need in the way that is most helpful to them.

Questions for reflection

To what extent are you able, in your practice, to ensure the participation of children, parents and carers in assessment, planning and direct work?

What actions can you take to make sure your practice acknowledges children's and families' strengths and builds upon them?

Part III

Complex challenges in the workplace

Sarah Matthews

In Part III we continue to focus on social work practice and in particular the emerging challenges which the social work student faces when they arrive in the workplace as a qualified worker. This part of the book encourages all social workers to engage in activities which develop and protect themselves and their practice. Throughout, the authors acknowledge the twenty-first-century context of social work practice, build upon the positive contributions which social workers make and look ahead to the new capabilities that the social worker should consider and use to grow. Each author identifies new learning and directions that social workers could take in order to continually develop their own knowledge, values and skills and constantly improve their social work practice.

First, Davis, Gordon and Walker (Chapter 20) engage the reader in a journey made in the workplace from learner to newly qualified practitioner, and in particular they discuss the positive impact which learning in practice can have. The authors argue that there are constant themes which are crucial to each part of this journey, including the importance of very good preparation and induction for learning, the need for employers to understand the student role and its demands, and the requirement for both work-based and academic support. The learning journey is one which should continue throughout the life of a practitioner and is further explored in the following chapters.

Nix (Chapter 21), writing on technology-enhanced learning in social work, continues this travel metaphor with a call to all learners and practitioners alike to engage with information and communication technology (ICT). The chapter explores the evolving journey of technology in both the study and practice of social work and provides first-hand accounts from learners who have become practitioners and who are using ICT in their day-to-day practice. Nix concludes that the technological skills developed can have a generic application to core tasks in social work practice.

Building upon the call to engage with information and communication technology, Fraser (Chapter 22) encourages all social work practitioners to engage with ICT in order to study and practise social work values. Fraser describes the use of one internet-based tool and the experiences of those who are using it in both study environments and practice settings. The chapter puts forward the notion that information technology and the specific tool he describes can be used to identify, analyse and discuss the values that underpin practice and in turn support relationship building. Failure to do the latter is often seen as a negative consequence of the use of technology. Fraser concludes that such virtual learning environments can be included into the study of social work and practice and these mechanisms will themselves also need to change and be modified over time to accommodate and assimilate new developments.

A more traditional communication tool skill is discussed by Rai (Chapter 23) who reflects on writing in social work education and practice as a central – yet often overlooked – part of social work education and practice. Rai discusses the primary medium of writing through which student social workers are assessed, and asks the reader to consider how qualified social workers can transfer these academic skills into their practice to good effect. Writing for social work practice reflects the institution for whose purpose it is being created, just as in an academic setting. Its impact is also affected by the degree to which the writer takes account of the purpose of writing and the potential audience. Rai argues for a critical and reflective stance to the production of writing in all areas of social work.

Seden and McCormick (Chapter 24) ask the reader to consider the importance of social workers caring for themselves, being managed and engaging in professional development. This triangulation, they propose, is highly relevant for newly qualified social work practitioners if they are to stay in the role and grow their expertise. The responsibility for all three sides of their triangle lies not just with the individual but should be shared with managers and organizations. All should be aware of and address barriers to being able to successfully achieve the balance between caring for oneself and others. Such strategies, they conclude, should not be left to chance but should be in place from the outset.

The theme of professional development is reinforced by both Cooper (Chapter 25) and Blewett (Chapter 26) whose work draws this part and the book to a close. Both examine why and how social workers should engage in continuing professional development (CPD). Cooper 'careers' through CPD with seven metaphors. He asks the reader to consider the central role which CPD should have in social work and suggests that the approach individual workers take is a strong indicator of their approach to practice. CPD can be an opportunity for lifelong learning, challenge and growth. Cooper illustrates the idea of the relationship between a career in social work and professional development with a series of metaphors which reflect the complex association between employers' requirements and individuals' life-cycles and priorities.

Blewett echoes Cooper's discussion of the reasons why social workers should undertake continuing professional development but also suggests further strategies that practitioners can employ in supporting their professional development. Among the themes he discusses are the development of critically reflective practice and the use of research. He describes the models of research outlined in the literature, namely the research-based practitioner model, the embedded research model and the organizational model as a useful framework for continuing professional development. Both strategies he suggests will develop self-confident and professionally assertive practitioners. Blewett concludes by suggesting that focusing on these elements, both as a practitioner and as an organization, will have a positive impact on social work as it is practised on an individual level, and in the wider environment; which is timely given the debates regarding the nature and future of social work in the first decade of the twenty-first century.

20 Learning in practice

Some reflections on the student's journey

Roger Davis, Jean Gordon and Gill Walker

> What this chapter has done is rekindle my interest in my professional development in respect of my Post Qualifying Award. I am hoping once the 'dust settles' and I 'find my feet better' in this new service I am now working in, I will begin the process of applying to commence my Practice Teaching Award.
>
> (Social worker – Children and Families, Area Team)

Introduction

Learning in practice has 'long been recognized as an important part of developing and maintaining high standards of practice' (Thompson 2006: 1). Much of this learning necessarily takes place 'live', in the workplace where social work practice actually happens. Work-based learning provides opportunities for social care workers to gain experience to enable entry to social work training programmes, for social work students to demonstrate evidence of their ability to apply their academic learning to practice, and for qualified practitioners at every stage of development to learn directly from critical reflection on their day-to-day work.

This chapter takes a look at the journey of the social worker as a learner in practice from entry to qualifying training, through student Practice Learning Opportunities (PLOs) in their own workplace, to the first six months of qualified practice. The authors are social work educators, based in Scotland and England, with experience of facilitating both academic and practice learning. In this chapter we will variously be setting the research examples within an English or Scottish policy context. We hope this will allow readers to gain an understanding of different influences on learning in practice in different parts of the United Kingdom (UK).

The beginning of the journey: embarking on a social work degree

The introduction of a degree level qualification for social workers in 2003/4 has been recognized as providing a key strength of the profession, required to meet the 'growing and increasingly complex demands' faced by social workers in the twenty-first century in Scotland (Scottish Executive 2006b: 3) as well as other parts of the UK. At the same time, UK policy has stressed the importance of widening participation in social work education so that the qualified workforce reflects the diversity of the population (Scottish Executive 2006b: 64). The development of credit transfer systems, such as the Scottish Credit and Qualifications Framework (SCQF 2007), has been one response to this policy objective, promoting opportunities for individuals to gain credit towards social work training from prior study such as Higher National Certificate (HNC), and including work-based qualifications such as the National (and Scottish) Vocational Qualifications.

A study to examine the experiences of social work students with 'advanced entry' (Dumbleton *et al.* 2008) explored the extent to which students felt that their previous experience and training prepared them for social work training, and identified the support required for successful transition into the second year of a four-year honours degree programme (the Scottish social work degree is one year longer than its counterparts in other parts of the UK). The findings of the study suggested that these students were able to make a successful transition onto the social work programme.

Despite having very diverse employment and educational backgrounds, the students who participated in the study described some very similar experiences as they embarked on social work training. Interviewed towards the end of their first year of study, all twenty-four students were positive about their achievements and of the experience of participating in the social work programme, but they also experienced some challenges as they adjusted to becoming students.

Students who had come through work-based vocational training routes, who had gained credit for SVQ and HNC qualifications, tended to perceive themselves as being at a disadvantage in relation to other students with previous degrees or other experience of previous university study. This created anxiety for many of these students at first and a sense that 'we would be dunces in class ...' (Dumbleton *et al.* 2008: 11). However, these differences seemed to become less significant as students settled into the programme and became more confident about their abilities. There appeared to be a number of key factors that supported them in managing this transition: the importance of both life and previous practice experience to their entry to social work education was highlighted by all the students (Dumbleton *et al.* 2008: 6). These experiences enabled students to integrate their learning, about social work theory for example, during the programme with their 'live' experience of practice. It appeared that students developed increasing confidence that they could transfer knowledge, skills and values from their practice experience in the workplace to social work education as they progressed through their first year of the qualification. For many, this transition was supported by the development of skills in reflection and reflective writing that enabled them to identify their own personal capabilities as practitioners and enhanced their ability to learn from ongoing practice (Dumbleton *et al.* 2008: 12).

The participants also suggested a number of ways in which social work programmes can improve the support they offer to students. A central theme was the need to support student confidence and self belief, both as learners embarked on their training and as they progressed through the programme. Good-quality inductions, and an effective learning environment that builds confidence to support independent learning, taking account of students' needs for both work-based support and academic support, were seen as crucial elements in that transition (Dumbleton *et al.* 2008).

Dumbleton *et al.*'s research highlights the importance of a wide range of prior experience, both personal and professional, to the social worker embarking on social work education, and identifies some of the supports students need to make best use of that experience. We now move on to look at learning in practice during the social work degree.

Moving on: the journey through qualification

The social work degree requires students to have 200 days of learning in practice: it also requires students to undertake this practice in at least two different settings and to provide services to two different service user groups (Department of Health 2002). As a result the drive to extend the number and range of sites where learning in practice can take place became a key objective in all parts of the UK. In England this work was taken forward by the Department of Health-funded Practice Learning Taskforce 2003–6, the Learning Resource Networks, and the more recently formed Social Work Development Partnership (Skills for Care 2009). In a review of practice learning following the introduction of the degree in England, Doel* (2005: 8) referred to the emergence of a 'new landscape'. To date this landscape had continued to move and shift, reflecting a diverse range of contexts and locations as the drive to address a national shortage of PLOs continues to challenge both employers and Higher Education providers.

Although there has been very little research on students undertaking employment-based PLOs, there is a prevailing perception that students are less satisfied with placements in their own employing agency than 'external' PLOs. Dunworth (2007: 163), for example, suggests that students prefer PLOs with their employing organization so they can gain new experience. Two research studies provide some interesting insights into the experiences of students undertaking practice learning in their workplace and, more broadly, help us to begin to gain a better understanding of how practice, learning and employment interact. First, Walker (2004) explored the strengths and weaknesses of undertaking a PLO in a student's own work base from the perspective of thirty students. She then went on to investigate good practice in workplace-based PLOs from the employer's perspective in relation to a sample of six personnel who were involved in practice learning (Walker 2006).

The findings of the 2004 study suggested that student satisfaction was strongly related to clarity about student identity, a restricted and adjusted workload, and support and awareness of the student role from supervisors, colleagues and practice assessors. When these prerequisites were in place there was evidence to suggest that a student's own workplace can be an effective location within which to undertake a PLO. These findings were further substantiated by the 2006 study in which employers identified successful examples of own workplace PLOs. Taken together the studies suggested that own work-base PLOs are not necessarily a poorer learning opportunity but can only be as good as the quality of support and understanding provided by both employers and educational systems.

Other research has pointed in the same direction, for example, Hopkins *et al.** (2005: 573) found that social work students in their own employment-based PLOs reported positive and different learning experiences. They suggest that familiarity with the setting had enabled the students to negotiate suitable and different learning opportunities.

Significantly, Walker (2004: 35) also found that students did not perceive themselves as passive recipients of support. They frequently identified themselves as playing an active function in achieving a positive learning environment, also described by Barron (2004: 35) as the ability to be 'self directing'. Students believed that they should and could take responsibility for developing support networks with student colleagues and becoming assertive and proactive learners.

Walker's research highlights the importance of both the personal capabilities of individual students, and the capacity of both employers and education providers to support effective use of practice for learning and development. This interplay between student and organizational capabilities is also identified in the last section of this chapter as key to student progression as they embarked on social work training (Dumbleton *et al.* 2008), and is one we will return to later.

The end of the journey? Post-qualifying learning

Learning, of course, does not come to an end when social workers complete qualifying training, and since the 1990s there has been a growing emphasis on ensuring that social work practitioners and managers continue to prioritize their work-based professional development. These requirements are now built into Codes of Practice for the UK social services workforce with workers in Scotland, for example, being required to ensure that they take responsibility for 'maintaining and improving their knowledge and skills' (SSSC 2005: 15). UK social work registration requirements for post-registration teaching and learning are designed to cement a new ethos of continuous professional development into the structure of social work practice and service delivery and it is further recognized that this needs to be supported by employers (SSSC 2008b: 8). There is also increasing appreciation of the context in which learning takes place, and the need for social services agencies to take responsibility for developing as 'learning organizations' which can learn from experience and adapt to changing circumstances (see, for example, Gould and Baldwin 2004). This growing emphasis on continuous learning is not unique to social services work, or even to the workplace. Social work learning in practice has an important contribution to make, both to meet these policy objectives and, through the growing body of research about what supports learning in practice, to suggest some effective ways to achieve these aims.

The final part of this chapter will focus on some early findings of a research project *Prepared for Practice? Exploring and evaluating the first six months of post-qualified practice in social work* (P4P) that explores how prepared a small group of these graduates felt for their first six months of professional practice (Nix *et al.* 2009). The P4P study seeked to investigate what happened during these students' degree studies that helped develop them from skilled workers to reflective, professional practitioners.

As is the case with some social work students, those in the study brought a variety of skills and knowledge with them but acknowledged that at programme entry there was an awareness that they still had a lot to learn and reflect on:

> I ... know I've got all this experience, I know I do a good job, because my boss tells me I do, but there's something missing ... that thing that I know I do but I don't know why I do it.
>
> (Graduate A, Nix *et al.* 2009: 11)

All students in the P4P study talked about the importance and relevance of their PLOs in helping to crystallize the relationship between theory and practice, by and large regardless of whether the PLO was within or without the sponsoring agency. Most of these newly qualified social workers are, in their first six months of practice, working with more complex cases and managing greater risk than in their pre-qualifying roles, even where they are continuing to work in the same team as before. Unsurprisingly most are also being allocated work that requires a qualified social worker to carry out, such as court and child protection work, as their employers seek to capitalize on their employees' new status. Most graduates understood from the outset of their training that their employer/sponsor would expect them to take on increased levels of responsibility after graduating and that this might involve moving to positions within the agency that would require social worker qualification as an essential job specification.

With only a few exceptions what was evident from these graduates was the clear sense of confidence they felt in their role whatever the setting:

> I stepped into the degree course and I've stepped out the other side, and I'm very different as a result. Still ... in essence the same woman that I was but I'm now somebody who can really, I think, quite easily argue

> for what I'm trying to say, and to know that there's a lot of evidence, there's a lot of research behind ... what I'm saying.
>
> (Graduate I, Nix *et al.* 2009: 17)

While some students reported a shift in identity conferred upon them by service users, carers or colleagues, what was significantly more important and relevant was that this new-found confidence emerged from an academic appreciation of the value of reflection on the social work process, built up on a sound knowledge base and developed through learning in practice. This emerging confidence was evident in relation to developing a professional identity as well as the confidence to challenge and advocate for service users and carers, negotiate role and task, and own professional assessments and definitions of situations.

Osmond and O'Connor (2006) found that qualified child protection social workers in Australia did not routinely employ a research or theory base to underpin their practice. They suggest that social work students need to develop a style of learning that utilizes best practice and which they take with them into their employment as qualified workers. The early findings from the P4P project (Nix *et al.* 2009) is capturing some heartening evidence that this group of newly qualified social workers may indeed have developed an appreciation of the importance of research and learnt the Information Literacy skills required to engage with evidence-informed practice.

The qualification journey

This chapter has travelled with the social work student through the social work degree qualification and out the other side into qualified practice. What does this journey tell us about what works in learning in practice? Research used to investigate the roads to and through qualification finds students who are highly motivated, persistent and self-directed in their approach to learning in practice. Student contributions to these different research projects appear to chart a steady development of confidence in their ability to critically reflect on past and present experience, and to integrate this new learning with their developing skills, knowledge and professional values. Their accounts of these changes highlight the importance of both their own motivation and abilities, and the capacity of both employers and educational providers to support this learning in practice.

Scotland's *Framework for Continuous Learning in Social Services* (SSSC/ Institute for Research and Innovation in Social Services 2008) also stresses many of the personal capabilities highlighted by students as significant to learning from practice in these studies, such as motivation to learn, confidence and the ability to critically evaluate their practice and that of others. The framework, which seeks to embed a structured approach to lifelong learning in Scotland also, importantly, stresses the importance of the organizational environment in supporting social services staff to realize their personal capabilities. The need for such organizational capabilities is evident from the student and practitioner perspectives in the research summarized for this chapter. They include the importance of very good preparation and induction for learning, the need for employers to understand the student role and its demands and for both work-based and academic support for student learning through qualification and beyond. Crisp and Maidment (2009) suggest that, far from seeing practice learning as being 'what students do', we need to reconceptualize practice learning as just one step of a lifelong professional learning process which requires both proactive learners and the expertise and insight of supportive employers and the education providers. Both these personal and organizational capabilities are needed to develop the 'confident and competent workforce' (Scottish Executive 2006b: 7) required for social work in the twenty-first century.

Questions for reflection

How are you able to be an active learner in your workplace?

What specific support (for example, through induction, supervision and training opportunities, etc.) can you call on from employers and colleagues to remain actively engaged in learning?

21 Technology-enhanced learning for social work education and practice

Ingrid Nix

> The chapter provides a good overview of the difficulties and more positive aspects of Technology-Enhanced Learning and Information and Communication Technology skills within learning opportunities and social work practice. It encourages practitioners to relate information to their practice.
>
> (Social worker – Community Mental Health Team)

Contexts

A feature of twenty-first-century social work practice is that practitioners are spending large amounts of time on technology-enhanced tasks. Work practices are changing not just to accommodate developments within the 'digital age', but are also being driven by government imperatives such as the Modernising Government agenda (Cabinet Office 1999) and E-government strategy (Cabinet Office 2000). These policies stipulated that all services be e-accessible by 2005 to improve public access to services and engage with citizens and their communities. Inevitably, educational providers and employers face the challenge of identifying how best to teach capability in Information and Communication Technology (ICT) and how it can best be utilized to enhance social work practice. Social workers, who previously would not have expected ICT to be part of their skill-set, will need to become engaged both as learners and as practitioners.

To address teaching capability, the care councils of Scotland, Wales and England incorporated ICT into their social work degree qualifications, requiring ECDL (European Computer Driving Licence) equivalent skills. In 2009 after consultation, the English care council made revisions to the requirements for the social work degree in England, removing ECDL equivalence. Instead, along with some specific ICT requirements, the benchmarks (Quality Assurance Agency 2008: section 6.4) explicitly included skills achieved through blended learning:

> Approaches to support blended learning should include the use of ICT to access data, literature and resources, as well as engagement with technologies to support communication and reflection and sharing of learning across academic and practice learning settings.

Instead of teaching a separate syllabus of ECDL skills, this revision suggests that 'blended learning' (or technology-enhanced learning – TEL) can provide opportunities to develop generic ICT skills of use to work-based learners as well as social work practitioners. While engaging in learning about social work, learners will simultaneously be using and developing skills in the technologies that help deliver that learning and which may be equally useful in their practice.

This chapter explores an example of integrated ICT skills development incorporating ECDL skills requirements and TEL on an open and distance learning social work degree. It draws on the project *Prepared for Practice?* (P4P) (Cooper *et al.* 2009; Nix *et al.* 2009), a small-scale study of graduates which investigated the experiences of work-based learners during their studies as social work degree students and how, once graduated and working as social work practitioners, they perceive their studies in preparing them for technology-enhanced social work practice. The chapter considers the successes and limitations of the integrated ECDL and TEL approach encountered, focusing especially on the views of the more confident P4P participants, who reveal the evolving role of technology within their professional practice and their attitudes towards it.

E-learning approaches

E-learning emphasizes the electronic or digital nature of learning materials and tools to deliver learning, including websites, electronic documents and media on DVD-ROM. Blended learning highlights the nature of the mix involved, often indicating a combination of face-to-face with digital technology. Since technological horizons are continually broadening, learning can take place with the help of a growing list of technologies, including mobile devices and social networking tools. Technology-enhanced learning emphasizes the intention that the learning experience be supported and enriched by the contribution of technology. Technology-enhanced social work practice refers to any equivalent developments which support and bring benefit to social work practice and improve or enrich the experience of service users and carers.

The introduction of technologies into the workplace may be disruptive. As Rafferty and Steyaert* point out (2009: 590–3), during the policy era 'of accountability and monitoring' staff perceived computerized systems as less about enhancing practice and more about managerialism, producing 'unreflective people-processing' (White 2009: 129), and taking practitioners away from their face-to-face contact with service users and carers (Peckover *et al.* 2008; Shaw *et al.* 2009). Others have argued that technologies could improve practice, provide better information sharing and save time (Ousley *et al.** 2003: 194). However, since the 1990s additional arguments have been emerging, affirming the potential of technologies to enrich the quality of peoples' lives, learning and practice (Rafferty and

Steyaert 2009: 589–91). There are encouraging signs that this is starting to occur among graduates in the United Kingdom. Some P4P participants are now actively pursuing how best to employ technologies to benefit service users and carers. Indeed, some are sufficiently interested to want to help design improvements in their own work-based computerized systems. Since poor uptake can have potentially devastating effects on outcomes for service users and carers, there is interest in research which explores how work-based learners come to accept and use technologies, and the links to home and educational use (Thorpe and Edmunds 2009).

Technology-enhanced learning tends to be delivered through an online virtual learning environment (VLE) or learning management system (LMS) – basically a one-stop website. Courses within it will be made up of a blend of content using a variety of media and computer-based or electronic facilities, sometimes accessible via course websites. By being regularly required to use these facilities the learner, therefore, has the potential to develop and maintain the relevant skills (Oliver and McLoughlin 2001). The motivation to use a VLE comes partly through necessity to engage with course materials but also through the benefits it offers, such as the convenience of resources provided in one location.

TEL features depend on choices made by educational providers (Ayala* 2008) but may include all of these facilities:

- course websites containing electronic course materials (to access information in a variety of ways);
- online communication forum and discussion tools (to reflect and communicate interactively with peers bringing a range of perspectives);
- library facilities – online journals, databases, recommended websites (to retrieve and evaluate information to support practice such as decision making);
- media-rich case studies, interactive simulations – online/offline (to interrogate diverse practice examples and perspectives);
- applications to locate, capture, store, share and present information.

The programme of ICT skills development evaluated in the P4P study was designed for students to develop across three years (or levels) of study, from awareness-raising, to applying, to critically evaluating the skills, corresponding to their development as reflective and critical practitioners in social work practice.

Student perspectives

The following student perspectives are drawn from twelve P4P participants who were interviewed in 2009, six months into their post-qualifying social work practice. The interviewees, who had volunteered to participate in follow-up evaluation before graduating, represented a range of experience both in terms of ICT and social work practice. All had combined being employed in social work during their degree studies. The examples discussed demonstrate how the participants engaged with TEL evaluating the usefulness of the learning and how they selected out what was relevant to immediate tasks, roles and responsibilities.

In terms of adjusting to TEL, the majority of P4P participants perceived that they started the degree already confident in basic ICT skills. Whatever their original starting point, the majority of P4P participants agreed they emerged from using TEL during their degree with higher confidence levels in ICT and Information Literacy (IL) skills. Several P4P participants indicated they found TEL useful as work-based learners because they were able to use its flexibility to select activities to suit their work or travel arrangements, and it therefore prepared them for independent learning. For some, being in the workplace sometimes proved a barrier to learning, hence having additional flexibility to learn away from work via TEL offered distinct advantages.

The motivation of participants was influenced both by the importance given to ICT within their practice settings and by recognition given within the educational qualification, for instance, by the proportional weighting of marks given in assessments. Activities, such as communicating in online forums, received variable levels of commitment due to lack of marks awarded. Likewise, some found the detailed work required for the bibliographic database too time-consuming and complex compared with their own preferred techniques. Despite the principles it highlighted regarding detailed record-keeping, it would appear that the rationale for the bibliographic database's use was too remote from an equivalent application in their particular social work practice setting.

Most P4P participants disliked ICT skills activities which did not have immediate relevance to their studies or were couched in a social work practice they did not recognize. Participants also reported that they wanted systems such as online communication systems provided for study to resemble as closely as possible those they encountered in their social work practice, perceiving any switch between educational and work systems as disorientating as well as time consuming. Some P4P participants were able to extrapolate and transfer skills from one system to another, but if pressured by lack of time or confidence they were unlikely to make connections and therefore perceived the activity or skill as fruitless.

The issue of whether to provide generic or customized and contextualized activities highlights a dilemma for educators. Confident and already skilled, P4P participants valued opportunities to select their own route through learning materials, self-assessing their need and deciding when to study something. As one participant put it, 'there is not enough time to learn everything in case it might be necessary' (Nix 2009: 26). Less confident participants preferred step-by-step guidance and integrated activities to provide regular practice. The majority of participants reported receiving in-house training for in-house systems. This therefore suggests that degrees need not teach service-specific skills. Practitioner motivation is then also likely to be higher, and timing and support more appropriate. Nonetheless, one participant felt it would be helpful to be given authentic examples by educational providers, for instance, of systems in neighbouring local authorities, to broaden their understanding of underpinning principles and uses.

So, having encountered technology enhancements during their learning, how did participants see these enhancements transforming their own social work practice and the practice of others, and what were their attitudes? To contextualize their motivation, the P4P participants almost unanimously agreed that ICT has a crucial role to play in their work. They indicated that as well as the subtle benefits ICT can bring to practice, such as imparting information in more accessible ways to service users, a key driver is the fundamental task of accurately recording and sharing information and avoiding gaps – thus helping to manage risk.

Examples which participants gave of their recent social work practice incorporating ICT or IL skills included:

- Managing their workload using tools such as an online calendar, spreadsheets, or saving template documents to be used more efficiently.
- Using search skills to locate information on behalf of service users or to make a case to colleagues in support of a particular decision.
- Producing clear, legible, professional-looking reports and documentation to share with others.
- Using in-house database systems effectively and swiftly, thereby allowing more time to be spent with service users.

This suggests that there is indeed considerable synergy between the skills needed for TEL and technology-enhanced social work practice.

For both study and social work practice, computer systems need to be user friendly, intuitive to understand and tasks straightforward to achieve in order to optimize time spent on the computer. It was evident that among the more confident participants some took a particularly proactive approach, engaging with TEL and adapting it to add value to their practice. Information literacy skills can provide a clear link to core functions of practice, such as evidence gathering and evaluating and interpreting information. For example, a former IT manager now working in a Children in Care Team indicated that the degree took away her fear about where to look for information. When asked to work with applications using different methods than her norm on course activities she found it required additional concentration and was sometimes frustrating. However, she noted that she learnt different and sometimes more effective techniques. In one case when an activity did not suit her approach, she instead came up with her own method, which in itself she found useful. She attributed her ability to take on learning two new computerized record systems in two different practice learning opportunities to her growing confidence.

The importance of effectively capturing and sharing information was widely recognized by the P4P participants, many of whom work in social work settings where a particular computerized system is already embedded. Although some appeared to be satisfied, others were critical of the design of the systems and practices developing around their use. Three of the twelve participants stood out as being particularly reflective about the quality of the ICT systems and usage in their workplaces, and since developing their skills while studying for the social work degree were interested in bringing about improvements. Comments from two of them are summarized next.

One participant had strong views about the dangers of people entering incomplete data into the system, thus leaving the possibility of others entering data into the wrong location in the system. She felt this introduced risks and she speculated that it was caused by people finding the systems difficult or unworkable. She also experienced different practices working in different teams: in a Referral and Assessment team and later in a Children and Care Team where she discovered information had been inputted in different ways, leading to inconsistencies.

Another participant commented on the frustration of data not flowing from one system into another by default, which is a common issue (Shaw *et al.* 2009: 621). For example, data from scanned health documents could not be copied and pasted into social work care plans and therefore required typing in. At her own request and as a result of her increased confidence, she spent extra training time with the IT department to evaluate any new system to gain a holistic understanding and to better support her colleagues.

It appears that strengthening confidence and the ability to critique their own and others' practice enabled these participants to engage with ICT systems. It is reassuring to discover that 'champions' are emerging who are prepared not only to support their less confident colleagues, but also motivated enough to address their concerns about less than effective systems, and willing to help inform design improvements to those systems to change practices.

Technologies also bring benefit to people who use services, providing up-to-the-minute information and research and allowing the speedy sharing of information. One participant referred to methods of communication she selects to suit different service users. She may, for example, use mobile phone text messaging with teenagers (in her view their preferred way to contact her), and with a mother with learning difficulties and another with hearing difficulties (for whom the text format allows greater accessibility). Her use appears to be discerning. Another participant, working for a drug and alcohol service, revealed that her agency uses a combination of their own website and links to social networking sites to attract young people to revisit their website regularly to view updates to drug-related information.

Several participants mentioned new working practices on their horizons, including smart-working, mobile-working using smartphones and home access to work networks; and using the new database, ContactPoint, which is being introduced in some social work departments. Their concerns included managing employers' expectations of employee work–life balance, which can include the assumption, for example, that staff and resources can be reached at all times using mobile technologies, including at home. Some participants commented on a reluctance to use a smartphone, believing that practitioners can fall into the trap of overusing them – for example, checking their emails even during a break in a training session. As educators we may wish to consider how best in future to investigate and monitor practice needs and create a match with TEL, so that the practitioner can simultaneously keep abreast of emerging technologies while engaged in social work education.

Conclusion

This chapter has discussed the use of TEL and ICT skills within one social work education programme in order to prepare learners for current technology-enhanced practice. The 'snapshots' of the views of P4P participants have highlighted the kinds of issues that arise in such preparation. The examples given illustrate that the skills developed by using TEL have a generic application to core tasks in social work practice, both in terms of working effectively with computerized systems and processes, but also regarding the quality of the information that can be found and shared, and how best it can be communicated, including with service users and carers. This has demonstrated that rather than view this as a happy coincidence, we should explicitly recognize that TEL has a role to play in preparing practitioners for practice.

As technological tools for learning and practice evolve, practitioners will need to keep abreast of change and be open-minded about future innovations. Involvement with and evaluation of such tools will ensure that new systems and approaches are fit for purpose, including for social work practice, and are neither inappropriate nor imposed. Such ongoing appraisal is crucial to ensure technology is indeed enhancing practice.

Questions for reflection

How far do the experiences and perceptions of the interviewees resonate with your own experiences of e-learning?

What would be two or three key messages about the use of ICT in the workplace that you would want social worker employers and educators to take away from this evaluation?

22 An innovative approach to the study and practice of social work values

Sandy Fraser

I learned about the importance and application of social work values and how the Values Exchange can provide a twenty-first-century forum to discuss social work values in a non-threatening and participative manner.

(Inspector – Health and Social Care)

Introduction

This chapter does not discuss the nature of social work values per se, rather it suggests a different way to study and practise social work values using new technology. It features an examination of one web-interactive system that aims to allow detailed reflection and iterative inspection of values when they arise in interdisciplinary practice situations. The context for social work practice is changing and web-based Information Communication Technology (ICT) is likely to become a part of the study and practice of the social work process itself and will always throw up challenges. The use of new technologies in the study and practice of social work practice can give rise to Orwellian or Frankensteinian fears, and equally to misplaced enthusiasm for gadgets and electronic trickery. The latter may reflect a desire to avoid or escape from the necessity generating valid relationships with service users – often the difficult heart of the social work role (Gorman 2003).

For example, a criticism that has been levelled at the 'electronic Common Assessment Framework' provided for childcare social workers in England, is that it takes social workers away from direct client contact (Pithouse *et al.* 2009; White *et al.* 2009). Both in the Laming Report (Cm 5730 2003: 32–5) and also in the *Report of the Social Work Task Force* (DCSF 2009b: 3) there has been substantial criticism of ICT systems which provide a basis for consistent record keeping and multidisciplinary communication. Yet the prospect of using new technologies in social work is not necessarily an aspect of Orwellian 'Newspeak', nor is it monstrous. It is perhaps a question of balance and judging how to make the best use of what ICT offers in the context of social work practice.

We therefore need to adopt a view which sees the use of ICT in professional practice as part of 'real' social work (Chapter 21) while at the same time we need to evaluate the utility of each software application, as there is certainly no technological 'magic bullet' that can substitute for building relationships with service users. That said, we may also need to avoid antagonistic dualism between 'real' social work and ICT in the (social work) workplace. Failing to do so could perhaps adversely prejudice attitudes to new developments where new technology offers the prospect of collaborative learning for practice. This chapter introduces and discusses an example of how ICT can be used to identify, analyse and discuss the values that underpin practice to support rather than avoid building relationships.

Values are fundamentally a collection of ideas, beliefs and suppositions that people have about themselves and the social world they live in. Yet values can be slippery:

> the concept 'values' is one of those portmanteau concepts which chases after meaning, like 'community'. It derives its popularity and legitimacy from the fact that it is an apparently simple, universally accessible concept which has a simple unexceptional primary meaning (a value is something people value) which conceals a large number of secondary meanings and understandings ... The notions of value can easily slip, chameleon-like, between users and utterances, delighting all and offending none because most people do not take the trouble to think about what they actually mean in their own lives and those of others.
>
> (Pattison 2004: 1)

Social work often promotes itself as a value-based profession:

> it has long been felt that it is social work's distinctive value base that best exemplifies and advances the profession's identity and historic purpose.
>
> (Barnard *et al.* 2008: 1)

Of course the profession does have various values built into its Codes of Practice provided by each regulatory body for social work in the UK (CCW undated; GSCC 2002a; NISCC 2002; SSSC 2009), but actually these only represent one possible focus. With the exception of some academic authors, such as Banks* (2006), the language used in social work to discuss values is of a restricted kind. Values inherent in the Codes of Practice provide a message in broad terms of what social workers ought not to do – as an aspect of professional discipline, with punitive consequences if such rules are transgressed – for example, the possibility of de-registration (see Chapter 5). Values inherent in occupational standards are more positive, but also relate to the technical idea of competence. Again, failure to act in compliance with standards identifies incompetence. Values-based social work, both before and after the emergence of the undergraduate social work degree as the main professional qualification, is expressed in terms such as anti-oppressive practice and anti-discriminatory practice, thus positing general behaviour that social workers ought and ought not to do.

However, it can be argued that realizing social work values in either the study or practice of social work cannot be just about working out what characterizes the behaviour of an incompetent social worker. Equally, the corollary of these negative terms are more affirmative sounding concepts like empowerment, person-centred practice – concepts which follow classic Biestekian values (Biestek 1961). These tend to focus on individual needs, while the negative terms seem more concerned with the social and cultural. The point argued here is that for the most part, in the study of social work and everyday social work practice, however much practitioners are regularly confronted with problems involving value-conflict, there is neither a sufficient vocabulary nor enough discursive space (see Chapter 4) given to values and their ethical application. The use of web-based ICT applications can help in this field.

I have already argued (Chapter 4) that the language needed to resolve these value-based problems is not highly developed either in social work practice or in social work education; but the language required cannot emerge outside of a practice-based or pedagogical discursive space. It cannot be 'parachuted' into practice from the 'heavens' of academia. Asking social work students and practitioners to buy a primer in moral philosophy for social workers, or some kind of 'rough guide' on values for beginners can only be the start of any journey towards effectively using values for practice. Values cannot exist outside of debate and dialogue, as values shift. For example, it can be argued that it is not possible to have a value about anything without a human and social context composed of relationships with others. That said, it is also possible for us to have values without reflection, leaving them unexamined, unthought through and unrecognized. Dialogue establishes or confirms our values whether that involves what we think about a soap opera or the work of academics. There is a limit to classroom-based applications and tutorials based on text. Supervision and team-based discussion are just some ways to discuss value-based problems. Discussion of values for practice perhaps can benefit from other platforms to make it useful. An example of one such innovative tool is described next.

An interactive way of discussing values

The Values Exchange is an example of an interactive web-based software application. The architecture and infrastructure of the site is based on the ideas of Seedhouse, a New Zealand-based academic. He has written extensively about health care ethics and most of the ideas behind the Values Exchange can be found in his writings (Seedhouse* 2005, 2009f). In brief, Seedhouse argues that the Values Exchange can help its users to investigate their own and others' values through a series of case studies (Seedhouse 2009a), while the web system offers a means of opening up the discussion of values applied to hypothetical or actual practice situations. The case studies can be taken from the public domain; or alternatively Values Exchange can be used by practitioners to investigate and reflect upon their own and their immediate colleagues' values by considering people and situations in their practice environment. Therefore it can be used for study or to discuss real life in real time. In 2009, ten UK universities used the Values Exchange in practice settings in health. A number of others, including The Open University used the Values Exchange in regard to learning about social work practice (Seedhouse 2009b, 2009c). The Values Exchange is also used in other practice settings (Seedhouse 2009d) and in a number of Mental Health Trusts (Seedhouse 2009e). In these 'real life/real time' contexts staff can use a secure website where mental health practitioners, for example, can articulate their individual value positions and ethics regarding the treatment and care of individual patients and service users in real time. A practitioner can outline a moral dilemma and can show which kind of practice choice they have made and offer colleagues a chance to agree or disagree with their viewpoint, and more importantly offer a way of discussing their agreement or disagreement in an engaging and systematic way.

When a practitioner logs on to the system and engages with a Values Exchange case, they are invited to respond to a proposition, which gives a particular point of view on a subject. They can also explore various links to information about the subject at hand, such as newspaper reports or electronic journal articles, which act as a guide or stimulus for further thought. The user can either access these articles or can proceed to using the site. The user is then expected to complete a 'rings' analysis which captures initial reactions to the case before proceeding to the 'grid' analysis which prompts a more detailed response and line of reasoning by which the user agrees or disagrees with the initial proposition. Values Exchange prompts each user to reflect upon and analyse the values that they bring to bear on a given case, thus hopefully aiding reflective practice. There are further refinements of the task. The practitioner can be prompted to clarify their argument in support of their choice to agree or disagree with the proposition. Once both the 'rings' and 'grid' analyses are complete the user can submit the case. Up to that point the user can edit what they have said, but after a case has been submitted they cannot make further changes.

Following case submission the user is asked to select a report based on their submission. A number of different types of report are available; these compare the user's view with all other users' views in relation to the same case. Reports allow detailed analysis, exchange and dialogue about users' values. Until submission users are not able to see how other participants have responded to the case in question, so they do not see what other people have said until they have made a commitment to a point of view. The reports can then be used to review what the individual user has said or to identify trends in the overall pattern of responses. Reports can also be used to analyse how different participants value different kinds of argument to support a decision or view. They can be used with large or small numbers of people. In 2010, the website offers at least thirty-three different types of report per case that can be accessed to review how other users justified their decision. The Values Exchange also offers its own online forums where discussion can continue or further discussion can take place in face-to-face tutorials, education settings or in team discussions in the workplace.

Discussion

The Values Exchange can be used in a restricted way, to place a boundary around what a particular group of practitioners value in specific cases. Yet there is no practical barrier or principle why this kind of restriction should always apply. Service users as well as practitioners can easily use the same Values Exchange to explore and explain their perspectives (Seedhouse 2009e). For example, the South Staffordshire and Shropshire Healthcare National Health Service Foundation Trust Values Exchange is open to service users and carers as well as practitioners. My experience of its use in an academic context suggests that surprising differences and similarities of viewpoint may be reached. Practical solutions to complex issues may be discovered. Instead of ICT being regarded as something outside of and separate from the relational heart of social work it could become an important mediator of, and tool for exploring and explaining, differing values positions which impact directly on care; whether those perspectives derive from different professional perspectives or service users.

I would suggest that the Values Exchange offers a participatory and democratic opportunity to deal with the uncertainties and complexities that surround twenty-first-century social work practice. It suggests one practical way in which partnerships can be formed, thus increasing practitioner capabilities in communicating with services users as well as within and beyond specific practice teams. By its nature it not only allows discussion of values, it also allows opportunities to draw on empirical evidence as well as legal and policy developments to justify positions, it also offers a vehicle for collaborative learning.

The Values Exchange is not a magic bullet; there are no real shortcuts to building relationships. If it is treated only as a gadget it will not work, it has to be integrated into the study of social work and practice. Not only that but like any web-based application it will have to change, it will have to accommodate and assimilate developments in its own environment. At some point it may be superseded by an alternative way of exploring values and ethics. In the second decade of the twenty-first century it offers a facility for transcending boundaries and engaging in some emotionally and morally challenging issues which are central to practice.

Questions for reflection

First, go to the free Values Exchange website (http://www.values-exchange.com) and go through one of the cases there.

How did your values compare to other Values Exchange users' values and did you rethink your position?

Would the Values Exchange be a useful learning tool for you or your agency colleagues, providing the cases were appropriate for your context?

23 Reflections on writing in social work education and practice

Lucy Rai

> This chapter is about the writing needs of social work practitioners. I found the introduction to the debate on writing as a skill versus the social context, together with different expectations and norms, very interesting.
>
> (Service manager – older people)

Introduction

Writing is a central, although often overlooked, part of social work education and practice. Within education, students' learning and competence is assessed through writing, while in practice much of social work practice is conducted through and recorded in writing. By identifying the importance of writing in social work, this chapter offers some reflections on the ways in which a more conscious awareness of the relationship between the author, their reader, the context in which writing takes place and the final text produced can improve 'practice' in its widest sense.

A bundle of skills or a social practice?

Academic writing is at the heart of higher education, forming the primary medium through which students are assessed. In the context of a highly selective higher education system, the ability of students to convey their understanding through the medium of academic writing is a basic expectation. Responses to demands to address the standard of academic writing in the UK to date have primarily been either in the form of remedial support for individual students focused through libraries or study support centres, or where student need is perceived more broadly through study support modules (Lea and Street 2000; Lillis 2001). Such support draws upon a 'skills deficit' model which relies on students supplementing 'deficits' in writing skills via support offered through workbooks, toolkits, electronic skills labs and teaching which focuses on teaching surface elements of written language such as punctuation and spelling. Social work education in the UK has taken a similarly skills-based approach to writing in as far as competence in literacy (assessed though successful completion of GCSE or equivalent in English) has been built into the entry requirements for qualifying training (GSCC 2002b).

There is an emerging body of research in the UK exploring academic and professional writing through drawing on a *social practices* approach to writing (Lea and Street 2000; Lillis 2001; Rai 2004, 2006). This approach moves away from limiting writing to a set of discrete acquirable skills and more towards viewing it as 'a communication process which is embedded in social contexts, interactions and relationships' (Rai 2006: 790), or an activity embedded in social and interpersonal ways of being (Bazerman 1981, 1988; Lea and Street 2000). The significance of this shift in emphasis is that it opens up the possibility of exploring writing in the social and interactional contexts in which it takes place. The purpose of the text, the author and the reader all become relevant in understanding how a particular piece of writing is created.

Within an academic context, for example, a social practices approach recognizes the significance the diversity of writing requirements across disciplines and the extent to which academic writing is local to institutions, courses and even individual tutors. Whilst it may seem obvious that 'writing physics' is different from 'writing social work', students can find it more difficult to understand why 'writing social work' differs from 'writing sociology' and, more perplexing, why the expectations of 'writing social work' might differ between universities and individual tutors. These differences are common in higher education and arise in part from the belief or assumption that the academic essay is a commonly understood way of writing with clear or commonsense 'rules'. In her research on student writing, Lillis (1997) suggests that student writing frequently labelled as an 'essay' can disguise complex expectations of students' writing (Lillis 1997: 186). The essay in fact represents a very particular way of constructing knowledge which, whilst frequently presented as transparent, is both implicit and complex. Writing in social work education commonly encompasses a range of assessed academic writing tasks, including 'essays', reflective writing and portfolios, alongside the writing undertaken during fieldwork to assess practice competence (I use 'fieldwork' here in place of 'practice' due to the potentially confusing multiple uses of the term practice). The writer's success in any task will rely significantly upon their understanding of the expectations of the course and assessor in each task.

Essay or reflective writing?

It is common in social work education for students to be assessed through a combination of 'essays' and various forms of reflective writing, such as reflective essays, journals or commentaries in portfolios. Although these are also considered to be academic writing, the expectations of how students present their ideas may be very different. One of the most significant differences is that in more reflective writing the author is expected to focus more on themselves in their writing, a process which can create tensions with some assumptions about how an academic essay should be constructed. An essay, for example, is typically expected to present evidence from authoritative sources (such as published books or journals) in order to build an objective, dispassionate argument. A piece of reflective writing may share all these expectations, but in addition the author is required to include subjective reflections on their own experience, values or practice as a key part of building an argument or reasoned position. There are also some linguistic challenges presented by some forms of reflective writing, such as making a judgement about the use of the first person singular pronoun (I). Although the acceptability of the use of 'I' has shifted in academia, its use remains questioned in an academic essay whilst being unavoidable in reflective writing, without the use of cumbersome linguistic techniques. A more significant issue, however, is the importance of 'I' to enable the author to use a personal voice in their writing in order to offer true reflective insights. The rules or expectations about specific writing tasks may differ, so it is important for a student writer to seek as much clarity as possible and for educators to ensure that guidance is explicit, as unspoken assumptions can be unhelpful for writer and reader.

At undergraduate level, guidance is commonly provided at the level of university or faculty regulations and also at course level. At university or faculty level there may be common regulations about issues such as plagiarism and styles of referencing, whilst at the individual course level more detailed guidance might be provided about expected content and perhaps style of writing or structure. It is where guidance addresses issues such as 'style' and 'structure' that there can be assumptions made about what the writer should take for granted as accepted conventions in academic writing where in fact no such commonsense or uniform conventions necessarily exist between courses, faculties or universities.

Reflective writing in social work education provides a medium for students to demonstrate that they can offer a commentary on their practice; as such it is the link between academic learning and fieldwork. Where an 'essay' is a tool through which the student demonstrates his or her ability to comprehend and marshal theoretical knowledge into an argument or reasoned position, most reflective writing uses the same theoretical knowledge to evaluate and justify practice. The inclusion of this added dimension, your own practice, makes reflective writing very challenging for many students. It requires the ability to précis an account of practice without slipping into lengthy description. It also requires the writer to demonstrate their understanding of theory by applying it critically to an evaluation of their own practice. Reflective writing can also be personally challenging where it requires the author to discuss their own values and beliefs, for example, in relation to professional ethics. The thinking skills involved in reflective writing, therefore, provide a very good assessment of a student's ability to be a self-critical, evidence-based practitioner. Is there a link, however, between the writing skills used in an educational context and those used in the field?

Writing in fieldwork

Writing plays two key roles in social work practice. It is a method for recording what happens and it can also *be* what happens. Case note recording is primarily a space where factual events can be documented, but it is also a space where social workers can record their professional view and plan future action. Such records are vital not only as a statutory verification of practice but also as a method through which information can be shared with colleagues and monitored by supervisors or managers. As with academic writing, specific expectations of writing in practice are locally defined and so may vary from agency to agency or service to service. Writing, as all practice in social work, will be guided by relevant legislation, policy and local good practice. Healy and Mulholland suggest that

> Your institutional context shapes your writing practices in so far as it shapes both your professional purpose, and the expectations of the audiences for your writing. An understanding of the influence of the institutional context can enhance your credibility and effectiveness as a communicator.
>
> (Healy and Mulholland* 2008: 13)

Healy and Mulholland continue by reminding social work writers that the conventions of writing can vary in terms of style, language and structure and that such conventions should be observed in order to maximize the effectiveness of writing (Healy and Mulholland 2008: 27). One very significant impact on writing in social work has been the introduction of electronic recording and the use of specific software for entering data, such as for assessment work. Such software prescribes to a very great degree the structure and style of writing, and to a lesser extent also prescribes the content. In contrast, where case recording allows 'free writing', or writing out with the constraints of specialized software (Chapters 21 and 22), any constraints arise only from the expectations of the employing agency.

Determining expectations for effective writing

In both academic and practice writing, there are four key factors to consider in order to achieve effective writing – context, audience, purpose and writer. These factors are each discussed in turn next.

Context

Context can be loosely understood as incorporating 'audience' and 'purpose' discussed later. Context also relates to all factors which have an impact on the writer creating a text. These might range from the institutional constraints, such as relevant rules and regulations to where the writing takes place. Imagine for yourself the difference in completing a piece of assessed writing on paper in examination conditions compared with writing at home on a computer, perhaps with the family in the background and interruptions such as the telephone. The environment itself can distract from the task but equally can stimulate ideas that feed into the content or style.

Similarly in the workplace, writing is constrained and directed by relevant legislations, policy and expectations. These might be fairly obvious, such as agency procedures on case recording, but they might arise from workplace culture or practices. Paré* (2000: 163) suggests that students and newly qualified social workers pass through an apprenticeship into professional writing practices through which they are infused by the institutional and organizational ideologies of the practice environment. These kinds of cultural issues might influence how case recording in the workplace might include the attitude of the social work staff towards the value of recoding and how it is used both by colleagues and by senior staff or line managers. Where the writing is accepted as a valuable and constructive task it may receive more positive attention than if it is perceived as a tool for accountability or control. It is also important that the writing is perceived as relevant to the core role of delivering quality services rather than as a bureaucratic obstacle to 'getting on with the job'. There can also be very subtle influences on writing, such as relationships between team members or between individual team members and their manager. Paré (2000) suggests that students need to be assisted in becoming 'critically literate' in order to play a part in challenging established professional writing practices which might be ineffective or unhelpfully ideologically driven. He concluded that addressing change at an individual or even team level was unhelpful and that writing practices could most effectively be changed from within an organization by challenging the workplace culture.

Audience

The audience refers to the person or people you are writing for. This can be more complex than it sounds as texts frequently have multiple audiences. A personal letter or an email may be written and addressed to a single individual with no intention that it should be shared more widely. In an academic or professional context, however, you are frequently writing for multiple and/or unknown audiences. A piece of assessed writing may be written with the knowledge that the primary audience is the tutor who will assess it. However, academic conventions would not encourage a conversational style in which a student writer addressed a known tutor personally. Northedge (2005: 275) suggests that students should write for an anonymous *intelligent person in the street*, or in other words, that although the reality is their work will be read by a known individual who has specialist knowledge of the topic, the text should be constructed as if it was to be read by an interested, intelligent outsider. For the author, the implication is that the audience, to some degree is an imaginary one, and that an element of role playing is needed in order to write an essay which meets the expected conventions.

In a practice context the audience involves less role playing, but is no less of a challenge due to the extensive number of audiences. For a piece of case recording the potential audiences could include: social work colleagues; service users; non-social work colleagues; line managers; service users' family or advocates; police; solicitors/barristers/judges; or auditors.

Each of these audiences may read the recording from a different perspective and with different levels of understanding or knowledge and with different purposes. A good example of recording, therefore, should be written in such a way as to address its key functions in relation to each audience. Effective case recording should, therefore, be written in language accessible to all audiences, when it is reporting on events where different views were expressed, each should be noted alongside who expressed them and, perhaps most importantly, the professional view of the author should be included, ideally alongside theoretical or legal justifications. It is here that reflective writing and practice writing can be seen to reconnect, through the demonstration of critical evidence-based practice.

Purpose

'Purpose' in relation to academic writing may seem obvious – to demonstrate academic competence. Essentially this is the case, and requires a careful observance by the author that he or she has met the assignment brief and learning outcomes. In many academic institutions, assignments (the research in preparation and the feedback on them) are intended to constitute a key part of the students' learning. Professional courses, such as social work, have the added dimension of assessing professional competence and suitability. The consequence of this is that, although it is unlikely that an assessment would meet the learning outcomes well and contravene good or ethical practice, this kind of dichotomy is theoretically possible. Student writers in social work, therefore, need to be aware of the dual purpose of assessing academic understanding and skill alongside judging professional competence and suitability.

In a practice context, the purpose of a text is often prescribed through the procedures into which it falls, for example, an assessment or a review document. Even within these parameters it is worth an author considering the wider purpose of a document. Returning to the case recording, the purposes could potentially include documenting events:

- as a statutory record of services provided or interventions made;
- as a planning or assessment tool for current or future workers;
- as evidence for legal teams (for or against the agency);
- to enable transparency for service users or their advocates to be offered access to records;
- to enable accountability on behalf of individual workers and the agency.

This range of purposes for one document illustrates the challenge for social workers in carrying out what might appear a very routine task.

Writer

The final issue to consider is yourself, the writer, and your own relationship with writing. This may appear to be a rather odd issue to consider, but it is possibly the most important. Each of us have travelled an individual road to literacy which will have included our own language and educational histories. For some of us our language history is very simple and involves (in the UK) learning English as a first language as an infant which we continue to use throughout adult life and which forms the basis of developing literacy skills. For many, however, this first language differs to a greater or lesser extent from the standard English required in academic or professional writing. This may be because we speak a non-standard variety of English (some might refer to this as a dialect) or because English is a first, second or even third language. Even for speakers of English as a first language there is a process of familiarization to move from spoken to academic or professional writing. For those with a more complex and challenging journey to travel from spoken to written language, there may be many emotive and practical hurdles to face when engaging in complex writing tasks. Similarly, each writer will have developed literacy skills in varied educational contexts, some of which will have been creative, supportive and rewarding whilst others have involved criticism, demotivation and even discrimination. These personal journeys to becoming a writer remain relevant for student and professional writers and the interplay between these personal journeys and the more immediate issues of audience, purpose and context can have a significant influence on the success of a text.

Conclusion

Social workers are familiar with the need to consider a wide range of issues in planning effective communication. Their professional training prepares them for thinking about the communication needs of the people they are working with in terms of meta-communication and the influence of the environment and task. It would also be a familiar approach to consider the relevant interpersonal issues which may impact upon an exchange of face-to-face communication. Such a holistic consideration of effective communication practice, incorporating the social and physical environment as well as the interpersonal, is equally relevant to writing. Developing the ability to write effectively in the context of social work does not rely upon learning a new set of skills; it relies upon the ability to transfer the skills of critically reflective social work practice to writing.

Questions for reflection

When you are writing for academic assignments or in your practice how much are you able to consider the significance of audience, purpose, context and writer?

Who are the people that make up the audience for your fieldwork writing and how does thinking of their responses influence the way you write?

24 Caring for yourself, being managed and professional development

Janet Seden and Mick McCormick

> This chapter conveys a realistic overview of the reality of the complexity of contemporary social work practice and measures that should be in place to support practitioners at all levels. I felt that the authors' observations really resonated with many issues I was struggling to deal with as a newly qualified practitioner. I feel that it gave me permission to take action.
>
> (Social worker/Care manager – Adult Care)

Introduction

Caring for yourself, being managed and professional development are three interrelated topics which are highly relevant for newly qualified practitioners if they are to stay in social work and expand their expertise through practice, further training and the proactive support of their colleagues and managers. It may seem counter-intuitive to place caring for yourself ahead of being managed and professional development in a chapter for practitioners aiming to enhance the lives of others through their work. However, it has become apparent, for example, in reports that have followed inquiries into child deaths (e.g. Cm 5730 2003*), that individuals often carry case loads which are too high, or are asked to undertake complex work without adequate supervision, management and support (Cm 5730 2003; Chapter 6). The situation of Lisa Arthurworrey is a powerful example.

Lisa was 'blamed' for Victoria Climbié's death and her name placed on the Protection of Children Register by the (then) Home Secretary as if she had directly harmed a child herself. The care tribunal overturned that decision, saying her mistakes were due to lack of experience, lack of training and a lack of supervision. The impact on her was devastating and she was left uncertain as to whether to stay in social work or indeed whether the GSCC would accept her for registration (*Guardian Society* 2005). Of course, Lisa was not the only professional to have seen Victoria or to have missed opportunities to intervene. Nonetheless she bore the brunt of the media criticism and the impact of the inquiry. It is also appears that she was practising without proper support, supervision or a professional support network (Cm 5730 2003).

Caring for yourself and others

In caring work, if you are not able to care for yourself and obtain the relevant support for your professional actions there will inevitably be repercussions for others. Service users are not best served by social workers who are near to burnout, too tired to care or who have become indifferent and cynical through overload, poor management or poor agency practices. Often social workers are faced with some of society's most challenging issues which not only require them to be knowledgeable about the law, professional practice and a whole range of skills and methods of working (Trevithick 2008), but also to be able to use themselves in emotional and often highly charged meetings with others. As Trevithick (2000: 1) says:

> The context of social work is changing rapidly. However one fundamental element remains the same, namely that social work is located within some of the most complex problems and perplexing areas of human experience, and for this reason, social work is, and has to be a highly skilled activity.

Unfortunately, as a result of rapid change and increasing role complexity, as well as a chronic lack of resources in some agencies, social workers may still find themselves with high case loads, pressure to take on the most complex work early in their careers, little support from managers and inadequate supervision. Nonetheless, for well intentioned reasons, they continue trying to do their best for their service users. Often this is at personal cost and they can inadvertently find themselves out of their professional depth.

Therefore, a social worker's sense of personal well-being about occupying their role, together with necessary support, is critical for their service users and for their own mental health. It is important that, given the challenging nature of the work, social workers can make conscious and accountable professional judgements and decisions, and still retain enough capacity to care for themselves, their families and friends and enjoy their leave, weekends and free time. These sources of renewal outside of work are essential for personal well-being. One sign of stress and overload is an ability to find time for family, friends and the activities that give you a sense of well-being. It is also important that the stresses associated with the job are supported by employers and not consistently taken home for families to resolve.

Self-care in complex contexts

So what are the blocks and barriers that prevent social workers from caring for themselves? What kind of management and professional development opportunities are needed to ensure that individuals are able to maintain their equilibrium and emotional availability? This chapter considers this, arguing that self-care needs constant attention throughout a professional's career and should not be left to chance. As Brechin (2000: 142) says:

> For the carer personally, whether professional or unpaid, to care at all is, in a sense, to be continually open and vulnerable to challenge. Learning to be respectful and supportive of others, often in very difficult circumstances may be the biggest challenge of all.

The role of social work in society seemed assured at the turn of the twentieth century as the degree level qualification was introduced, registration was required and various reviews defined and codified what it means to be a social work professional – a title protected in law and codes of practice (Chapter 5). The twenty-first century review in Scotland identified the 'reserved' functions of social work:

> Social workers should assess, plan, manage the delivery of care and safeguard the well-being of the most vulnerable adults and children.
>
> (Scottish Executive 2006b: 30)

The reserved functions included responsibilities for those who are in need of protection, and/or in danger of exploitation or significant harm and/or at risk of causing significant harm to themselves and others and/or are unable to provide informed consent. It also included responsibilities for developing, monitoring and implementing protection plans, with an awareness of risks and the identification of changing circumstances which require a revised plan. This definition is one that focuses on the daily experiences of practitioners: that they are responsible for managing some of society's most complex issues.

However, no sooner did the ground for social work seem more secure when a series of incidents led to more media scrutiny and government doubt in England about the social work degree's fitness for purpose. This is the case despite research that identifies the complexities of evidencing the degree's outcomes (Orme *et al.* 2009). Social work yet again became a political football as another Task Force was convened to inquire into the social work role. Social work training has been subject to almost continual review and changes since the 1990s and has always had an image problem when compared with other professionals. Doctors are 'saviours' and nurses are 'angels', while social workers are at best 'do-gooders' and 'busybodies' and at worst 'baby-snatchers'. More recently they have been described in the press as 'incompetent' and 'bungling'. There will inevitably be 'mistakes' in practice (Burton 2003), social work is an imprecise activity but one which can be done accountably and through work that can be defended. However, the global nature of some unrealities in public perception is almost entirely down to media stereotyping and hard to work against. It is rare that positive media coverage is seen (*Community Care* 2009: 4–5).

These negative images appear to persist despite the efforts of professional associations such as the British Association of Social Workers. The barrage of negative media coverage creates tension which impacts on social workers' day-to-day activities, as public perception is influenced by these stereotypes. Further, campaigns against social work in the media can distort perception to the point where children and adults are put at further risk, if communities are reluctant to engage with social work practitioners as a result. This is particularly undermining when service users, communities and social workers in reality share a joint interest in combating social injustice and inequalities (see Beresford and Croft* 2004). Part of self-care, therefore, may involve engagement with those bodies which positively seek to clarify and communicate the role of social work for society. An accurate understanding of what the profession can and cannot do is needed by service users and their communities.

This is an issue which was taken up in 2009 by *Community Care* magazine which has worked to promote social work positively through the 'Stand Up Now for Social Work' Campaign. In May 2009 (4–5) the magazine reported the outcome of a study which was undertaken into the media coverage of social work. It found that not only was there almost universally a 'critical tone' but that also 'four in ten failed to give a right of reply to all parties, thus breaching editorial guidelines'. Although there were exceptions, with papers such as *The Times* and *Guardian* carrying the more positive articles compared with *The Sun* and *The Mail,* overall the media coverage of social work is predominantly negative and inaccurate. *Community Care* concludes that social workers are not able to get their side of the story covered and that

> One way or another, this must change, if the situation is to improve for the profession. And social workers themselves must be part of the solution by talking more about their successes.
>
> (*Community Care* 2009: 5)

The campaign has called for:

- the media to portray social workers in an accurate and balanced way;
- the government to support and promote respect for the social work profession;
- employers to promote positive images of social work and support staff to tell their successes.

(*Community Care* 2009: 5)

However, the other salient point to communicate is that there cannot always be 'successes' when social workers operate in such challenging and complex environments. Also, while it is welcome to have such a campaign, the influence of the press that supports social work positively is less than the influence of the tabloids that denigrate it. It will need sustained implementation on the back of the campaign to make a difference. We would, therefore, suggest that it is part of the social work role to communicate to the community in which it works and to local media just what social work can and cannot achieve, what its role is, and to challenge the negative descriptions used in the tabloid press. This is also part of caring for ourselves, our team and our professional identity.

This leads us to consider the role of organizations in supporting staff. It is essential that government is positive about the role of social work and supports it financially. It is also the case that the organizations which are funded to employ social workers and provide services have themselves become more complex places in which to work. Since the rise of managerialism (Harris 2007; Harris and White 2009) social workers can find themselves working in pressured environments where scant attention is given to supervision and professional development and where the culture is simply one of pressure throughout and the achievement of targets. They may find themselves struggling to hold on to the values, ethics and ideals which brought them in to social work in the face of business models.

Many have argued that it remains possible for sound management in social work and social care to remain congruent with a service user focused approach to enable the participation of practitioners in the process (Martin and Henderson 2001; Henderson and Atkinson 2003; Seden and Reynolds 2003; Aldgate *et al.* 2007). Early career practitioners can themselves examine the management practice in agencies where they apply for jobs and where possible choose those posts where there is a commitment to sound and ethical management practices which support workers to perform to the best of their ability. Where the necessary support for the work is not forthcoming it can be difficult to challenge oppressive management practice and it may be necessary to act as a team, make requests for supervision in writing and engage union support.

It can also be difficult when newly qualified and starting to develop your sense of professional role if you find yourself working in a multidisciplinary environment. As it is increasingly likely that social workers will find themselves in multi-agency environments (Morris 2008), this section considers some issues of identity that this raises. In such settings it can be difficult to hold on to your identity as a social worker. However, doing so can only enhance the service provided to the service user and the agency in which you are working.

So, what particular contribution can social work and social workers bring to muliti-agency settings? As well as the unique knowledge, skills and values which social workers bring as a result of their training, we would suggest that social workers' orientation and training enables them to place the service users at the centre of their practice. Beresford (2007), writing about what service users value in social workers, identifies this person-centeredness as:

- *the social approach* – a way of working with individuals which locates the issues that they face in the social context of their lives;
- *relationships* – a way of working that places value on establishing a relationship through which trust and understanding can be built;

- *personal qualities* – a way of working which focuses on warmth, respect, being non-judgemental, listening and treating people as equals.

(Beresford 2007: 5–6)

Given this unique, social and holistic approach, how can you as a social worker ensure that this approach shapes practice in multi-agency environments?

Nix *et al.* (2009) suggest that social workers who are prepared for practice through their undergraduate training and who feel supported to continue to practise reflectively and pursue post-qualifying education feel confident both in their identity as a social worker and in the unique contribution they can bring to the multi-agency setting:

> The main thing and a lot of people have commented on it, is my increased confidence is dealing with other members of the team ... speaking up and challenging.
>
> (Nix *et al.* 2009)

There are also personal issues which impact on your ability to work, illness in the family, for example, or caring responsibilities. In these circumstances the work/life balance often becomes extremely difficult unless you have a proactive Human Resources section in your agency and good management support to make the necessary adaptations for your work. Employer policies and procedures for managing stress and for providing the means for teams to support each other are essential if the organization is to support staff to give their best. The next section of the chapter considers roles and responsibilities in staff support.

Roles and responsibilities

Writing in 1982, Payne and Scott (1982) sought to clarify the purpose of supervision. They argued that one major purpose of supervision was to establish accountability, but that supervision was not 'merely a vehicle for accountability to the organization' (Payne and Scott 1982: 8). They suggested that there were three major purposes of supervision: a management or administrative function; an educative or teaching function; and a supportive or enabling function. Jumping forward twenty years it seems that the identified purposes of supervision have changed little.

Cree and Myers* (2008) also suggest that the main aim of social work supervision is to 'provide efficient and effective services to clients' (2008: 138) and that there are three basic functions for supervision. These functions still remain those as suggested by Payne and Scott all those years ago. In addition to the three functions, Cree and Myers begin to explore ways in which social workers might make better use of supervision, and we would suggest that a social worker who is an active rather than a passive participant in the supervision process is key to both personal development and the provision of a quality social work service. In particular it is important to bring your own personal development needs as well as issues of case management to the supervision table and, if needed, to be assertive about these being addressed.

Whilst Wilson *et al.* (2008) point to a changing climate in which supervision tends towards case management and gives limited regard to education and support, they acknowledge that where supervision is more balanced (offering case management, support and education) then this is an enriching experience for the social worker – offering opportunities for reflection and development. Social workers committed to improving and developing as capable practitioners must be prepared to negotiate space in supervision for support and education – a more balanced experience of supervision would seem to produce a more reflective practitioner who feels supported and more prepared for practice.

It seems important that social work retains the new-found sense of specialism, created by the protected role of the social worker. There are clear mandated functions for social work in twenty-first-century society and a body of knowledge about how to practise (Trevithick 2008). Campaigns such as 'Stand Up Now for Social Work' and organizations such The Social Work Action Network (SWAN) (*Guardian Society* 2009) have identified some of the issues. It is also a complex judgement to know when to assert your identity as a social work professional and when perhaps to stand back in the interests of others. However, we argue that it is essential to have thought through your own strategies for maintaining your well-being as a practitioner from the beginning. The relationship between self-care, being managed and professional development is an important triangulation for the practitioner's career and thinking about the responsibilities for continuing professional development which are shared between practitioner and agency.

Questions for reflection

What responsibilities do my employer, my line manager and my colleagues have towards me?

What agency and personal resources can I draw in to support my own well-being?

25 Careering through social work

Metaphors of continuing professional development

Barry Cooper

> This chapter has been useful in encouraging me to consider the metaphors I use to understand my own CPD and the impact this may have on my learning and practice. It enabled me to consider social work through a more creative lens.
>
> (Team manager – Intermediate Care Team)

Introduction

At some point in most people's social work career they find themselves asking questions such as 'how did I get into this?' and 'where am I going?' Existential introspection is not the sole preserve of social work, of course, although there is perhaps something exceptional about the complexities and demands of social work practice that leads to just this kind of self-questioning on a rather more regular basis than other professions. The responses to these heartfelt questions are often metaphorical, such as 'I feel trapped', 'I've lost my way' or 'this is a window of opportunity'. This chapter explores continuing professional development (CPD) and careers through an examination of these kinds of questions and seven metaphorical ways of making sense that can be used. For example, over the years I have been struck by how many times social workers have described their post-qualification study experiences as 'jumping through hoops': an interesting circus metaphor! In an earlier publication on this subject I began by proposing that the attitudes of professional workers to their CPD are a strong indicator of their approach to practice. I ended by asking readers whether professional practice is a 'minimum-requirements activity' or 'an opportunity for lifelong learning, challenge and growth?' (Cooper 2008c: 235), pointing out that the responsibility for choice lay with the individual. In essence, I think the choice remains the same but this chapter arrives there through a different kind of discussion.

The idea of social work as a career is related to its development as a profession which, in the UK, has been largely situated within the organizational structures and cultures of public service local authorities. This is not necessarily the case in other Western industrialized societies or other countries around the world. In a growing age of globalization this is an important point, as a UK-centric view of social work can lead to comfortable public bureaucracy assumptions such as 'career ladders' and 'promotional pathways' (more metaphors!). However, it is debatable whether the unique demands of social work lend themselves to these kinds of career certainties. An indication of this is the growing problem of staff retention (Unison 2009) which has given rise to unprecedented multimedia government advertising and recruitment campaigns. In the twenty-first century, changes have been made to strengthen the institutional position of social work through increased regulation and registration through the devolved Care Councils in the nations of the UK. All social workers in the different nations of the UK must register with their regulatory Care Councils and maintain their registration every three years to be able to practise. In England, these arrangements for CPD and a future system of 'licence to practise' have come under scrutiny as part of a far more fundamental, root and branch review of social work as a whole (DCSF 2009b). The role of employers continues to be given a high profile by government and any future reforms will have to be shaped through the organizations that employ social workers.

Social work in the UK is now delivered by an increasingly diverse range of organizations and it has been argued that the style and character of social work services are strongly influenced by the nature of the organization that delivers them (Warham 1977; Kakabadse 1982; Pithouse 1987). These three authors developed innovative ways of examining the complex, multi-layered relationships of personal, professional and institutional interests that combine to produce social work. A very different, and equally ground-breaking, approach to understanding organizations and the careers that interlink them has been developed through the use of metaphor (Morgan 2006; Inkson 2007). I often recall that a social work tutor on my own social work qualifying course in the 1980s described his view of social work education as a 'springboard' to further development. By this metaphor he meant that social work would benefit from people entering and leaving at different times in their life and that qualification should be the start of a process of CPD that might develop in different directions both within and without social work. Whatever the shape of post-qualification CPD in the future, there can be little doubt that it will remain an individual responsibility to initiate, pursue and maintain areas of continued professional learning and competence development. In doing this, the adoption of a 'strategic approach' argued by Sobiechowska (2007) is a good start. The self-evaluation checklists on motivation and approaches to learning, drawn from Entwhistle and Peterson (2004), help to focus attention upon the learner-centred aspects of self-managed CPD. However, checklists have their limitations.

Much broader considerations are offered through an exploration of 'career as metaphor' that link the individual and their CPD in the contexts of their personal history, family circumstances, current employment and future aspirations. Morgan's (2006) concept of 'multiple metaphors' is particularly useful in recognizing the many different interests and perspectives in social work that range from public policy through to private lives. Inkson (2007) develops this approach in understanding careers generally and I have drawn upon this to provide different illustrations of the relationship between social work careers and attitudes towards CPD. The seven metaphors I consider are: craft (constructing your career and CPD); seasons and cycles (career and CPD as life course); matching (career and CPD as 'fit'); journey (career and CPD as pathways); network (career and CPD through relationships); economic (career and CPD as resource); and narrative (career and CPD as stories).

Craft: constructing your career and CPD

The metaphor of social work as 'craft' is a good place to start. Learning and CPD in practice combines two central professional tensions between functional competence and personalized creativity (Poehnell and Amundson 2002) that have underpinned the major debates about social work. *A Framework for Continuous Learning* in Scotland (SSSC 2008a) and the *The Post-Qualifying Framework for Social Work Education and Training* in England (GSCC 2009) are good examples of institutional attempts to pave the way for CPD whilst allowing scope for individuals to find their own routes and develop their own particular interests. 'Carving out a career' is a common craft metaphor with underpinning assumptions about purposeful, individual choices made on a rational basis having considered and weighed up alternatives within a well-ordered system.

However, it has rarely been clear why people embark on social work as a career, how they continue or why they decide to leave. This uncertainty often seems to reflect the popular vagueness or misconceptions within society about what social workers actually do. Nonetheless, the problems of retention within the profession and the need to create a viable and attractive career framework are recognized and there are plans to address this (DCSF 2009b). In 2010, the current advice issued to provide guidance on post-qualifying CPD in social work often appears weighted towards functional decision making. I would argue that this needs to be leavened by reasons based within different rationalities, and an example of this underpins the next metaphor.

Seasons and cycles: career and CPD as life course

Social work is a part of wider welfare services provided to individuals and families throughout their lives. This complex range of provision has to be reflected through multicultural sensitivities and a diversity of approaches to people with different needs at different seasons of their life-cycle and family-cycles (Robinson 2003). These same considerations offer different ways of thinking about patterns of social work careers and CPD. The 'right time' to engage in social work, from a life course perspective, becomes a decision based within a higher set of priorities derived from the lifeworld of peoples' lived experience rather than just the systems in which they work (Cooper 2010). In Chapter 3, I argued for the vital importance of reflexivity to social work where core values reside in the demonstration of actions that matter to both service user and social worker. This is not the language of check-lists and requirements, although it doesn't necessarily exclude them, but places priority upon personal meaning and significance. The next metaphor addresses a different approach.

Matching: career and CPD as 'fit'

'You can't put a square peg in a round hole.' This everyday metaphor underpins the continuing, and controversial, question of suitability for social work. The qualification for entry onto the register of professional social work in the UK (see Chapter 5) remains a generic one. However, since the 1990s social work practice has become increasingly specialist and it is arguable that not everyone qualified to practise is necessarily suited to this. The Social Work Task Force (DCSF 2009b: 15) recommends for England 'a new regime for testing and interviewing candidates that balances academic and personal skills' along with 'a new supported and assessed first year in employment, which would act as the final stage in becoming a full, practising social worker'. In these new proposals, examining the suitability of candidates' entry to and progression within the profession makes the assessment of social workers as important as the assessment of service users and just as problematic (Cooper and Nix 2009). The problem of assessing the suitability of people as practitioners raises fundamental questions about the nature of the conceptualization of the future for social work roles and tasks; the characteristics of people that really matter and questions of how personal attributes can be reliably measured. These are hugely contested areas. Perhaps the metaphor of 'fit', as in pegs and holes, is too static an image to reflect the complex and changing nature of social work with people, relationships, social situations and definitions of problems. The next metaphor is more fluid.

Journey: career and CPD as pathways

The 'journey through life' is a common metaphor that is also often applied to experiences of work within a professional career. This metaphor characterizes a sense of movement and change of career over time and place. Such is the power of the assumptions of change and progress through a career that a prolonged and unwelcome lack of movement in an occupation is frequently described as 'being stuck'. Post-qualification CPD has been promoted through changing frameworks as an opportunity, or pathway, for practitioners to initiate movement and influence the direction of change through a purposeful plan of professional studies, retraining and reappraising current and future prospects. Journeys can be seen as both travel and destination. The vertical journeys implied by 'career ladders' and 'getting to the top' suggest an upward promotion within organizational structures that reward greater responsibility, experience and qualifications. In social work this has often meant a destination away from practice and into management. The damaging repercussions of this trend for the consolidation of professional practice has finally been recognized by the Social Work Task Force in England who recommend making 'progression routes available to high quality, specialist practitioners which do not remove them from frontline practice' (DCSF 2009b: 37). This welcome focus upon the need to recognize, reward and maintain expertise in social work practice offers the potential for CPD and career progression to be shaped less by organizational boundaries (Arthur and Rousseau 1996) and influenced more by different considerations, such as professional enjoyment and fulfilment (Mirvis and Hall 1994). For some this might include a sense of personal 'vocation' – a word lost to social work in the twenty-first century? If the career can be seen as a journey then it is a social one. The importance of personal and professional relationships as influences upon the travel experience are explored next.

Network: career and CPD through relationships

Social work has historically recognized the importance of relationships as the basis for a professional engagement between worker and service user (Wilson *et al.* 2008). However, the influence of relationship-based social work with service users has waxed and waned over the years along with an understanding of the dynamics of the 'parallel processes' that can be reflected within colleague and supervisory relationships (Mattinson 1975). In a small-scale study of a local authority social work service, although 63 per cent of those surveyed cited their manager as being 'encouraging' towards their post-qualification studies candidature, the same proportion perceived the attitude of their team colleagues as being 'indifferent or unhelpful' (Cooper and Rixon 2001: 708). If time and space is to be found within social work service organizations for CPD, then the Social Work Task Force recommendation to 'encourage a shift in culture which raises expectations of an entitlement to ongoing learning and development' (DCSF 2009b: 12) will require some powerful mechanisms to create, support and encourage professional learning relationships. The frameworks for CPD requirements stress an individual's responsibility, but it is not theirs alone. This implied spirit of employment partnership is recognized with the task force recommendations (DCSF 2009b: 7) for 'clear, universal and binding standards for employers' in addition to those expected of employees as social workers. It is an explicit statement of social work as a resource that needs optimizing by all stakeholders and the next metaphor addresses this.

Economic: career and CPD as resource

As noted earlier, the retention of social workers is increasingly problematic. It makes little economic sense to expensively train social workers who leave when they cannot be persuaded to make a career within the profession. So, whose career is it? The answer, of course, is that it is yours; but both employer and employee have a responsibility to develop and grow the social worker as a key human resource for the service agency. It is in the individual social workers' interests to develop their curriculum vitae in order to be in a position to maintain their registration to practise and construct their career path in the direction that suits their professional interests and life-cycle priorities. An enlightened employer would recognize their employees as assets to be retained and nurtured and so support opportunities for CPD and career enrichment. Both of these responsibilities are clearly stated in the current voluntary Codes of Practice in England and other nations. However, it is likely that future arrangements to support CPD in social work, will be on a far more regulated and mandatory basis. In such circumstances I would argue that social work needs more stories of what works well as the basis for best practice in careers and CPD. The last metaphor takes this forward.

Narrative: career and CPD as stories

The narrative approach to social work stories is established in the United States (LeCroy 2002). In the UK as a whole this same approach, within the profession and among practitioners, supervisors, service users and carers, could lead to narrative accounts of 'best practice' as stories of what routinely works well in social work (Jones *et al.* 2008). CPD is about practice and the career stories of practitioners can provide powerful illustrations of the realities, journeys and aspirations of professional social work lives and experiences that combine all of the preceding metaphorical perspectives. A first step is taken by Thomas and Spreadbury (2008) who talked to social workers about their experiences of supervision and support. At a time when opportunities for social networking and communication are greater than ever before there seems no reason why social work cannot create its own communities of best practice in CPD and careers. Stories abound – we create, narrate and share them as ways of making sense of what we do and what happens.

Conclusion

While I'm sure it remains an individual's responsibility to develop their career and CPD, this need not be done alone. Such decisions need to reflect the complex associations between employer's requirements and individuals' life-cycles and priorities. I have argued that the metaphors and stories of practice realities help to explore and celebrate the richness and diversities of social work lives and experiences. Such approaches offer different and creative ways to understand the complexities, contributions and capabilities of best practice and CPD in social work.

Questions for reflection

Do you have a clear idea of where you are in your career and where you want to go in your CPD?

Which of the above metaphors of career and CPD are relevant to how you see your future development in social work?

26 Continuing professional development

Enhancing high-quality practice

James Blewett

> The chapter confirms for me the way in which reflective practice is important and essential to modern-day social work – skills and values are utilized, challenged and reconstructed to fit the dynamic nature of social work. I liked the fact that the need for reflective practice to be balanced with social work knowledge was addressed in relation to continuing professional development.
>
> (Senior practitioner – Adults' Intermediate Care Team)

Introduction

A requirement of professional registration in all four nations of the UK is that social workers must be accountable for the quality of their work and take responsibility for maintaining and improving knowledge and skills (CCW undated; GSCC 2002a; NISCC 2002; SSSC 2005). Against what has increasingly been recognized as a challenging backdrop for social workers, this chapter seeks to look at some of the issues that arise from meeting the new requirements for both practitioners and employers. It seeks to offer some strategies that practitioners can employ in supporting their continuing professional development and in so doing contribute to the wider discussion about the changing roles and identities of contemporary social work.

A changing professional context

The Care Standards Act 2000 was an important watershed in the development of social work in the UK and is central in setting the context to a discussion of continuing professional development in contemporary social work. The Act introduced professional registration that brought with it an aspiration for enhanced professional status and new accountability structures. Codes of Practice were introduced as the basis of this registration, serving as both an articulation of this aspiration for a more robust professional identity and to serve in effect as a code of conduct for practitioners (Chapter 5). In all four nations there were two Codes of Practice: one for workers and one for employers. An important component of the Codes of Practice has been how continuing professional development (CPD) is central to maintaining high standards of practice. Agencies in all four nations are expected to provide opportunities for CPD to be realized and support the continuing professional development of practitioners who work within their organizations (CCW undated; SSSC 2008b; GSCC 2009).

Formalizing the requirement for CPD might well raise the status of training and other developmental activity of social workers in the workplace and, therefore, may represent a step forward in recognizing the 'expert' nature of the profession with regard to acknowledging the ever-evolving knowledge base that informs practice. However, enshrining CPD in professional codes does not, in itself, overcome the considerable barriers that exist to embedding this dimension of the professional role in everyday practice.

The reports from the Social Work Taskforce (DCSF 2009b) reflect the analysis of a number of policy-related publications that have highlighted the difficulties facing social work (Utting 1997; Cm 5730 2003; Laming 2009). These reports recognize that there are profound systemic problems at a national level and within the local agencies in which social work is delivered. However, the challenges facing social work are more complex than, for example, not having the time or resources to do the job. They are also closely related to the role and nature of CPD. The registration requirements reflect a desire to create a high-status social work profession. Conversely, throughout the first decade of the twenty-first century, social work practitioners have also faced a growing curtailment of their professional autonomy and ability to exercise individual professional discretion that should come with such status (Munro 2004; Tilbury 2004). This apparent contradiction can create a very real tension for practitioners and their employers. This tension is reflected in a number of ways such as the degree to which practitioners are given responsibility for decision making but also the role and nature of CPD in their day-to-day practice.

This tension is all the more significant as it comes in a period when the trajectory of policy in both adult and children's services raises questions about the role of social work. In children's services the policy drivers have been towards an increasingly integrated workforce in which there are diffuse professional boundaries, and services for particularly vulnerable children are 'joined up' (DCSF 2008). Likewise in adult services the move towards the personalization of services (Department of Health 2007) is having a major impact on the role and tasks of social work. This uncertainty about the role of social work has significant implications for how agencies, and indeed practitioners themselves, are able to attend to their professional development. It is difficult to construct coherent career pathways and professional development programmes when there is a lack of clarity about the role of social workers in fast-evolving services and, therefore, the nature of practice itself.

Reflective practice and continuing professional development

In some senses social work has always been a profession in flux, sensitive to and responding to the ebb and flow of social policy (Chapters 2 and 3). Activities that seek to promote practitioners' CPD, therefore, need to recognize that social work is simultaneously stimulating and rewarding but also challenging and possibly, at times, overwhelming. They need to take account of the challenging context in which practitioners are working (Gupta and Blewett 2007; DCSF 2008, 2009b). This is particularly because the work in all areas of practice can involve engaging with complex, emotive issues which challenge the boundary between the personal and professional and require a capacity to act decisively while not losing sight of the ambiguities and ethical and moral dilemmas that can often arise (Chapter 3).

A social work practitioner, therefore, requires a sophisticated and responsive combination of values, skills and knowledge. It is perhaps for this reason that the idea of reflective practice has had a particular resonance within social work and has been at the heart of discussion in the profession about the role and nature of CPD (Fook 2007). Reflective practice is a concept that has been embraced across the caring services and indeed beyond (Boud 2010; Frost 2010). Based originally on the influential work of Schön (1983), reflective practice is a conceptual framework that recognizes the interaction between the activity of practice and the analytic mindset of the practitioner. Kolb (1984) understood this interaction as a four-stage cyclical process whereby the reflective practitioner is able to constantly learn and re-appraise their activity on the basis of the impact that it is having. This dynamic, therefore, means that CPD in social work is much more than learning new technical knowledge on formal courses. As Banks (2006: 142) notes:

> Developing a capacity for critical reflection is much more than simply learning procedures or achieving particular competencies. Part of the process of becoming a reflective practitioner is the adoption of a critical and informed stance towards practice.

The notion of reflective practice and its relationship to CPD has become widely perceived as a positive and beneficial approach to social work practice (Chapter 3). Banks (2006), however, uses the adjective 'critical' in relation to reflection, arguing that reflection does not in itself challenge a mechanistic, technocratic approach to practice. This a theme that has been taken up by a number of writers who believe that while it is of course helpful to be reflective as opposed to non-reflective when thinking about the process of practice this in itself is not enough when making sense of the social work task (Fook 2007, Chapter 3). They argue that the ongoing professional development of social workers must be based upon a conceptual framework that challenges the assumptions about the way people live their lives.

This is particularly important in an era when so much of social policy is based on helping vulnerable citizens live 'normal lives' (Jordan 2000). While this may be a positive aspiration for many individuals and their families, it does, nevertheless, require practitioners to be aware of the assumptions that underpin a notion of 'normal'. Furthermore, a critical approach to practice is based on recognition of the structural inequalities that shape ours and other societies and indeed state intervention, even when well intentioned does not always have a benign impact. Social workers often have to exercise their professional authority within a non-voluntary relationship with people who are at best reluctant or even hostile to the involvement of social workers in their lives (Dalrymple and Burke 2006).

This again raises real challenges for both practitioners and those attempting to support their professional development. Much of what has been perceived as the 'crisis in social work' has been related to the credibility of the competence of social work practice (Laming 2009). It has already been argued that this can reinforce a risk averse bureaucratized system, but this can also reinforce a culture of professional development that is solely based on the acquisition of technical knowledge rather than the development of a critically informed stance towards practice.

Continuing professional development in the workplace

What is common ground among social work theorists, and has been largely accepted by policy makers and regulators (DCSF 2009b; GSCC 2009) is that some degree of critical reflection is an important component of a professional culture that seeks to develop self-confident and professionally assertive practitioners. Recognition of the limitations and criticisms of administrative Information Technology systems that attempt to micro-manage practice have been increasingly accepted, for example, during the first decade of the twenty-first century (Shaw *et al.* 2009). Producing such a workforce partly depends upon attracting high-quality recruits to the profession. However, it is also dependent upon a high-quality CPD for those who are attracted to social work. Within any continuing professional system there is a balance between what are the expectations of individual practitioners in meeting their developmental needs and to what extent is it the responsibility of their employing agencies. The requirements in both the *Code of Practice for Social Care Workers* and the *Code of Practice for Social Care Employers* in England (GSCC 2002a) represent this tension. While both parties clearly have responsibilities, the nature of those respective responsibilities and the dynamic between the two is important to consider. In essence the debate is how practitioners update their knowledge and skills.

The formal way of achieving this update has been through undertaking university-based post-qualifying programmes. There have been a number of attempts to reform this system, culminating in England, in a revised

Post-Qualifying (PQ) framework being introduced (GSCC 2009). However, Brown *et al.* (2008) note that, while little research has been undertaken into the impact of post-qualifying training, implementation of the PQ framework has been piecemeal. Galpin (2009) further argues that attendance on post-qualifying training does not in itself necessarily address developmental needs. Doel *et al.* (2008) argue that formal training is most effective when delivered in conjunction with 'in house' mentoring and real workload relief.

There are, though, less formal but nevertheless more fundamental mechanisms by which the CPD needs of social workers are met in the workplace, the most important being supervision. The relationship between the social work practitioner and their employing agency is mediated through this supervisory relationship. This relationship has been recognized also as a key forum in which the CPD of the practitioner can potentially be addressed (Chapter 24); supervision at its best combines professional accountability with support and development. It is in this supervision where reflection can be promoted and modelled, and critical thinking encouraged and supported through exploring the assumptions underpinning practitioners' case work (Thomas and Spreadbury 2008). Nevertheless, utilizing supervision to support CPD is not always easy in the current context of practice. Supervision has come under increasing pressure in terms of capacity, both in terms of workload but also, as Harris (2007) argues, in the increasing influence of managerialism which has resulted in a focus on the accountability and performance management components of supervision at the expense of the developmental and supportive functions. Munro (2004) argues that it is, however, ultimately counterproductive, and accountability is enhanced by the critical capacities of the practitioner

The Social Care Institute of Excellence (SCIE) in England has explored the tension between the respective responsibilities between employer and practitioner when they explored knowledge needs of social care organizations in a systematic review of the literature. Walter *et al.* (2004) identified three models for developing the use of research by professionals in this sector. These models are a helpful framework for also thinking about models of CPD. The first of these models, the research-based practitioner model, envisages practitioners as relatively autonomous, taking a high degree of personal responsibility for their professional development and maintaining their own research mindedness. Professional training and education, obtained on the initiative of the individual, plays a key role in providing knowledge which practitioners can then use to modify and develop their practice.

The embedded research model, by contrast, sees the ownership of research mindedness as residing almost solely with national and local policy makers, and managers, in care agencies. Research use is ensured by embedding it in policies and procedures that can then be implemented through regulatory standards and regulatory mechanisms. The *Framework for the Assessment of Children in Need and their Families* (Department of Health *et al.* 2000) is a good example of the way that research can be embedded in this way. This guidance, which is based on child development, resilience and ecological research, requires that assessments are based upon a conceptual 'triangle' that reflects this research. The guidance further requires that assessments are carried out within strict timescales, and these are enforced by including them as government performance indicators. In the embedded research model, therefore, 'The use of research is both a linear and instrumental process: research is translated into practice change' (Walter *et al.* 2004: 25). This model attaches little importance to the direct influence of professional expertise of individual practitioners, and implies little need for the professional development of practitioners. On the contrary, in many respects this model can be seen as a way of mitigating the weak practice of some individual workers.

The third model identified by the SCIE review is the organizational excellence model. This also puts agencies 'at the centre', and the crucial role they play is in developing a research-minded culture through the use of training, supervision and clear leadership. Research and other associated knowledge is seen as contributing to service development but it is recognized that findings need to be adapted to the local context. Translatory organizations, such as Making Research Count or Research in Practice, are seen as having an important part to play in supporting the management of agencies in developing this culture and assisting practitioners to work in a critically reflective and sophisticated manner.

Each model, the review argues, has its strengths but each also has limitations with regard to supporting continuing professional development of practitioners. The research-based practitioner model can place unrealistic responsibility on the individual practitioner and absolve employers from ownership of their staffs' professional development or the development of research-minded services. Conversely, the embedded research model can absolve individuals from responsibility for both their professional development and their practice. It also can undermine professional skill and judgement, implying that the application of research is an ideologically neutral, technical process.

Conclusion

Professional registration has formalized and increased the responsibility placed upon individual practitioners to maintain and enhance their literacy with the knowledge base and proactively seek out developmental opportunities. In so doing registration has promoted a professional identity that transcends practitioners' employment with a specific agency. However, social workers are practising within systems that are overstretched and which, in many respects, do not promote professional autonomy. There are debates currently taking place about giving a statutory basis to the Employers Code of Practice (DCSF 2009b). This reflects a belief that the increased expectations placed on practitioners must be matched by a corresponding commitment on the part of policy makers, regulators and employers. The raised expectations on practitioners will only be met if a 'whole systems approach' is adopted and social workers are provided with sophisticated developmental opportunities that include access to post-qualifying courses, high-quality and coherent internal training programmes and reflective professional supervision. Such a strategy will only succeed, however, if it is predicated on manageable workloads if the aspiration for an enhanced learning culture in social work is to be realized. This is not only crucial in maintaining the morale of the workforce but will also go a long way to determining the experience of social work practice on the part of those who use services.

Questions for reflection

What is your view of the balance of respective responsibilities between employers and practitioners with regard to the professional development of social workers?

What helps or hinders the professional development of social workers?

Endnote

The editors

Social work has existed as a profession for over 60 years in the UK. Its fortunes have fluctuated, but over that time is has had a key role in work in government-funded criminal justice, children's services and adult's mental health, disability and older people's services. Social workers have had a presence in hospitals, prisons, the courts and other institutions, and key roles in private, voluntary and charitable and community social work agencies. In these settings they have often lead the development of new services, taken a lead to combat injustices and to counter discrimination and been in the foreground of significant changes such as the closure of large institutions and the development of community-based services.

Across that time, a distinct body of knowledge, expertise and skills has been both accumulated and developed which can be charted through the history of the professional journals such as the *British Journal of Social Work* and through the activities of the professional body, the *British Association of Social Workers*. It can be argued that much has been borrowed from law, sociology, psychology, politics, management and other disciplines, but the way social work has formulated its use of knowledge in practice, sometimes termed 'practice wisdom', is distinctly its own. We would argue that if social work did not exist in the four countries of the UK it would need to be reinvented, for issues of poverty, marginalization, injustice and disadvantage still need addressing in the UK. Additionally, social work is arguably an international profession and is certainly challenged to respond to the impact of globalization in the UK.

This book has considered the interacting contexts within which individual practitioners work at the beginning if the twenty-first century and the issues created by this complexity. It has also considered social workers' responses to the roles, relationships and responsibilities they have and the learning in and challenges of the workplace. In our view, what emerges is that despite the criticisms of social work by the media, there is good cause to be optimistic about what social work can achieve for society. However, social workers can only do their tasks with supported opportunities for training and environments in the workplaces where they practise which supports further learning, from both successes and, on some occasions, mistakes. Like all professionals charged with complex tasks, social workers cannot be effective in their endeavours without the active support of government, other care professionals and communities.

References

Aarons, N. and Powell, M. (2003) 'Issues related to the interviewer's ability to elicit reports of abuse from children with an intellectual disability: a review', *Current Issues in Criminal Justice*, 14(3): 257–68.

Adams, P. (2008) 'The code of ethics and the clash of orthodoxies: a response to Spano and Koenig', *Journal of Social Work Values and Ethics*, 5(2), www.socialworker.com (accessed 14 January 2010).

Adams, R. and Payne, M. (2009) 'Ethical tensions and later life: choice, consent and mental capacity', in R. Adams, L. Dominelli and M. Payne (eds) *Critical Practice in Social Work*, 2nd edn, Basingstoke: Palgrave Macmillan.

ADSS (2005) *'Safeguarding Adults' – a National Framework of Standards for Good Practice and Outcomes in Adult Protection Work*, London: ADSS.

Ager, W., Dow, J., Ferguson, I., McPhail, M. and McSloy, N. (2006) *Service User Involvement at the Heart of Social Work Education: good practice guidelines*, www.sieswe.org (accessed 31 August 2009).

Ahmadi, N. (2003) 'Globalisation of consciousness and new challenges for international social work', *International Journal of Social Welfare*, 12(1): 14–23.

Ahmed, M. (2007) 'BASW chief slams regulator for being too soft on social worker misconduct', *Community Care*, 10 May: 5.

Ahmed, M. (2009) 'Baby Peter case in Haringey', *Community Care Online*, www.communitycare.co.uk (accessed 1 November 2009).

Aldgate, J. and McIntosh, M. (2006a) *Looking After the Family: a study of children looked after in kinship care*, Edinburgh: Social Work Inspection Agency.

Aldgate, J. and McIntosh, M. (2006b) *Time Well Spent: a study of well-being and children's daily activities*, Edinburgh: Social Work Inspection Agency.

Aldgate, J. and Seden, J. (2006) 'Direct Work with Children', in J. Aldgate, D.P.H. Jones, W. Rose and C. Jeffery (eds) *The Developing World of the Child*, London: Jessica Kingsley Publishers.

Aldgate, J. and Simmonds, J. (1992) *Direct Work with Children*, London: Batsford.

Aldgate, J., Healy, K., Malcolm, B., Pine, B., Rose, W. and Seden, J. (eds) (2007) *Enhancing Social Work Management*, London: Jessica Kingsley Publishers.

Al-Krenawi, A. and Graham, J.R. (2003) 'Principles of social work practice in the Muslim Arab World', *Arab Studies Quarterly*, 25(4): 75–91.

Allnock, D., Akhurst, S., Tunstill, J. and NESS Research Team (2006) 'Constructing and sustaining Sure-Start Local Programme partnerships: lessons for future inter-agency collaborations', *Journal of Children's Services*, 4(3): 7–29.

Alphonse, M., George, P. and Moffatt, K. (2008) 'Redefining social work standards in the context of globalization: lessons from India', *International Social Work*, 51(2): 145–58.

Alston, M. (2007) 'Globalisation, rural restructuring and health service delivery in Australia: policy failure and the role of social work?', *Health and Social Care in the Community*, 15(3): 195–202.

Anning, A., Cottrell, D., Frost, N., Green, J. and Robinson, M. (2006) *Developing Multi-professional Teamwork for Integrated Children's Services*, Maidenhead: Open University Press.

Arthur, M.B. and Rousseau, D.M. (eds) (1996) *The Boundaryless Career: a new employment principle for a new organisational era*, Oxford: Oxford University Press.

Atkinson, D., Jackson, M. and Walmsley, J. (1997) *Forgotten Lives: Exploring the History of Learning Disability*, Kidderminster: BILD Publications.

Atkinson, D., Nind, M., Rolph, S. and Welshman, J. (2005) *Witnesses to Change: families, learning difficulties and history*, Kidderminster: BILD Publications.

Ayala, J. (2008) *Blended Education in Social Work: a case study in teaching, learning and technology*, Saarbrucken: VDM Verlag.

Baginsky, M. (ed.) (2008) *Safeguarding Children and Schools*, London: Jessica Kingsley Publishers.

Bailey, J.R.D., Bruder, M., Carta, J., Defosset, M., Greenwood, C., Kahn, L., Mallik, S., Markowitz, J., Spiker, D., Walker, D. and Barton, L. (2006) 'Recommended outcomes for families of young children with disabilities', *Journal of Early Intervention*, 28(4): 227–51.

Baldock, J.C. and Hadlow, J. (2002) 'Self-talk versus needs-talk: an exploration of the priorities of housebound older people', *Quality in Ageing*, 3(1): 42–8.

Baldry, E., Bratal, J. and Breckenridge, J. (2006) 'Domestic violence and children with disabilities: working towards enhancing Social Work practice', *Australian Social Work*, 59(2): 185–97.

Banks, S. (1995) *Ethics and Values in Social Work*, Basingstoke: Palgrave Macmillan.

Banks, S. (1998) 'Professional ethics in social work: what future?' *British Journal of Social Work*, 28(2): 213–31.

Banks, S. (2004) *Ethics, Accountability and the Social Professions*, Basingstoke: Palgrave Macmillan.

Banks, S. (2006) *Ethics and Values in Social Work*, 3rd edn, Basingstoke: Palgrave Macmillan.

Banks, S. (2008) 'Critical commentary: social work ethics', *British Journal of Social Work*, 38(6): 1238–49.

Barclay, P.M. (1982) *Social Worker: their role and tasks*, London: NISW/Bedford Square Press.

Barnard, A., Horner, N. and Wild, J. (eds) (2008) *The Value Base of Social Work and Social Care*, Maidenhead: McGraw-Hill/Open University Press.

Barnardo's, Family Rights Group and NCH (2002) *Family Group Conferences – principles and practice guidance*, Barkingside: Barnardo's.

Barnett, R. (1997) *Higher Education: a critical business*, Buckingham: SRHE/Open University Press.

Barr, H. (1998) 'Competent to collaborate: towards a competency-based model for interprofessional education', *Journal of Interprofessional Care*, 12(2): 181–7.

Barrett, L.L. (2008) 'Healthy @ Home', AARP Knowledge Management. http://assets.aarp.org/rgcenter/il/healthy_home.pdf (accessed 22 January 2010).

Barron, C. (2004) 'Fair play: creating a better learning climate for social work students in social care settings', *Social Work Education*, 23(1): 25–37.

Batty, D. (2003) 'Registration scheme launched for social workers', www.guardian.co.uk/society (accessed 17 October 2007).

Bazerman, C. (1981) 'What written knowledge does: three examples of academic discourse', *Philosophy of Social Sciences*, 11(3): 361–87.

Bazerman, C. (1988) *Shaping Written Knowledge: the genre and activity of the experimental article in science*, Maddison: University of Wisconsin Press.

Bećirević, M., Dowling, M., Seden, J. and Buchanan, I. (2010 in press) *A Qualitative Study of Children with Disabilities and their Families in Bosnia and Herzegovina and Bulgaria*, Innocenti Research report: UNICEF.

Beck, U. (1992) *Risk Society: towards a new modernity*, London: Sage.

Beresford, P. (2007) *The Changing Roles and Tasks of Social Work: from Service Users' Perspectives: a literature informed discussion paper*, London: Shaping Our Lives.

Beresford, P. and Croft, S. (1993) *Citizen Involvement: a practical guide to change*, Basingstoke: Palgrave Macmillan.

Beresford, P. and Croft, S. (2003) 'Involving service users in management; citizen access and support', in J. Reynolds, J. Henderson, J. Seden, J. Charlesworth and A. Bullman (eds) *The Managing Care Reader*, London: Routledge.

Beresford, P. and Croft, S. (2004) 'Service users and practitioners reunited: the key component for social work reform', *British Journal of Social Work*, 34(1): 53–68.

Beresford, P., Croft, S. and Adshead, L. (2008) '"We don't see her as a social worker": a service user case study of the importance of social workers' relationship and humanity', *British Journal of Social Work*, 38(7): 1371–88.

Biestek, F.P. (1961) *The Casework Relationship*, London: Allen & Unwin.

Bingham, J. (2008) 'The social worker who warned of another Climbié-style tragedy in Haringey', www.telegraph.co.uk (accessed 14 January 2010).

Blaschke, C.M., Freddolino, P.P. and Mullen, E.E. (2009) 'Ageing and technology: a review of the research literature', *British Journal of Social Work*, 39(4): 641–56.

Blewett, J., Lewis, J. and Tunstill, J. (2007) *The Changing Roles and Tasks of Social Work: a literature informed discussion paper*, London: GSCC.

Boddy, J. and Statham, J. (2009) *European Perspectives on Social Work: models of education and professional roles. A briefing paper*, London: Thomas Coram Research Unit.

Bokhari, K. (2008) 'Falling through the gaps: safeguarding children trafficked into the UK', *Children and Society*, 22(3): 201–11.

Boud, D. (2010) 'Relocating reflection in the context of practice', in H. Bradbury, N. Frost, S. Kilminster and M. Zukas (eds) *Beyond Reflective Practice: new approaches to professional lifelong learning*, London: Routledge.

Bowles, W., Collingridge, M., Curry, S. and Valentine, B. (2006) *Ethical Practice for Social Work*, Maidenhead: Open University Press.

Bowling, A. and Gabriel, Z. (2007) 'Lay theories of quality of life in older age', *Ageing and Society*, 27(6): 827–48.

Brady, B. (2006) *Evaluation of The Children's Parliament*, Glasgow: Education for Global Citizenship Unit, University of Glasgow.

Brae, S. (2000) 'Participation and involvement in social care', in H. Kemshall and R. Littlechild (eds) *User Involvement and Participation in Social Care: research informing practice*, London: Jessica Kingsley Publishers.

Brammer, A. (2010) *Social Work Law*, 3rd edn, Harlow: Pearson Education.

Brandon, M., Belderson, P., Warren, C., Howe, D., Gardner, R., Dodsworth, J. and Black, J. (2008) *Analysing child death and serious injury through abuse and neglect: what can we learn? A biennial analysis of serious case reviews 2003–2005*, London: DCSF.

Brandon, M., Thoburn, J., Lewis, A. and Way, A. (1999) *Safeguarding Children with the Children Act 1989*, London: The Stationery Office.

Brearley, J. (2007) 'A psychodynamic approach to social work', in J. Lishman (ed.) *Handbook for Practice Learning in Social Work and Social Care*, London: Jessica Kingsley Publishers.

Brechin, A. (2000) 'The challenges of caring relationships', in A. Brechin, H. Brown and M.A. Eby (eds) *Critical practice in health and social care*, London: Sage/The Open University.

Brindle, D. (2007) 'Questionable punishment', *The Guardian*, 1 August, www.guardian.co.uk (accessed 17 October 2007).

Brindle, D. (2008) 'Registering disapproval', *The Guardian*, 2 July, www.guardian.co.uk (accessed 27 October 2008).

British Association of Social Workers (2002) *Code of Ethics*, Birmingham: BASW.

British Institute of Learning Disabilities (2004) *Factsheet – what is a learning disability?*, Kidderminster: BILD Publications.

Brown, H. (2009) 'Safeguarding adults', in R. Adams, L. Dominelli and M. Payne (eds) (2009) *Critical Practice in Social Work*, 2nd edn, Basingstoke: Palgrave Macmillan.

Brown, K., McCloskey, K., Galpin, D., Keen, S. and Immins, T. (2008) Evaluating the impact of post-qualifying social work education, *Social Work Education*, 27(8): 853–67.

Browne, D. (2009) 'Black communities, mental health and the criminal justice system', in J. Reynolds, R. Muston, T. Heller, J. Leach, M. McCormick, J. Wallcraft and M. Walsh (eds) *Mental Health Still Matters*, Basingstoke: Palgrave Macmillan.

Burns, R. (1994) *The Works of Robert Burns*, Hertfordshire: Wordsworth Editions.

Burt, M. and Worsley, A. (2008) 'Social work, professionalism and the regulatory framework', in S. Fraser and S. Matthews (eds) *The Critical Practitioner in Social Work and Health Care*, London: Sage/The Open University.

Burton, J. (2003) 'Managing mistakes and challenges', in J. Seden and J. Reynolds (eds) *Managing Care in Practice*, London: Routledge/The Open University.

Butler, I. and Drakeford, M. (2003) *Scandal, Social Policy and Social Welfare*, 2nd edn, Bristol: Policy Press/BASW.

Bytheway, B., Ward, R., Holland, C. and Peace, S. (2007) *Too Old: Older People's Accounts of Discrimination, Exclusion and Rejection: a report from the Research on Age Discrimination Project (RoAD) to Help the Aged*, London: Help the Aged.

Cabinet Office (1999) *Modernising Government*, London: Cabinet Office.

Cabinet Office (2000) *E-government: a strategic framework for public services in the information age*, London: Cabinet Office.

Care Council for Wales (2008) *Annual Review 2007/08*, www.ccwales.org.uk (accessed 25 January 2010).

Care Council for Wales/Cyngor Gofal Cymru (Undated) *Code of Practice for Social Care Workers*, Cardiff, www.ccwales.org.uk (accessed 25 January 2010).

CareSpace: the Online Community for Social Care (2008), www.communitycare.co.uk/carespace/forums (accessed 31 October 2009).

Care Standards Tribunal (2006) *YD* v *The General Social Care Council*, www.carestandardstribunal.gov.uk (accessed 27 October 2009).

Care Standards Tribunal (2007) *Christopher Bradford* v *The General Social Care Council*, www.carestandardstribunal.gov.uk (accessed 27 October 2009).

Carr, S. and Dittrich, R. (2008) *Personalisation: a rough guide*, London: SCIE.

Case, S.P. (2007) 'Questioning the "evidence" of risk that underpins evidence-led youth justice interventions', *Youth Justice*, 7(2): 91–106.

CDCS – European Committee for Social Cohesion (2004) *User's Involvement in Social Services*, Strasbourg: CDCS.

Cemlyn, S. (2008) 'Human rights and gypsies and travellers: an exploration of the application of a human rights perspective to social work with a minority community in Britain', *British Journal of Social Work*, 38(1): 136–52.

Chase, E., Knight, A. and Statham, J. (2008) *Promoting the Emotional Wellbeing of Unaccompanied Young People Seeking Asylum in the UK*, London: Thomas Coram Research Unit.

China National Committee on Ageing (2008) *Dignity and Respect of Older People in Asia: MIPPA Implementation*, www.cnca.org.cn (accessed 22 January 2010).

Clark, C. (2000) *Social work ethics: politics, principles and practice*, Basingstoke: Palgrave Macmillan.

Clark, C. (2006) 'Moral character in social work', *British Journal of Social Work*, 36(1): 75–89.

Clarke, H., Gough, H. and Macfarlane, A. (2004) *It Pays Dividends: direct payments and older people*, Bristol: Policy Press.

Cleaver, H., Nicholson, D., Tarr, S. and Cleaver, D. (2007) *Child Protection, Domestic Violence and Parental Substance Misuse*, London: Jessica Kingsley Publishers.

Cm 5730 (2003) *The Victoria Climbié Inquiry*, London: The Stationery Office.

Community Care (2009) *'Social work 'failures' crowd out positive news, May 14: 4, 5.*

Compton, B.R. and Galaway, B. (1989) *Social Work Processes*, California: Brookes-Cole.

Cooper, B. (2001) 'Constructivism in social work: towards a participative practice viability', *British Journal of Social Work*, 31: 721–38.

Cooper, B. (2008a) 'Constructive engagement: best practice in social work interviewing – keeping the child in mind', in K. Jones, B. Cooper and H. Ferguson (eds) *Best Practice in Social Work: critical perspectives*, Basingstoke: Palgrave Macmillan.

Cooper, B. (2008b) 'Best practice in social work interviewing: processes of negotiation and assessment', in K. Jones, B. Cooper and H. Ferguson (eds) *Best Practice in Social Work: critical perspectives*, Basingstoke: Palgrave Macmillan.

Cooper, B. (2008c) 'Continuing professional development: a critical approach', in S. Fraser and S. Matthews (eds) *The Critical Practitioner in Social Work and Health Care*, London: Sage/The Open University.

Cooper, B. (2010) 'Educating social workers for lifeworld and system', in M. Murphy and T. Fleming (eds) *Habermas, Critical Theory and Education: International Studies in the Philosophy of Education*, London: Routledge.

Cooper, B. and Broadfoot P. (2006) 'Beyond description and prescription: towards conducive assessment in social work education', *International Studies in Sociology of Education*, 16(2): 139–57.

Cooper, B. and Nix, I. (2009) 'Prepared for practice? An approach for capturing graduates' perceptions', paper presented at the 11th UK Joint Social Work Education Conference and 3rd UK Social Work Research Conference, University of Hertfordshire, Hatfield.

Cooper, B. and Rixon, A. (2001) 'Integrating post-qualification study into the workplace: the candidates' experience', *Social Work Education*, 20(6): 701–16.

Cooper, B., Davis, R., Nix, I. and McCormick, M. (2009) 'Prepared for practice? Transitions from social work student to professional practitioner', paper presented at the 4th and final Open CETL Conference, the Open University, Milton Keynes, December, www.open.ac.uk/pbpl (accessed 25 November 2009).

Corner, L. and Bond, J. (2004) 'Being at risk of dementia: fears and anxieties of older adults', *Journal of Aging Studies*, 18(2): 143–55.

Council for Healthcare Regulatory Excellence (2009) *Report and Recommendations to the Secretary of State for Health on the Conduct and Function of the General Social Care Council*, London: CHRE.

Cree, V. (2002) 'Social work and society', in M. Davis (ed.) *The Blackwell Companion to Social Work*, 2nd edn, Oxford: Blackwell.

Cree, V. and Myers, S. (2008) *Social Work: making a difference*, Bristol: Policy Press.

Crisp, B.R. and Maidment, J. (2009) 'Swapping roles or swapping desks? When experienced practitioners become students on placement', *Learning in Health and Social Care*, 8(3): 165–74.

Curtice, L. (2006) *How is it Going? A survey of what matters most to people with learning disabilities in Scotland today*, Glasgow: Enable.

Dalrymple, J. and Burke, B. (2006) *Anti-Oppressive Practice: social care and the law*, 2nd edn, Maidenhead: Open University Press.

Daniel, B., Wassell, S. and Gilligan, R. (1999) *Child Development for Child Care and Protection Workers*, London: Jessica Kingsley Publishers.

Danso, R. (2009) 'Emancipating and empowering skilled immigrants: what hope does anti-oppressive practice offer?', *British Journal of Social Work*, 39(3): 539–55.

Davidson, S. and King, S. (2005) *Public Knowledge of and Attitudes to Social Work in Scotland*, Edinburgh: Scottish Government.

Davis, M. (2006) 'The Marxism of the British New Left', *Journal of Political Ideologies*, 11(3): 335–58.

Dennis, J. (2007) 'The legal and policy frameworks that govern social work with unaccompanied asylum seeking children in England', in R. Kohl and F. Mitchell (eds) *Working with Unaccompanied Asylum Seeking Children*, Basingstoke: Palgrave Macmillan.

Department for Children, Schools and Families (2008) *Revised Every Child Matters Outcomes Framework*, London: DCSF.

Department for Children, Schools and Families (2009a) *Integrated Children's System*, London: DCSF, www.dcsf.gov.uk (accessed 24 September 2009).

Department for Children, Schools and Families (2009b) *Building a Safe, Confident Future: the final report of the Social Work Task Force*, London: Department of Health/DCSF.

Department for Communities and Local Government (2008a) *Online Social Networks: research report*, Wetherby: DCLG.

Department for Communities and Local Government (2008b) *Understanding Digital Exclusion: research report*, Wetherby: DCLG.

Department for Education and Skills (2004a) *Every Child Matters: change for children*, London: The Stationery Office.

Department for Education and Skills (2004b) *Every Child Matters: next steps*, London: The Stationery Office.

Department for Education and Skills (2007) *Every Child Matters, Change for Children: common assessment framework*, www.everychildmatters.gov.uk (accessed 1 December 2009).

Department for Work and Pensions (2005) *Opportunity Age – Opportunity and Security Throughout Life: section five – keeping in touch – the importance of social networks*, London: DWP.

Department of Health (1998) *Modernising Social Services: promoting independence, improving protection*, London: The Stationery Office.

Department of Health (1999) *Report of the Expert Committee: review of the Mental Health Act 1983*, London: The Stationery Office.

Department of Health (2000a) '*No Secrets: guidance on developing and implementing multi-agency policies and procedures to protect vulnerable adults from abuse*', London: The Stationery Office.

Department of Health (2000b) *A Quality Strategy For Social Care*, London: The Stationery Office.

Department of Health (2000c) *Assessing Children in Need and their Families: practice guidance*, London: The Stationery Office.

Department of Health (2001a) *The Children Act Now: messages from research*, London: The Stationery Office.

Department of Health (2001b) *Valuing People: a new strategy for learning disability for the 21st century*, London: The Stationery Office.

Department of Health (2002) *Requirements for Social Work Training*, London: The Stationery Office.

Department of Health (2003) *Fair Access to Care Services: guidance on eligibility criteria for adult social care*, London: The Stationery Office.

Department of Health (2007) *New Ways of Working for Everyone – a best practice implementation guide*, London: The Stationery Office.

Department of Health (2008) *Code of Practice; Mental Health Act 1983*, London: The Stationery Office.

Department of Health, Cox, A. and Bentovim, A. (2000) *The Family Pack of Questionnaires and Scales*, London: The Stationery Office.

Department of Health, Department for Education and Employment and Home Office (2000) *Framework for the Assessment of Children in Need and Their Families*, London: The Stationery Office.

Department of Health, Social Services and Public Safety (2007) *Bamford Review of Mental Health and Learning Disability*, Northern Ireland: DHSSPS.

De Shazer, S. (1988) *Clues: investigating solutions in brief therapy*, New York: Norton.

Disability Rights Commission (2007) *Maintaining Standards, Promoting Equality: professional regulation within nursing, teaching and social work and disabled people's access to those profession*, www.maintainingstandards.org (accessed 16 March 2009).

Doel, M. (2005) *New Approaches to Practice Learning*, London: Skills for Care.

Doel, M., Nelson, P. and Flynn, E. (2008) 'Experiences of post-qualifying study in social work', *Social Work Education*, 27(5): 549–71.

Donzelot, J. (1988) 'The promotion of the social', *Economy and Society* 17(3): 395–427.

Douglas, A. and Philpot, T. (1998) *Caring and Coping: a guide to social services*, London: Routledge.

Dowling, M. (2006) 'Translating theory into practice? The implications for practitioners and users and carers', *Translating Theory into Practice*, 18(1): 17–30.

Dowling, M. and Dolan, L. (2001) 'Families with Children with Disabilities – Inequalities and the Social Model', *Disability and Society*, 16(1): 21–35.

Dumbleton, P. (1998) 'Words and numbers', *British Journal of Learning Disabilities*, 26(4): 151–3.

Dumbleton, S., Gordon, J., Kelly, T., Miller, T. and Aldgate, J. (2008) *Making Advanced Entry Work: the experience of social work education in Scotland*, Dundee: SSSC.

Duncan, B. (2007) 'Inspecting for improvement in Scotland', *Journal of Care Services Management*, 2(1): 17–27.

Dunn, J. (2008) *Family Relationships, Children's Perspectives*, London: One Plus One.

Dunworth, M. (2007) 'Growing your own; the practice outcomes of employment based social work training. An evaluative case study of one agency's experience', *Social Work Education*, 26(2): 151–69.

Dutton, W.H., Helsper, E.J. and Gerber, M.M. (2009) *The Internet in Britain: 2009*, Oxford: Oxford Internet Institute, University of Oxford.

Duvell, F. and Jordan, B. (2000) *'How Low Can You Go?' Dilemmas of social work with asylum seekers in London*, Exeter: Department of Social Work, Exeter University.

Eby, M. and Gallagher, A. (2008) 'Values and ethics in practice', in S. Fraser and S. Matthews (eds) *The Critical Practitioner in Social Work and Health Care*, London: Sage/The Open University.

Emerson, E. (2007) *The Mental Health of Children and Adolescents with Learning Disabilities in Britain*, Lancaster: The Institute for Health Research.

Enable (1999) *Stop It! Bullying and harassment of people with learning disabilities*, Glasgow: Enable.

Entwhistle, N.J. and Peterson, E.R. (2004) 'Conceptions of learning and knowledge in higher education: relationships with study behaviour and influences of learning environments', *International Journal of Educational Research*, 41(6): 407–28.

Evers, A. (2006) 'European perspectives and future challenges of welfare services', in A. Matthias (ed.) *Nordic Civic Society Organisation and the Future of Welfare Services: a model for Europe?* Copenhagen: Tempa Nord.

Fahlberg, V. (1984) 'The child who is stuck', in M. Adcock, and R. White (eds) *Working with Parents*, London: British Agencies for Adoption and Fostering.

Family and Parenting Institute (2007) *Listening to parents: a short guide*, London: FPI.

Feeley, M. and Simon, J. (1994) *Actuarial Justice: the emerging new criminal law. The futures of criminology*, London: Sage.

Ferguson, I. (2007) 'Increasing user choice or privatizing risk? The antinomies of personalization', *British Journal of Social Work*, 37(3): 387–403.

Ferguson, I. (2008a) 'Concluding thoughts: frustrations and possibilities', in M. McPhail (ed.) *Service User and Carer Involvement, Beyond Good Intentions*, Edinburgh: Dunedin Academic Press.

Ferguson, I. (2008b) *Reclaiming Social Work: Challenging neo-liberalism and Promoting Social Justice*, London: Sage.

Ferguson, I., Lavalette, M. and Whitmore, E. (2005) *Globalisation, Global Justice and Social Work*, Abingdon: Taylor & Francis.

Findlay, A., Fyfe, N. and Stewart, E. (2007) 'Changing places: voluntary sector work with refugees and asylum seekers in core and peripheral regions of the UK', *International Journal on Multicultural Societies*, 9(1): 54–74.

Fitzpatrick, T. (2008) *Applied Ethics and Social Problems*, Bristol: Policy Press.

Fook, J. (2007) 'Reflective practice and critical reflection', in J. Lishman (ed.) *Handbook for Practice Learning in Social Work and Social Care*, London: Jessica Kingsley Publishers.

Foster, M., Harris, J., Jackson, K., Morgan, H. and Glendinning, C. (2006) 'Personalised social care for adults with disabilities: a problematic concept for frontline practice', *Health and Social Care in the Community*, 14(2): 125–35.

Foucault, M. (1975) *Discipline and Punish*, Harmondsworth: Penguin.

Frost, N. (2010) 'Professionalism and social change – the implications of social change for the "reflective practitioner"', in H. Bradbury, N. Frost, S. Kilminster and M. Zukas (eds) *Beyond Reflective Practice: new approaches to professional lifelong learning*, London: Routledge.

Galpin, D. (2009) 'Who really drives the development of post-qualifying social work education and what are the implications of this?', *Social Work Education*, 28(1): 65–80.

Gamble, A. (1991) 'The weakening of social democracy', in M. Loney, B. Robert, J. Clarke, A. Cochrane, P. Graham and M. Wilson (eds) *The State of the Market*, 2nd edn, London: Sage.

Gardner, R. (2003) 'Working together to improve children's life chances: the challenge of inter-agency collaboration', in J. Weinstein, C. Whittington and T. Leiba (eds) *Collaboration in Social Work Practice*, London: Jessica Kingsley Publishers.

Gee, M. and McPhail, M. (2008) 'The voice of service users and carers in Universities', in McPhail, M. (ed.) *Service User and Carer Involvement: Beyond Good Intentions*, Edinburgh: Dunedin Academic Press.

General Social Care Council (2002a) *Code of Practice for Social Care Workers and Employers*, London: GSCC.

General Social Care Council (2002b) *Accreditation of Universities to Grant Degrees in Social Work*, www.gscc.org.uk (accessed 1 August 2009).

General Social Care Council (2003) *The General Social Care Council (Conduct) Rules 2003 and Explanatory Notes*, www.gscc.org.uk (accessed 27 October 2009).

General Social Care Council (2004) *Code of Practice for Social Care Workers and Code of Practice for Employers of Social Care Workers*, London: GSCC.

General Social Care Council (2008) *Raising Standards: social work conduct in England 2003–2008*, London: GSCC.

General Social Care Council (2009) *The Post-Qualifying Framework for Social Work Education and Training*, London: GSCC.

General Social Care Council/Joint Universities Council Social Work Education Committee (2007) *Suitability for Social Work*, www.gscc.org.uk (accessed 24 February 2008).

Geser, H. (Release 3.0 2004) 'Towards a sociological theory of the mobile phone', in *Sociology in Switzerland: sociology of the mobile phone*, Zurich, http://socio.ch/mobile/t_geser1.htm (accessed 22 January 2010).

Giddens, A. (2002) *Runaway World: how globalisation is reshaping our lives*, London: Profile Books.

Gilleard, C. and Higgs, S. (2005) *Contexts of Ageing: class, cohort and community*, Cambridge: Polity Press.

Gillen, S. (2008) 'Views of the boundaries', *Community Care*, 4 September: 16–17.

Gilligan, R. (2000) 'Adversity, resilience and young people: the protective value of positive school and spare time experiences', *Children and Society*, 14(1): 37–47.

Ginsburg, N. (2009) 'Race, ethnicity and social policy', in H. Bochel, C. Bochel, R. Page and R. Sykes (eds) *Social Policy Themes, Issues and Debates*, Harlow: Pearson Education.

Glaister, A. (2008) 'Introducing critical practice', in S. Fraser and S. Matthews (eds) *The Critical Practitioner in Social Work and Health Care*, London: Sage/The Open University.

Glasby, J. and Littlechild, R. (2009) *Direct Payments and Personal Budgets: putting personalisation into practice*, Bristol: Policy Press.

Glisson, C. and Hemmelgarn, A. (1998) 'The effects of organisational climate and inter organisational co-ordination on the quality and outcomes of children's service systems', *Child Abuse and Neglect*, 22(5): 402–21.

Goddard, J., Leht, R. and Lapadat, J. (2000) 'Parents of children with disabilities: telling a different story', *Canadian Journal of Counselling*, 34(4): 273–89.

Gorman, H. (2003) 'Which skills do care managers need? A research project on skills, competency and continuing professional development', *Social Work Education*, 22(3): 245–59.

Gould, N. and Baldwin, M. (2004) *Social Work, Critical Reflection, and the Learning Organisation*, Farnham: Ashgate.

GoWell (2007) 'Baseline findings 2006', in *Community Health and Well-being Survey*, Glasgow: University of Glasgow and MRC Social and Public Health Sciences Unit, www.gowellonline.com (accessed 14 September 2009).

Gray, M. and Webb, S.A. (eds) (2010 forthcoming) *International Social Work*, London: Sage.

Gray, M., Coates, J. and Yellow Bird, M. (eds) (2009) *Indigenous Social Work around the World*, Farnham: Ashgate.

Guardian Society (2005) '*Social workers "more protected" after Climbié care worker ruling*', 9 June, www.guardian.co.uk/society (accessed 8 April 2009).

Guardian Society (2009) '*Time is of the essence*', 11 March, www.guardian.co.uk/society (accessed 24 March 2009).

Gupta, A. and Blewett, J. (2007) 'Change for children? The challenges and opportunities for the children's social work workforce', *Child and Family Social Work*, 12(2): 172–81.

Habermas, J. (1986) *Knowledge and Human Interests*, Cambridge: Polity Press.

Hallett, C. and Birchall, E. (1992) *Co-ordination and Child Protection, a review of the literature*, Edinburgh: The Stationery Office.

Hallett, C. and Stevenson, O. (1980) *Child Abuse: aspects of interprofessional co-operation*, London: Allen & Unwin.

Hardey, M. and Loader, B. (2009) 'Older people and the role of digital services', *British Journal of Social Work*, 39(4): 657–69.

Hardiker, P. and Barker, M. (2007) 'Towards social theory for social work', in J. Lishman (ed.) *Handbook for Practice Learning in Social Work and Social Care*, 2nd edn, London: Jessica Kingsley Publishers.

Harris, J. (2003) *The Social Work Business*, London: Routledge.

Harris, J. (2007) 'Looking backward, looking forward: current trends in human services management', in J. Aldgate, L. Healy, B. Malcolm, B. Pine, W. Rose and J. Seden (eds) *Enhancing Social Work Management*, London: Jessica Kingsley Publishers.

Harris, J. and White, V. (eds) (2009) *Modernising Social Work*, Bristol: Policy Press.

Harrison, K. and Ruch, G. (2007) 'Social work and the use of self, on becoming and being a social worker', in M. Lymbery and K. Postle (eds) *Social Work: a Companion to Learning*, London: Sage.

Hatfield, B. (2008) 'Powers to detain under mental health legislation in England and the role of the approved social worker: an analysis of patterns and trends under the 1983 Mental Health Act in six local authorities', *British Journal of Social Work*, 38(8): 1553–71.

Hayes, D. (2008) 'Confused on conduct', *Community Care*, 4 September, 18–19.

Hayes, D. and Humphries, B. (eds) (2004) *Social Work Immigration and Asylum: debates, dilemmas and ethical issues for social work and social care practice*, London: Jessica Kingsley Publishers.

Healy, K. and Mulholland, J. (2008) *Writing Skills for Social Workers*, London: Sage.

Healy, L.M. (2001) *International Social Work: professional action in an interdependent world*, New York: Oxford University Press.

Heller, T. (2009) 'Doing being human', in J. Reynolds, R. Muston, T. Heller, J. Leach, M. McCormick, J. Wallcraft and M. Walsh (eds) *Mental Health Still Matters*, Basingstoke: Palgrave Macmillan.

Helsper, E. (2009) 'The internet's conscientious objectors', *BBC online news magazine*, 6 August, www.news.bbc.co.uk (accessed 22 January 2010).

Henderson, J. and Atkinson, D. (eds) (2003) *Managing Care in Context*, London: Routledge/The Open University.

Hendrick, H. (2003) *Child Welfare*, Bristol: Policy Press.

Hendrick, H. (2006) 'Histories of youth crime and justice', in B. Goldson and J. Muncie (eds) *Youth Crime and Justice*, London: Sage.

Hessle, S. (2007) 'Globalisation: implications for international development work, social work and the integration of immigrants in Sweden', in L. Dominelli (ed.) *Revitalising Communities in a Globalising World*, Farnham: Ashgate.

Hester, R. (2008) 'Power, knowledge and children's rights in the teaching of youth justice practice', *IUC Journal of Social Work – Theory and Practice*, 17: 2, www.bemidjistate.edu (accessed 11 November 2009).

Higham, P. (2006) *Social Work: introducing professional practice*, London: Sage.

Hill, M. and Hopkins, P. (2009) 'Safeguarding children who are refugees or asylum seekers: managing multiple scales of legislation and policy', in K. Broadhurst, C. Grover and J. Jamieson (eds) *Critical Perspectives on Safeguarding Children*, London: Wiley-Blackwell.

Hodgson (2002) *Youth participation*, 29/4/02, issue 44, Edinburgh: Scottish Executive.

Holland, C. and Katz, J. (2010) 'Cultural identity and belonging in later life: is extra care housing an attractive concept to older Jewish people living in

Britain?', *Journal of Cross-Cultural Gerontology*, Online First – DOI 10.1007/s10823-009-9107-9.

Holland, D. (2008) 'The current status of disability activism and non-governmental organizations in post-communist Europe', *Disability and Society*, 23(6): 543–55.

Holloway, M. and Lymbery, M. (2007) 'Caring for people: social work with adults in the next decade and beyond', editorial, *British Journal of Social Work*, 37(3): 375–86.

Home Office (2008) *UK Border Agency Code of Practice for Keeping Children Safe from Harm*, London: Home Office, www.ukba.homeoffice.gov.uk (accessed 14 September 2009).

Hopkins, K.M., Deal, K.H. and Bloom, J.D. (2005) 'Moving away from tradition: exploring the field experiences of part time, older and employment-based students', *Journal of Social Work Education*, 41(3): 573–89.

Horwath, J. (2009a) *The New Child's World: the comprehensive guide to assessing children in need*, London: Jessica Kingsley Publishers.

Horwath, J. (2009b) 'Working effectively in a multi-agency context', in H. Cleaver, P. Cawson, S. Gorin and S. Walker (eds) *Safeguarding Children: a shared responsibility*, London: Wiley-Blackwell.

Howe, D. (1996) 'Surface and depth in social work practice', in N. Parton (ed.) *Social Theory, Social Change and Social Work*, London: Routledge.

Howe, D. (2006) 'Disabled children, parent-child interaction and attachment', *Child and Family Social Work*, 11(2): 95–106.

Howe, D. (2009) *A Brief Introduction to Social Work Theory*, Basingstoke: Palgrave Macmillan.

Howitt, D. (1992) *Child Abuse Errors: when good intentions go wrong*, New York: Harvester Wheatsheaf.

Hudson, B. (2000) 'Inter-agency collaboration – a sceptical view', in A. Brechin, H. Brown and M.A. Eby (eds) *Critical Practice in Health and Social Care*, London: Sage/The Open University.

Hudson, B. (2002) 'Interprofessionality in health and social care: the Achilles' heel of partnership?', *Journal of Interprofessional Care*, 16(1): 7–17.

Hudson, B., Hardy, B., Henwood, M. and Wistow, G. (1999) 'In pursuit of inter-agency collaboration in the public sector: what is the contribution of theory and research?', *Public Management: an international journal of research and theory*, 1(2): 235–60.

Hugman, R. (2009) 'But is it social work? Some reflections on mistaken identities', *British Journal of Social Work*, 39(6): 1138–53.

Humphries, B. (2004a) 'An unacceptable role for social work: implementing immigration policy', *British Journal of Social Work*, 34(1): 93–107.

Humphries, B. (2004b) 'The construction and re-construction of social work', in D. Hayes and B. Humphries (eds) *Social Work Immigration and Asylum Debates: dilemmas and ethical issues for social work and social care practice*, London: Jessica Kingsley Publishers.

Huxley, P., Evans, S., Webber, M. and Gately, C. (2005) 'Staff shortages in the mental health workforce: the case of the disappearing Approved Social Worker', *Health and Social Care in the Community*, 13(6): 504–13.

Ingham, N. (ed.) (2002) *Gogarburn Lives*, Edinburgh: Living Memory Association.

Ingleby, D. (1985) *Professionals as Socialisers: the 'psy complex'*, New York: JAI Press.

Inkson, K. (2007) *Understanding Careers: the metaphors of working lives*, London: Sage.

International Association of Schools of Social Work (2009) www.iassw.aiets.org (accessed 30 September 2009).

International Federation of Social Workers (2002) *Ethics in Social Work, Statement of Principles*, Berne: IFSW.

International Federation of Social Workers (2008) www.ifsw.org (accessed 19 September 2008).

Jackson, M. (2007) 'Thinking about loss to make sense of our self', in W. Tovey (ed.) *The Post-Qualifying Handbook for Social Workers*, London: Jessica Kingsley Publishers.

Johnston, L. (2008) *Missed out: missing out adults with learning disabilities who live in the family home and their right to recognition and resources*, Bridge of Weir: Quarriers.

Jones, C. (1996) 'Anti-intellectualism and the peculiarities of British social work education', in N. Parton (ed.) *Social Theory, Social Change and Social Work*, London: Routledge.

Jones, D.P.H. (2006) 'Communicating with children about adverse experiences', in J. Aldgate, D.P.H. Jones, W. Rose and C. Jeffery (eds) *The Developing World of the Child*, London: Jessica Kingsley Publishers.

Jones, D.P.H. and Ramchandani, P. (1999) *Child Sexual Abuse: informing practice from research*, Oxford: Radcliffe Medical Press.

Jones, D.P.H., Hindley, N. and Ramchandani, P. (2006) 'Making plans: assessment, intervention and evaluating outcomes', in J. Aldgate, D.P.H. Jones, W. Rose and C. Jeffery (eds) *The Developing World of the Child*, London: Jessica Kingsley Publishers.

Jones, K. (1993) *Asylums and After: a revised history of mental health services, from the early 18th century to the 1900s*, London: Atholl Press.

Jones, K., Cooper, B. and Ferguson, H. (eds) (2008) *Best Practice in Social Work: critical perspectives*, Basingstoke: Palgrave Macmillan.

Jones, R.L. (2002) '"That's very rude: I shouldn't be telling you that": older women talking about sex', *Narrative Enquiry*, 12(2): 121–42.

Jones, R.L. and Ward, R. (2009) *LGBT Issues: looking beyond categories*, Policy and Practice in Health and Social Care Series, Edinburgh: Dunedin Academic Press.

Jordan, B. (2000) *Social work and the third way: tough love and social policy*, London: Sage.

Jordan, B. (2008) 'Social work and world poverty', *International Social Work*, 51(4): 440–52.

Jordan, B. and Jordan, C. (2000) *Social Work and the Third Way: tough love as social policy*, London: Sage.

Kakabadse, A. (1982) *Culture of the Social Services*, Aldershot: Gower.

Kang, T. (2009) 'Homeland re-territorialized: revisiting the role of geographical places in the formation of diasporic identity in the digital age', *Information, Communication and Society*, 12(3): 326–43.

Keeping, C. (2008) 'Practitioner research', in S. Fraser, and S. Matthews (eds) *The Critical Practitioner in Social Work and Health Care*, London: Sage/Open University Press.

Kemshall, H. (2002) *Risk, Social Policy and Welfare*, Maidenhead: Open University Press.

Kemshall, H. (2007) 'Risk assessment and risk management: the right approach?', in M. Blyth, E. Solomon and K. Baker (eds) *Young People and 'Risk'*, Bristol: Policy Press.

Khan, P. and Dominelli, L. (2000) 'The impact of globalization on social work in the UK', *European Journal of Social Work*, 3(2): 95–108.

Kim, T.K. (2009) 'Globalization and state-supported welfare: a test of curve-linear hypothesis in OECD countries', *International Social Work*, 52(2): 209–22.

Klein, R. (1993) 'O'Goffe's tale', in C. Jones (ed.) *New Perspectives on the Welfare State in Europe*, London: Routledge.

Kolb, D. (1984) *Experiential Learning: experience as the source of learning and development*, Englewood Cliffs, NJ: Prentice Hall.

Kubiak, C. and Hester, R. (2009) 'Just deserts? Developing practice in youth justice', *Learning in Health and Social Care*, 6(1): 47–57.

Lafrance, J. and Gray, E. (2004) 'Gate-keeping for professional social work practice', *Social Work Education*, 23(3): 325–40.

Laming, W.H. (2009) *The Protection of Children in England: progress report*, London: The Stationery Office.

Lavalette, M. and Ferguson, I. (2007) 'Towards a social work of resistance: international social work and the radical tradition', in M. Lavalette, and I. Ferguson (eds) *International Social Work and the Radical Tradition*, Birmingham: Venture Press.

Lawrence, S., Lyons, K., Simpson, G. and Huegler, N. (eds) (2009) *Introducing International Social Work*, Exeter: Learning Matters.

Layard, R. and Dunn, J. (2009) *A Good Childhood. The Landmark Report for the Children's Society*, Harmondsworth: Penguin.

Lea, M. and Street, B. (2000) 'Student writing and staff feedback in higher education: an academic literacies approach', in M. Lea and B. Stierer (eds) *Student Writing in Higher Education: new contexts*, Maidenhead: Open University Press.

Leadbeater, C. (2004) *Personalisation through Participation: a new script for public services*, London: Demos.

Leadbeater, C. (2005) *Personalisation and Participation: the future of social care in Scotland*, London: Demos.

Leadbeater, C. (2009) 'State of loneliness', *The Guardian*, 1 July, www.guardian.co.uk/society (accessed 22 January 2010).

Leadbeater, C., Bartlett, J. and Gallagher, N. (2008) *Making it Personal*, London: Demos.

LeCroy, C.W. (2002) *The Call to Social Work: life stories*, Thousand Oaks, CA: Sage.

Levin, E. (2004) *Involving Service Users and Carers in Social Work Education*, London: Social Care Institute for Excellence.

Levi-Strauss, C. (1987) *The View From Afar*, trans. J. Neugroschel and P. Hoss, Reading: Peregrine Books.

Lewis, V. (2003) *Development and Disability*, Oxford: Blackwell.

Lillis, T. (1997) 'New voices in academia? The regulative nature of academic writing conventions', *Language and Education*, 11(3): 182–99.

Lillis, T. (2001) *Student writing: access, regulation and desire*, London: Routledge.

Longley, P.A. and Singleton, D. (2009) 'Linking social deprivation and digital exclusion in England', *Urban Studies*, 46(7): 1275–98.

Lord P. and Hutchinson, P. (2003) 'Individualised support and funding: building blocks for capacity building and inclusion', *Disability & Society*, 8(1): 71–86.

Loucks, N. and Talbot, J. (2007) *No-one Knows: identifying and supporting prisoners with learning difficulties and learning disabilities: the views of prison staff in Scotland*, London: Prison Reform Trust.

Lovell, C. (2007) 'Tribunal finds GSCC guilty of discrimination', *Community Care*, 30 August, 8.

Lovelock, R., Lyons, K. and Powell, J. (2004) *Reflecting on Social Work: discipline and profession*, Farnham: Ashgate.

Lundeby, H. and Tossebro, J. (2008) 'Family structure in Norwegian families of children with disabilities', *Journal of Applied Research in Intellectual Disabilities*, 21(3): 246–56.

Lymbery, M. (2006) 'United we stand? Partnership working in health and social care and role of social work in services for older people', *British Journal of Social Work*, 36(7): 1119–34.

Lyons, K., Manion, K. and Carlsen, M. (2006) *International Perspectives on Social Work: global conditions and local practice*, Basingstoke: Palgrave Macmillan.

MacIntyre, G. (2008) *Learning Disability and Social Inclusion*, Edinburgh: Dunedin Academic Press.

MacKay, K. (2008) 'The Scottish adult support and protection legal framework', *The Journal of Adult Protection*, 10(4): 25–36.

Madoc-Jones, I., Bates, J., Facer, B. and Roscoe, K. (2007) 'Students with criminal convictions: policies and practices in social work education', *British Journal of Social Work*, 37(8): 1389–403.

Magito-McLaughlin, D., Spinosa, T. and Marsalis, M. (2002) 'Overcoming the barriers: moving towards a service model that is conducive to person-centred planning', in S. Holburn and P. Vietze (eds) *Person-Centred Planning: research, practice and future directions*, Baltimore, MD: Paul H. Brookes Publishing.

Mahoney, G. and Wiggers, B. (2007) 'The role of parents in early intervention: implications for social work', *Children and Schools*, 29(1): 7–15.

Mann, K. (1992) *The Making of an English 'Underclass'? The social divisions of welfare and labour*, Maidenhead/Philadelphia: Open University Press.

Marchant, R. and Jones, M. (2000) 'Assessing the needs of disabled children and their families', in Department of Health *Assessing Children in Need and their Families*, London: The Stationary Office, 73–112.

Margolin, L. (1997) *Under the Cover of Kindness: the invention of social work*, Charlottesville, VA: University Press of Virginia.

Martin, V. and Henderson, E. (eds) (2001) *Managing in Health and Social Care*, London: Routledge.

Matthias, A. (ed.) (2006) *Nordic Civic Society Organisation and the Future of Welfare Services: A model for Europe?*, Copenhagen: Tempa Nord.

Mattinson, J. (1975) *The Reflective Process in Casework Supervision*, London: Institute of Marital Studies/Tavistock Institute of Human Relations.

McCormick, M. (2009) 'Introduction', in J. Reynolds, R. Muston, T. Heller, J. Leach, M. McCormick, J. Wallcraft and M. Walsh (eds) *Mental Health Still Matters*, Basingstoke: Palgrave Macmillan.

McInnes, A. and Lawson-Brown, V. (2007) '"God" and other "Do-Gooders": a comparison of the regulation of services provided by General Practitioners and Social Workers in England', *Journal of Social Work*, 7(3): 341–54.

McLaughlin, K. (2007a) 'Revisiting the public/private divide: theoretical, political and personal implications of their unification', *Practice*, 19(4): 241–53.

McLaughlin, K. (2007b) 'Regulation and risk in social work: the General Social Care Council and the Social Care Register in context', *British Journal of Social Work*, 37(7): 1263–77.

McLean, T. (2007) 'Interdisciplinary Practice', in J. Lishman (ed.) *Handbook for Practice Learning in Social Work and Social Care: knowledge and theory*, 2nd edn, London: Jessica Kingsley Publishers.

McMillan, S., Johnson, J., Avery, E. and Macias, W. (2008) 'From have nots to watch dogs: understanding internet health communication behaviours of online senior citizens', *Information Communication and Society*, 11(5): 675–97.

McNeill, F., Batchelor, S., Burnett, R. and Knox, J. (2005) *21st Century Social Work: reducing re-offending – key practice skills*, Edinburgh: Social Work Inspection Agency, www.scotland.gov.uk (accessed 2 November 2009).

McPhail, M. (ed.) (2008) *Service User and Carer Involvement: beyond good intentions*, Edinburgh: Dunedin Academic Press.

Midgely, J. (1981) *Professional Imperialism: social work in the Third World*, London: Heinemann.

Midgley, J. (2009) 'Promoting reciprocal international social work exchanges: professional imperialism revisited', in M. Gray, J. Coates, and M. Yellow Bird (eds) *Indigenous Social Work around the World: towards a culturally relevant education and practice*, Farnham: Ashgate.

Miller, C. and Freeman, M. (2003) 'Clinical teamwork: the impact of policy on collaborative practice', in A. Leathard (ed.) *Interprofessional Collaboration: from policy to practice in Health and Social Care*, Hove: Brunner-Routledge.

Mills, C.W. (1970) *The Sociological Imagination*, Harmondsworth: Penguin.

Mirvis, P.H. and Hall, D.T. (1994) 'Psychological success and the boundaryless career', *Journal of Organisational Behavior*, 15(4): 365–80.

Mittler, P. (1979) *People not Patients: problems and policies in mental handicap*, London: Methuen.

Mohan, B. (2005) 'New internationalism: social work's dilemmas, dreams and delusion', *International Social Work*, 48(3): 241–50.

Morgan, A. and Fraser, S. (2009) 'Looked after young people and their social work managers: a study of contrasting experiences of using computer-assisted-self-interviewing (A-CASI)', *British Journal of Social Work*, http://assets.aarp.org/rgcenter/il/healthy_home.pdf (advance access published online 12 February).

Morgan, G. (2006) *Images of Organisation*, London: Sage.

Morris, J. (1999) 'Disabled children, child protection systems and the Children Act 1989', *Child Abuse Review*, 8(2): 91–108.

Morris, K. (ed.) (2008) *Social Work and Multi-Agency Working – making a difference*, Bristol: Policy Press.

Munk, R. (2005) *Globalization and Social Exclusion: a transformationalist perspective*, Bloomfield, CT: Kumarian Press.

Munro, E. (2004) 'The impact of audit on social work practice', *British Journal of Social Work*, 34(8): 1075–95.

Myers, S. (2007) *Solution-Focused Approaches*, Lyme Regis: Russell House.

Nash, M., Wong, J. and Trlin, A. (2006) 'Civic and social integration: a new field of social work practice with immigrants, refugees and asylum seekers', *International Social Work*, 49(3): 345–63.

National Institute for Mental Health in England (2008) *Mental Health Act 2007: New Roles*, London: National Institute for Mental Health in England.

National Mental Health Development Unit (2009) *New Roles Early Implementer Site Report*, London: National Mental Health Development Unit.

Nellis, M. (2001) 'The new Probation training in England and Wales: realising the potential', *Social Work Education*, 20(4): 415–32.

Nix, I. (2009) 'Windows into the workplace: capturing learner perceptions of their practice-learning needs', paper presented at Making Connections Conference at the Open University, Milton Keynes, June, www.open.ac.uk/pbpl (accessed 25 November 2009).

Nix, I., Cooper, B., Davis, R. and McCormick, M. (2009) 'Prepared for practice', Unpublished PBPL CETL research project, Milton Keynes: The Open University.

Northedge, A. (2005) *The Good Study Guide*, Milton Keynes: The Open University.

Northern Ireland Social Care Council (2002) *NISCC Code of Practice for Social Care Workers*, www.niscc.info (accessed 25 October 2010).

Northern Ireland Social Care Council (2007) www.niscc.info (accessed 4 October 2007).

Office for National Statistics (2009) *Pension Trends – Chapter 11: pensioner income and expenditure*, London: ONS.

Oliver, R. and McLoughlin, C. (2001) 'Exploring the practise and development of generic skills through web-based learning', *Journal of Educational Multimedia and Hypermedia*, 10(3): 207–26.

Open University, The (2006) *K113 Foundations for Social Work Practice*, CDA7, Track 8, Milton Keynes, The Open University.

O'Reilly, D., Cunningham, L. and Lester, S. (1999) 'Introduction', in D. O'Reilly, L. Cunningham and S. Lester (eds) *Developing the Capable Practitioner: Professional Capability through Higher Education*, London: Kegan Paul.

Orme, J. and Rennie, G. (2006) 'The role of registration in ensuring ethical practice', *International Social Work*, 49(3): 333–44.

Orme, J., MacIntyre, G., Green Lister, P., Cavanagh, K., Crisp, B.R., Hussein, S., Manthorpe, J., Moriarty, J., Sharpe, E. and Stevens, M. (2009) 'What (a) difference a degree makes: the evaluation of the new social work degree in England, *British Journal of Social Work*, 39(1): 161–78.

Orr, D. (2009) 'My day with mental health professionals', *The Guardian*, 9 December, www.guardian.co.uk (accessed 22 January 2010).

Osei-Hwedie, K. (1993) 'The challenge of Social Work in Africa: starting the indigenisation process', *Journal of Social Development*, 8(1): 19–30.

Osmond, J. and O'Connor, I. (2006) 'Use of theory and research in social work practice: implications for knowledge-based practice', *Australian Social Work*, 59(1): 5–19.

Ousley, M., Rowlands, J. and Seden, J. (2003) 'Managing information and using new technologies', in J. Seden and J. Reynolds (2003) *Managing Care in Practice*, London: Routledge/The Open University.

Owusu-Bempah, K. (2007) 'Children and separation: socio-genealogical connectedness perspective', in J. Aldgate, D.P.H. Jones, W. Rose and C. Jeffery (eds) *The Developing World of the Child*, London: Jessica Kingsley Publishers.

Parckar, G. (2008) *Disability Poverty in the UK*, London: Leonard Cheshire Disability.

Paré, A. (2000) 'Writing as a way into social work: genre sets, genre systems, and distributed cognition', in P. Dias and A. Paré (eds) *Transitions: writing in academic and workplace settings*, Cresskill, NJ: Hampton Press.

Parton, N. (1994) '"Problematics of government", (post)modernity and social work', *British Journal of Social Work*, 24(1): 9–32.

Parton, N. (1996) 'Social theory, social change and social work: an introduction', in N. Parton (ed.) *Social Theory, Social Change and Social Work*, London: Routledge.

Parton, N. (2003) 'Rethinking professional practice: the contributions of social constructionism and the feminist "ethics of care"', *British Journal of Social Work*, 33(1): 1–16.

Parton, N. (2006) *Safeguarding Childhood: early intervention and surveillance in a late modern society*, Basingstoke: Palgrave Macmillan.

Parton, N. (2007) 'Constructive social work practice in an age of uncertainty', in S.L. Witkin and D. Saleebey (eds) *Social Work Dialogues*, Alexandria, VA: Council on Social Work Education.

Parton, N. (2008) 'Changes in the form of knowledge in social work: from the "social" to the "informational"?', *British Journal of Social Work*, 38(2): 253–69.

Pattison, S. (2004) 'Understanding values', in S. Pattison and R. Pill (eds) *Values in Professional Practice: lessons for Health, Social Care and other professions*, Oxford: Radcliffe Medical Press

Payne, M. (2006) *What is Professional Social Work?* Bristol: Policy Press.

Payne, M. and Askeland, G.A. (2008) *Globalization and International Social Work: postmodern change and challenge*, Farnham: Ashgate.

Payne, M. and Scott, T. (1982) *Developing Supervision of Teams in Field and Residential Social Work – Part 1*, Paper No 12, London: National Institute for Social Work.

Peace, S., Holland, C. and Kellaher, L. (2006) *Environment and Identity in Later Life*, Maidenhead: Open University Press.

Peckover, S., White, S. and Hall, C. (2008) 'Making and managing electronic children: e-Assessment in child welfare', *Information, Communication and Society*, 11(3): 375–94.

Penna, S., Paylor, I., and Washington, J. (2000) 'Globalization, social exclusion and the possibilities for global social work and welfare', *European Journal of Social Work*, 3(2): 109–22.

Phillipson, C., Bernard, M., Phillips, J. and Ogg, J. (1998) 'The family and community life of older people: household composition and social networks in three urban areas', *Ageing and Society*, 18(3): 259–89.

Pithouse, A. (1987) *Social Work: the social organisation of an invisible trade*, Aldershot: Avebury.

Pithouse, A., Hall, C., Peckover, S. and White, S. (2009) 'A tale of two CAFs: the impact of the electronic Common Assessment Framework', *British Journal of Social Work*, 39(4): 599–612.

Pitt, B. (1998) 'Coping with loss: loss in late life', *British Medical Journal*, 316(7142): 1452–4.

Pitts, J. (1988) *The Politics of Juvenile Crime*, London: Sage.

Poehnell, G. and Amundson, N. (2002) 'Career craft', in M. Peiperl, M.B. Arthur, R. Goffee and N. Anand (eds) *Career Creativity: explorations in the re-making of work*, Oxford: Oxford University Press.

Poole, L. and Adamson, K. (2008) *Report on the Situation of the Roma Community in Govanhill*, Glasgow: Oxfam, www.oxfam.org.uk (accessed 30 September 2009).

Poole, T. (2006) *Telecare and Older People*, www.kingsfund.org.uk (accessed 22 January 2010).

Postle, K. and Beresford, P. (2007) 'Capacity building and the re-conception of political participation: a role for social care workers', *British Journal of Social Work*, 37(1): 143–58.

Powell, F. (2001) *The Politics of Social Work*, London: Sage.

Prior, P.M. (1992) 'The Approved Social Worker – reflections on origins', *British Journal of Social Work*, 22(2): 105–9.

Prior, P., Lynch, M.A. and Glaser, D. (1999) 'Responding to child sexual abuse, an evaluation of social work by children and their carers', *Child and Family Social Work*, 4(2): 131–43.

Prynn, B. (2008) 'Reflections on past social work practice: the central role of relationship', in S. Fraser and S. Matthews (eds) *The Critical Practitioner in Social Work and Health Care*, London: Sage/The Open University.

Pugh, R., and Cheers, B. (forthcoming 2010) *Rural Social Work: international persepectives*, Bristol: Policy Press.

Purdie, N. and Ellis, L. (2005) *Literature Review: A review of the empirical evidence identifying effective interventions and teaching practices for students with learning disabilities in Years 4, 5 and 6,* Victoria: Australian Council for Educational Research.

Quality Assurance Agency (2008) *Subject benchmarks statement: social work*, Mansfield: Linney Direct.

Rafferty, J. and Steyaert, J. (2009) 'Social work in the digital age', *British Journal of Social Work*, 39(4): 589–98.

Rai, L. (2004) 'Exploring literacy in social work education: a social practices approach to student writing', *Social Work Education*, 23(2): 149–62.

Rai, L., (2006) 'Owning (up to) reflective writing in social work education', *Social Work Education*, 25(8): 785–97.

Rapaport, J. (2006) 'New roles in mental health: the creation of the Approved Mental Health Practitioner', *Journal of Integrated Care*, 14(5): 37–46.

Ray, M., Bernard, M. and Phillips, J. (2008) *Critical Issues in Social Work with Older People*', Basingstoke: Palgrave Macmillan.

Reel, K. and Hutchings, S. (2007) 'Being part of a team: interprofessional care', in G. Hawley (ed.) *Ethics in Clinical Practice: an interprofessional approach*, Harlow: Pearson Education.

Rees Jones, I., Hyde, M., Victor, C.R., Wiggins, R.D., Gilleard, C. and Higgs, P. (2008) *Ageing in a Consumer Society: from passive to active consumption in Britain*, Bristol: Policy Press.

Reiter, B. (2009) 'Fighting exclusion with culture and art: examples from Brazil', *International Social Work*, 52(2): 155–66.

Robinson, L. (2nd edn 2003) 'Social work through the life course', in R. Adams, L. Dominelli and M. Payne (eds) *Social Work: themes, issues and critical debates*, Basingstoke: Palgrave Macmillan.

Rose, N. (1996) 'Governing "advanced" liberal democracies', in A. Barry, T. Osborne and N. Rose (eds) *Foucault and Political Reason: liberalism, neo-liberalism and rationalities of government*, London: UCL.

Rose, W. (2006) 'The developing world of the child: children's perspectives', in J. Aldgate, D.P.H. Jones, W. Rose and C. Jeffery (eds) *The Developing World of the Child*, London: Jessica Kingsley Publishers.

Rose, W. (2010) 'The Assessment Framework', in J. Horwath (ed.) *The Child's World*, 2nd edn, London: Jessica Kingsley Publishers.

Rose, W. and Barnes, J. (2008) *Improving Safeguarding Practice: Study of Serious Case Reviews 2001–2003*, London: DCSF.

Rose, W., Aldgate, J. and Barnes, J. (2007) 'From policy visions to practice realities: the pivotal role of service managers in implementation', in J. Aldgate, L. Healy, B. Malcolm, B.A. Pine, W. Rose and J. Seden (eds) *Enhancing Social Work Management: theory and best practice from the UK and USA*, London: Jessica Kingsley Publishers.

Saito, Y. and Johns, R. (2009) 'Japanese students' perceptions of international perspectives in social work', *International Social Work*, 52(1): 60–70.

Saleebey, D. (ed.) (2006) *The Strengths Perspective in Social Work Practice*, New York: Longman.

Sanderson, H. (2003) 'Implementing person-centred planning by developing person-centred teams', *Journal of Integrated Care*, 11(3): 18–25.

Satyamurti, C. (1979) 'Care and control in local authority social work', in N. Parry (eds) *Social Work, Welfare and the State*, London: Edward Arnold.

Save the Children (2003) *My mum is my new best friend: young asylum seekers' views of life in Glasgow*, Scotland: Save the Children.

Schlossberg, N.K., Waters, E.B. and Goodman, J. (1995) *Counseling Adults in Transition: Linking Practice with Theory*, New York: Springer.

Schön, D. (1983) *The Reflective Practitioner: how professionals think in action*, London: Temple Smith.

Scottish Commission for the Regulation of Care (2003) *National Care Standards for Child Care Agencies*, Edinburgh: Scottish Executive.

Scottish Credit and Qualifications Framework (2007) *The Scottish Credit and Qualifications Framework*, www.scqf.org.uk (accessed 1 May 2009).

Scottish Executive (2000) *The Same As You? A review of services for people with learning disabilities*, Edinburgh: Scottish Executive.

Scottish Executive (2001) *New Directions: report on the review of the Mental Health (Scotland) Act 1984*, Edinburgh: Scottish Executive.

Scottish Executive (2003) *The Framework for Social Work Education in Scotland*, Edinburgh: Scottish Executive.

Scottish Executive (2004) *Protecting Children and Young People: the Charter*, Edinburgh: Scottish Executive.

Scottish Executive (2005) *Getting it Right for Every Child: consultation on proposals for changes to children's services including the Children's Hearings System*, Edinburgh: Scottish Executive.

Scottish Executive (2006a) *Getting it Right for Every Child: proposals for action, consultation with children and young people*, Edinburgh: Scottish Executive.

Scottish Executive (2006b) *Changing Lives, Report of the 21st Century Social Work Review*, Edinburgh: Scottish Executive.

Scottish Executive (2007) *National Guidance on Self Directed Support*, Edinburgh: Scottish Executive.

Scottish Government (2008a) *A Guide to Getting it Right for Every Child*, Edinburgh: Scottish Government.

Scottish Government (2008b) *National Guidance on the Implementation of Local Area Coordination*, Edinburgh: Scottish Government.

Scottish Institute for Excellence in Social Work Education (2003) *Briefing Paper*, Dundee: SIESWE.

Scottish Social Services Council (2005) *Codes of Practice for Social Services Workers and Employers*, Dundee: SSSC.
Scottish Social Services Council (2008a) *A Framework for Continuous Learning and Development*, Dundee: SSSC.
Scottish Social Services Council (2008b) *Post Registration Training and Learning Requirements for Newly Qualified Social Workers: guidance notes for employers*, Dundee: SSSC.
Scottish Social Services Council (2008c) *Report on the Scottish Social Services Council's Work in Relation to Initial and Continued Suitability for Registration, 1 April 2003 – 31 March 2008*, www.sssc.uk.com (accessed 27 October 2009).
Scottish Social Services Council (2009) *Scottish Social Services Council (Conduct) Rule*, www.sssc.uk.com (accessed 7 October 2009).
Scottish Social Services Council/Institute for Research and Innovation in Social Services (2008) *The Framework for Continuous Learning in Social Services*, Edinburgh: Scottish Government.
Scourfield, P. (2007) 'Social care and the modern citizen: client, consumer, service user, manager and entrepreneur', *British Journal of Social Work*, 37(1): 107–22.
Seden, J. (2005) *Counselling Skills in Social Work Practice*, Maidenhead: Open University Press/McGraw-Hill Education.
Seden, J. and Katz, J. (2003) 'Managing significant life events', in J. Seden and J. Reynolds (eds) *Managing Care in Practice*, London: Routledge/The Open University.
Seden, J. and Reynolds, J. (2003) *Managing Care in Practice*, London: Routledge/The Open University.
Seebohm Report (1968) *Report on the Committee on Local Authority and Allied Personal Social Services*, London: HMSO.
Seed, P. (1973) *The Expansion of Social Work in Britain*, London: Routledge & Kegan Paul.
Seedhouse, D. (2005) *Values-Based Decisionmaking for the Caring Professions: the fundamentals of ethical decisionmaking*, Chichester: Wiley.
Seedhouse, D. (2009a) *The Company Behind Values Exchange*, www.vide.co.nz (accessed 31 May 2009).
Seedhouse, D. (2009b) *Open University K315 Values Exchange*, http://open.values-exchange.co.uk (accessed 31 May 2009).
Seedhouse, D. (2009c) *Welcome to Staffordshire University Values Exchange: a unique brain trainer!* http://staffs.values-exchange.co.uk (accessed 31 May 2009).
Seedhouse, D. (2009d) *Welcome to the Redbridge NHS Values Exchange*, http://redbridgepct.values-exchange.co.uk (accessed 31 May 2009).
Seedhouse, D. (2009e) *South Staffordshire and Shropshire Healthcare NHS Foundation Trust*, http://southstaffshealthcare.values-exchange.co.uk (accessed 31 May 2009).
Seedhouse, D. (2009f) *Ethics: the Heart of Healthcare*, 3rd edn, London: Wiley-Blackwell.
Sellers, S.L., and Hunter, A.G. (2005) 'Private pain, public choices: influence of problems in the family of origin on career choices among a cohort of MSW students', *Social Work Education*, 24(8): 869–81.
Senior, B. and Loades, E. (2008) 'Best practice as skilled organisational work', in K. Jones, B. Cooper and H. Ferguson (eds) *Best Practice in Social Work: Critical Perspectives*, Basingstoke: Palgrave Macmillan.

Shaw, I., Bell, M., Sinclair, I., Sloper, P., Michell, M., Dyson, P., Clayden, J. and Rafferty, J. (2009) 'An exemplary scheme? An evaluation of the Integrated Children's System', *British Journal of Social Work*, 39(4): 613–26.

Sheldon, B. (1978) 'Theory and practice in social work: a re-examination of a tenuous relationship', *British Journal of Social Work*, 8(1): 1–22.

Shemmings, D. and Shemmings, Y. (1995) 'Defining participative practice in health and welfare', in R. Jack (ed.) *Empowerment in Community Care*, London: Chapman and Hall.

Sheppard, M. (1993) 'Theory for Approved Social Work: the use of the Compulsory Admissions Assessment Schedule', *British Journal of Social Work*, 23(3): 231–57.

Sheppard, M. (2006) *Social Work and Social Exclusion: the idea of practice*, Farnham: Ashgate.

Sidebotham, P. and Weeks, M. (2010) 'Multidisciplinary contributions to assessment of children in need', in J. Horwath (ed.) *The Child's World*, 2nd edn, London: Jessica Kingsley Publishers.

Skills for Care (2009) *Sustaining Practice Learning with Local Authorities*, www.skillsforcare.org.uk (accessed 22 July 2009).

Skills for Care and Children's Workforce Development Council (2009) *Social Work Development Partnership*, www.practicelearning.org.uk (accessed 20 July 2009).

Slevin, E., Truesdale-Kennedy, M., McConkey, R., Barr, O. and Taggart, L. (2008) 'Community learning disability teams: developments, composition and good practice', *Journal of Intellectual Disabilities*, 12(1): 59–79.

Smale, G. (1977) *Prophecy, Behaviour and Change: an examination of self-fulfilling prophecies in helping relationships*, London: Routledge & Kegan Paul.

Smith, L. (2008) 'South African social work education: critical imperatives for social change in the post-apartheid and post-colonial context', *International Social Work*, 51(3): 371–83.

Sobiechowska, P. (2007) 'Adopting a strategic approach to post-qualifying learning', in W. Tovey (ed.) *The Post-Qualifying Handbook for Social Workers*, London: Jessica Kingsley Publishers.

Social Care Institute for Excellence (2006) *Guide 11: involving children and young people in developing social care*, London: SCIE.

Social Care Institute for Excellence (2009) *Guide 15: Dignity in care*, London: SCIE.

Spiers, J. (2008) *Who Decides Who Decides? Enabling choice, equity, access, improved performance and patient guaranteed care*, Oxford: Radcliffe Medical Press.

Staker, K. and Campbell, V. (1998) 'Person-centred planning: an evaluation of a training programme', *Health and Social Care in the Community*, 6(2): 130–42.

Staksrud, E. and Livingstone, S. (2009) 'Children and online risk: Powerless victims or resourceful participants?', *Information, Communication & Society*, 12(3): 364–87.

Stalker, K., Cadogan, L. and Petrie, M. (1999) *'If You Don't Ask You Don't Get' Review of Services to People with Learning Disabilities: the views of people who use services and their carers*, Edinburgh: Scottish Executive.

Stalker, K.O., Malloch, M., Barry, M.A. and Watson, J.A. (2007) *Evaluation of the implementation of local area co-ordination in Scotland*, Edinburgh: Scottish Executive.

Stalker, K.O., Malloch, M., Barry, M.A. and Watson, J.A. (2008) 'Local area co-ordination: strengthening support for people with learning disabilities in Scotland', *British Journal of Learning Disabilities*, 36(4): 215–9.

Steadman, H.J. (1992) 'Boundary spanners: a key component for the effective interactions of the justice and mental health systems', *Law and Human Behavior*, 16(1): 75–87.

Stevenson, O. (1963) 'Co-ordination reviewed', *Case Conference*, IX: 208–12.

Steyaert, J. and Gould, N. (2009) 'Social work and the changing face of the digital divide', *British Journal of Social Work*, 39(4): 740–53.

Stradling, B., MacNeil, M. and Berry, H. (2009) *Changing Professional Practice and Culture to Get It Right For Every Child: an evaluation overview of the development and early implementation phases of getting it right for every child in Highland 2006–2009*, Edinburgh: Scottish Government.

Stuart, O. (2006) *Will Community-Based Support Services Make Direct Payments a Viable Option for Black and Minority Ethnic Service Users and Carers?* London: SCIE.

Sullivan, P. and Knutson, J. (2000) 'Maltreatment and disabilities: a population-based epidemiological study', *Child Abuse and Neglect*, 24(10): 1257–73.

Tacchi, J. and Kiran, M.S. (2008) *Finding a Voice: themes and discussions: research from the Finding a Voice project*, New Delhi: UNESCO.

Tanner, D. (2009) 'Modernisation and the delivery of user-centred services', in J. Harris and V. White (eds) *Modernising Social Work: critical considerations*, Bristol: Policy Press.

Taylor, C. (2006) 'Practising reflexivity: narrative, reflection and the moral order', in S. White, J. Fook and F. Gardner (eds) *Critical Reflection in Health and Social Care*, Maidenhead: Macgraw-Hill.

Taylor, W., Earle, R. and Hester, R. (2010) *Youth Justice Handbook: theory, policy and practice*, Cullompton: Willan.

Tew, J. (ed.) (2005) *Social Perspectives in Mental Health: developing social models to understand and work with mental distress*, London: Jessica Kingsley Publishers.

Thatcher, M. (1987) 'No such thing as society', *Interview for Woman's Own*, www.margaretthatcher.org (accessed 18 November 2009).

Thoburn, J., Wilding, J. and Watson, J. (2000) *Family Support in Cases of Emotional Maltreatment and Neglect*, London: The Stationery Office.

Thomas, J. and Spreadbury, K. (2008) 'Promoting best practice through supervision, support and communities of practice', in K. Jones, B. Cooper and H. Ferguson (eds) *Best Practice in Social Work: critical perspectives*, Basingstoke: Palgrave Macmillan.

Thompson, N. (2006) *Promoting Workplace Learning*, Bristol: BASW/Policy Press.

Thompson, N. (2009) *Understanding Social Work*, 3rd edn, Basingstoke: Palgrave Macmillan.

Thorpe, D.H. (1980) *Out of Care: the community support of juvenile offenders*, Winchester, MA: Allen & Unwin.

Thorpe, M. and Edmunds, R. (2009) *Learners' Experiences of Blended Learning Environments in a Practice-based Context (PB-LXP)*, www.jisc.ac.uk (accessed 9 November 2009)

Tilbury, C. (2004) 'The influence of performance measurement on child welfare policy and practice', *British Journal of Social Work*, 34(2): 225–41.

Topss (2003a) *The National Occupational Standards for Social Work*, www.topss.org.uk (accessed 1 December 2003).

Topss (2003b) *Statement of Expectations from Individuals, Families, Carers, Groups and Communities who use Services*, www.topss.org.uk (accessed 1 December 2003).

Townson, L. and Chapman, R. (2003) 'Consultation: plan of action or management exercise', in J. Reynolds, J. Henderson, J. Seden, J. Charlesworth and A. Bullman (eds) *The Managing Care Reader*, London: Routledge and The Open University.

Trevithick, P. (2000) *Social Work Skills*, Maidenhead: Open University Press.

Trevithick, P. (2005) *Social Work Skills: a practice handbook*, 2nd edn, Maidenhead: Open University Press.

Trevithick, P. (2008) 'Revisiting the knowledge base for social work: a framework for practice', *British Journal of Social Work*, 38(6): 1212–37.

UNCRC (1989) *United Nations Convention of the Rights of the Child*, Geneva: United Nations.

UNICEF (2005) *Children and Disability in Transition in CEE/CIS and Baltic States*, Florence: Innocenti Research Centre.

UNICEF (2007) *Promoting the Rights of Children with Disabilities*, Florence: Innocenti Research Centre.

Unison (2009) *'Social Work Vacancies Hit Danger Point'*, www.unison.org.uk (accessed 6 November 2009).

United Nations (2006) *Convention on the Rights of Persons with Disabilities*, Geneva: United Nations.

Utting, W. (1997) *People like us: the report on the review of safeguarding for children living away from home*, London: The Stationary Office.

Valentine, C.W. (1956) *The Normal Child and Some of his Abnormalities*, Harmondsworth: Penguin.

Valtonen, K. (2001) 'Social work with immigrants and refugees: developing a participation-based framework for anti-oppressive practice', *British Journal of Social Work*, 31(6): 955–60.

Victor, C., Scrambler, S. and Bond, J. (2008) *The Social World of Older People: understanding loneliness and social isolation in later life*, Maidenhead: Open University Press.

Wagner, P. (1994) *A Sociology of Modernity: liberty and discipline*, London: Routledge.

Walker, G. (2004) *An Investigation into the Strengths and Weaknesses of Work-based Placements on the NOLP Dip.Sw.*, unpublished report, Milton Keynes: The Open University.

Walker, G. (2006) *Effective Practice Learning within the Context of Students' Own Workplace*, unpublished report, Milton Keynes: The Open University.

Walter, I., Nutley, S., Percy-Smith, J., McNeish, D. and Frost, S. (2004) 'Improving the use of research in social care practice', *Knowledge Review* 7, London: SCIE.

Walters, N. (2009) 'Asylum Seekers Speak: "Nothing can give us back the last seven years"', *The Guardian*, August 2009.

Ward, R. and Bytheway, W.R. (eds) (2008) *Researching Age and Multiple Discrimination*, Part 8 in The Representation of Older People in Research series, London: Centre for Policy on Ageing.

Warham, J. (1977) *An Open Case: the organisational context of social work*, London: Routledge & Kegan Paul.

Warren, J. (2007) *Service User and Carer Participation in Social Work Education*, Exeter: Learning Matters.

Webb, R. and Vulliamy, G. (2001) 'Joining up the solutions: the rhetoric and practice of inter-agency co-operation', *Children and Society*, 15(5): 315–32.

Webb, S.A. (2003) 'Local orders and global chaos in social work', *European Journal of Social Work*, 6(2): 191–204.

Webb, S.A. (2006) *Social Work in a Risk Society: social and political perspectives*, Basingstoke: Palgrave Macmillan.

Wellbourne, P., Harrison, G. and Ford, D. (2007) 'Social work in the UK and the global labour market', *International Social Work*, 50(1): 27–40.

Welsh Assembly Government (2004) *Children and Young People: Rights to Action*, Cardiff: Welsh Assembly Government.

White, S., Hall, C. and Peckover, S. (2009) 'The descriptive tyranny of the Common Assessment Framework: technologies of categorization and professional practice in child welfare', *British Journal of Social Work*, 39: 1197–217.

White, V. (2009) 'Quiet challenges? Professional practice in modernised social work', in J. Harris and V. White (eds) *Modernising Social Work*, Bristol: Policy Press.

Wigfall, V. and Moss, P. (2001) *More than the Sum of its Parts? A study of a multi-agency child care network*, London: National Children's Bureau.

Wiles, F. (2008) 'In work and outside work: the impact of professional registration on social work students' identities', research report, Milton Keynes: The Open University.

Wiles, F. (2009) 'Private lives and professional suitability: themes and discourses in Care Standards Tribunal decision about registered social workers', paper to Social Policy Association conference, Edinburgh, www.crfr.ac.uk (accessed 1 December 2009).

Wiles, F. (2010) 'The impact of professional registration on social work students' identities: progress report 11', research report, Milton Keynes: The Open University.

William, C.K., Tsui, M. and Yan, M. (2009) 'Social work as a moral and a political process', *International Social Work*, 52(3): 287–98.

Williamson, H. (2001) *Supporting Young People in Europe: principles, policy and practice*, Strasbourg: Council of Europe.

Wilson, K., Ruch, G., Lymbery, M. and Cooper, A. (2008) *Social Work: an introduction to contemporary practice*, Harlow: Pearson Education.

Yelloly, M. and Henkel, M. (1995) 'Introduction', in M. Yelloly and M. Henkel (eds) *Learning and Teaching in Social Work: towards reflective practice*, London: Jessica Kingsley Publishers.

Youth Justice Board (2009) *Youth Justice: The Scaled Approach – a framework for assessment and interventions* (post-consultation version two), London: Youth Justice Board.

Index